TIGHTROPE PASSAGE

TIGHTROPE PASSAGE

Along the Refugee Route to Canada

IVO MORAVEC

M&S

Canadian Cataloguing in Publication Data

Moravec, Ivo, 1948-
    Tightrope passage : along the refugee route to Canada

ISBN 0-7710-6500-0

1. Moravec, Ivo, 1948-   .   2. Refugees, Political – Czechoslovakia –
Biography.   3. Refugees, Political – Austria – Vienna – Biography.
4. Vienna (Austria) – Social conditions.   5. Refugees, Political – Canada –
Biography.   I. Title.

FC3099.L65Z49   1997   325'.21'092   C96-932526-6
FI059.5.L6M67   1997

The publishers acknowledge the support of the Canada Council and the
Ontario Arts Council for their publishing program. The publishers also
acknowledge the contribution of the Multiculturalism Programs of the
Department of Canadian Heritage.

Typesetting by M&S, Toronto
Printed and bound in Canada

McClelland & Stewart Inc.
The Canadian Publishers
481 University Avenue
Toronto, Ontario
M5G 2E9

1 2 3 4 5   01 00 99 98 97

For Jana and Ivo
and
for Stan

Contents

I

ON THE TRAIN

THE TRAIN JOLTED. Finally! We began inching forward on our trip to freedom. For the fifteenth or eighteenth time during the last couple of hours my sweat began to dry. I was standing in the corridor of the train, looking out a window that, despite the July haze, was closed. They had ordered it. They hadn't given a reason.

For two hours the train had been at the border station, an eerie place though the building was like any other in Bohemia. There was a stationmaster's office and a traffic office, a waiting room and a baggage room, even some geraniums in flowerpots on the window ledges. But there was no stationmaster, no dispatcher, no clerk in the ticket office, no luggage handler. Not a single passenger on the platform. Instead, three huge billboards dominated the view: Welcome to Czechoslovakia! Don't leave the train! Under the Party leadership we will achieve Socialism!

Along the length of the grey concrete platform stood soldiers in fatigues, their semi-automatic rifles at the ready. Though they looked uninterested, they were dangerous. Specially selected, reliable. Indoctrinated around the clock to see along their sights not a man but a would-be defector. For the two years of their compulsory military service, they had to wear the collar of discipline and were confined to their barracks somewhere behind the station. Each time they wanted to go out, to down a few beers, they had to humbly apply to the commander. Meanwhile, day after day, they watched trainloads of tourists leave for the West to enjoy a couple of weeks of freedom. They had no hope of going to the West, and their faces showed it. Somewhere at the bottom of their souls, envy, humiliation, and helplessness surely brewed. How much had to build up before one of them squeezed a trigger?

Since the train had pulled in I'd been moving back and forth between the corridor window and my seat beside my wife and son. I didn't have the patience to join their game of Battleship. I was fretting that in the station office the phone would ring, the commander would step out of the door and, with just a gesture of his index finger, motion me out of the train. He would have been told to confiscate my passport. My permission to travel was a joke. When the pressure on my nerves grew too great, I sat with my son, Ivo, and told him a fairy tale. But then my nervousness made me jump up and go to the window. *Come what may, but make it come fast.* I was soaked with sweat every time a telephone rang.

My thoughts tormented me:

If they come, should I run? How far is it to the border? They would shoot to kill. I am sure that many more of them are waiting farther down the rails. If I run, my wife and son would still be sitting here as hostages. I'd better continue with my story instead of showing them my face. I might look suspicious, I might irritate them somehow and make them pull me out of the train and lock me up in the luggage room. Sitting here, telling Ivo a fairy tale, I look more like a tourist slightly annoyed by the long waiting in the heat. No, I shouldn't look annoyed. It's safer to put on a mask of patient waiting, of respecting their complicated and responsible job. After all, checking three carriages and 120 people can't be done in two hours.

I have all the required documents. Otherwise I could not be this far. So incredibly close to the border.

★

Much earlier than I had expected it, some forty kilometres from the border, our compartment door slammed open. My son instinctively huddled to his mom, Jana. A grey uniform. No greetings. Piercing, cold eyes. His narrow lips barked, "Your passports!" He leafed through Jana's as if she had printed it herself. As if it hadn't been issued by his colleagues at the Ministry of the Interior in Prague! I would never forget that day six weeks ago.

During the five hours I waited in line at the ministry office, I progressed from the sidewalk along the hallway and up the stairs to the second floor of the old apartment building. At the top of the stairs were floor-to-ceiling bars, like in a jail. The sign above the narrow door read District Department of Passports and Visas. Behind the bars was a small anteroom, an ordinary wooden door, and beyond that a spacious, sunlit office. A counter with three windows and two clerks. I had already been here three times. The first was to hand in my application for an exit visa, a special supplement to the passport that would allow me to travel to the West. Then twice more on appointed days only to learn that nothing had been decided yet.

On hearing my name, the clerk reacted with a look that I had seen a few times before: a mixture of curiosity, apprehension, and sympathy. *So you are the Moravec. . . .* They had talked about me. This wouldn't make it easy to get the visa. She left. I waited. Three more clerks came to have a look at me under the pretext of checking something in a filing cabinet. A fourth didn't examine me at all, but lifted the counter, opened the door, and gestured me in.

A small room, no windows. A table, a couple of chairs, a portrait of the president, sharp light. No doubt a few microphones somewhere, perhaps a hidden videocamera. An official. His clothes didn't distinguish him from any other aging comrade. He wore crumpled grey pants, with shiny thighs and seat. His tweed jacket was shapeless. The shirt was blue-green checkered flannel and didn't match his loose GI-green tie. Unlike his clothes, his expression, especially the curve of his mouth with dropping corners, set him apart as a powerful comrade of great merit. He sat down and motioned me to take the other chair. We faced each other across the table. He offered me a cigarette. I took one. If I had declined, he would have interpreted it as a sign of my nervousness. I was doing my best to appear relaxed, as if we were going to have a friendly chat, though I knew that he knew almost everything about me from reading their secret files.

"Would you return if we let you travel?" he shot at me.

"I want to live in my country," I replied without hesitation.

"Prove it!" he yelled.

"How can I prove that I'm not going to emigrate?"

"What guarantees, then, do I have that you won't stay out there?" His eyes were X-raying me.

"My supervisor and his supervisor and the boss, the comrades from the union and from the party, the Special Procedures Department, all of them approved and recommended my application. Six people with whom I work and who know me well. Any of them could have turned me down without giving a reason. I have a good job in a research institute. I have a nice apartment and a family summer cottage. I have a good standard of living. I've had my script accepted by TV and my play by a theatre. Here I have the Czech language, which I can't write without. There's lots of money waiting for me when I return. My parents live here. My friends live here. I am happy living here. These are all the guarantees I can offer."

"Emigration is a felony," he warned.

"I know. I have never violated the law and I will not do so now. I respect the authorities."

I was scrutinizing every word I said, thinking half a sentence ahead. Does my voice sound natural? Relaxed? Fingers are drumming on the table. His fingers.

"How come they have given you a hard-currency allowance?"

Obtaining this allowance was a prerequisite for applying for the exit visa. If they hadn't given it to me, he would not have to make his annoying decision.

"I don't know their criteria. Perhaps the bank could give you more precise information." I was almost sure they would supply him with sound reasons. After all, accepting a substantial bribe is a crime, too.

"Do you think that life is better in the West?"

"I don't know what kind of life exists there," I answered truthfully, "but I have studied Marxism-Leninism, and as an economist I know their society is doomed. There's no future for them. The little I know about the West tells me this is true. Criminality, drugs, law of the jungle or none at all. Nothing for a decent person. You know best how many emigrants return home bankrupt and disillusioned when they discover they were taken in by the glitter." An exemplary ideological answer.

He was silent, trying to guess my thoughts. Living under socialism had taught me superb self-control. He reached for the heavy guns.

"What if we won't let you go?"

"I'd be disappointed because I haven't done anything to warrant your distrust, but my world would not collapse."

He left, but I didn't relax. I sensed that not only the president was watching me. Most likely the comrade had gone to consult with the expert at the tape-recorder. He returned.

"So we give it to you, after all."

"Thank you, comrade," I said with the appropriate humble gratefulness, though I felt like cursing him into the most hellish of all hells because he was mercifully granting me something that's guaranteed by the constitution.

"Wait at the counter. And do not forget," he wagged his index finger, "you've got your parents here, and your wife's sisters, and nephews and nieces. . . ."

The inevitable threat at the end. As if I hadn't been thinking for two years what their fate might be.

The clerk brought two pieces of paper with our exit visas. If they had been engraved in gold they wouldn't have been more precious.

"Good luck," she smiled.

Only when I was around two corners, safely out of sight, did I light two cigarettes at once.

The man in the grey uniform found Jana's passport in order. He checked mine. He watched me. Piercing eyes searched for any hint of nervousness, any signal that at the back of my mind was some intention incompatible with honourable tourism. I returned his gaze confidently.

"On your return, hand in the second part of the exit visa!" he snarled. Even though I could see only his back now, I didn't dare to think: Perhaps.

As soon as he left, a plump, uniformed woman, well into her fifties, burst into the compartment.

"Your customs and currency declaration!"

Decent people would say please, I thought.

"Here they are, if you please." One gets used to minor humiliations, and this might be the last one.

Packing had taken us a whole week. What would we really need? For each item there had to be not only a reason but also an alibi. The best combination of our future needs, weight and volume. Nothing suspicious, nothing prohibited.

"Show me that jewel!" Her eyes greedily examined the antique jewel that might one day pay for a few dinners or milk for our son.

"Why are you taking this on vacation?"

"We're visiting Paris." My wife offered the prepared answer. "Social life, theatres. I want to represent my country as best as I can."

There's not much she could do about such a politically correct intention.

"Open your luggage! Why do you need parkas in the summer?"

"We're going to the Alps, too. We'll sleep in a tent. Quite often there's snow, even in July," I explained.

Finally, she scored. "You haven't written down your sleeping bags!"

"I'll add them in now, if I may. The form says that only valuables like jewels, watches, cameras, fur coats need to be mentioned." Hastily I scribbled down three slightly used sleeping bags on the declaration that was supposed to guarantee we would bring them back and not barter them for a few cans of beer.

She left without a word. I won't miss you, dear, I wanted to say, but I didn't. She, too, could have pulled us off the train.

Perhaps they were really not all that powerful. But since childhood it had been beaten into our heads that they were. We had believed it, and so they didn't have to execute their power quite as ruthlessly.

When we finally made it to the border, to this eerie station, a pack of soldiers in black coveralls stormed the train. They scrutinized it inside, outside, above, below. They disassembled our three carriages almost to their nuts and bolts. They were searching for some desperate man who, having been denied all other means, might attempt to escape in a pressurized air tank or welded between two wall panels. They even checked the hollows where an infant wouldn't fit. They found no one.

The train jolted a second time. We were moving.

The station slid from view. A faint order of "At ease!" could be heard. At right angles to the rails was a wide strip of mown, yellow grass. No trees or bushes, no houses or haystacks. Nothing, though we were in a town. It was empty, controllable space. A potential shooting range. Next came a twenty-metre-wide strip of freshly ploughed soil that was hard to run on. And then the wires, the famous wires; the symbol and the pride of Czechoslovak socialism. Three parallel rows of three-metre-high barbed wire, perhaps charged with electricity. Every five hundred metres a watchtower, manned around the clock. The border between the world of progress and the world of decay. The guardians of Truth and Progress had no doubts which was which. Neither had I.

The train rattled over a railway bridge guarded by more sentries. A small river down below. Where was the exact border? Most likely in the middle. Here. Our lives broke into two halves.

No fence on the Austrian side. One was enough. Gardens descended to the riverbank. A fisherman quietly reeled in a fish. In the backyards were flowers, trees full of apples and cherries, rows of lettuce and radish. A suntanned man sat in an easy chair on his balcony, looking through binoculars at the Czech side. Maybe he hoped to catch a glimpse of his uncle or his sweetheart from a time when this town was whole, before the blade of the Iron Curtain chopped it in two.

Station Gmünd. A few hundred metres beyond Czechoslovakia and we were on a different planet. Everything was clean. Not a single soldier. Instead, a stationmaster, a dispatcher wearing a red cap, and passengers. And a restaurant with tables set out on the fine gravel of the first platform. People drank beer and sipped coffee, they laughed. I wouldn't have sat there for the world. Some block-head on the watchtower might shoot the beer mug out of my hand.

The Austrian formalities were over in thirty seconds, twenty of them spent wishing us happy holidays. I looked at Jana and I could tell she was thinking what I was thinking: How wonderful it would be to take little Ivo by the hand and to dance, all three of us, from the train to the restaurant, buy as many bottles of champagne as our arms could carry, sprinkle ourselves with it, invite everybody to be our guest, sing and happily weep on the shoulder of somebody who has no idea how lucky he is to live in a free country. And take a snapshot in front of the billboard advertising West cigarettes with the slogan "Go West!" What kind of coincidence put this slogan in my way? But – no cheering. No champagne. Still, my sweat dried up. Our muscles relaxed. The tension around our eyes and mouth eased. Our eyes were smiling. Only our eyes. We had yet to make it to Vienna, and maybe this Czech train had extra-territorial privileges, like a ship or an aircraft. Perhaps they still could come for us. Perhaps there was a washroom on this train, with a barred window and no inside doorknob.

"You should eat something," said Jana, handing me a bun and a slab of Hungarian salami. "It will do you good. And drink as much as you can."

She wanted me to wash the overdose of adrenalin out of my body. I forced myself to eat.

"Don't worry," she laughed, "we are travelling by train, aren't we?" She was alluding to an escape that had happened a few years ago and had become legend in Prague beer halls.

In the sixties he was the number-one acrobatic flyer, champion of the world. Then, in 1968, the Russian tanks rolled in, along with some half a million troops. He soon realized that everyday life with them would require an unacceptable level of moral acrobatics. When the borders were sealed and he was not able to escape, because they wouldn't grant him even a short vacation, he turned to what he did best. He squeezed his family into a small two-seater and headed for the West. They barely managed to take off in the overloaded plane, even though they took nothing with them but a full tank of gas. He flew as low as he could to avoid the radar, but in such a densely populated place as Bohemia no secret can be kept for long. They detected him, and when he ignored their landing orders they launched a jet fighter to shoot him down. He did his best – and it was the best in the world – with the overloaded plane, dogfighting the MiG, evading it again and again. In the end, the jet pilot, seeing what a great master of flying he was, honoured his skills and used neither guns nor missiles to shoot him down. After landing in Linz, he knew this performance beat in importance all the competitions he had ever won. Behind him, his green-faced family staggered onto the tarmac. They were no acrobats and entered Austria not only with empty pockets, but with empty stomachs as well. People say they settled somewhere in Canada.

"Give me a painkiller, please," I asked my wife.

"Your head again?"

For a number of years I'd suffered from migraine headaches. No physician could explain why. I fancied an explanation of my own: My headaches were the result of flirting with prohibited ideas, of my love affair with literature and philosophy, which resulted in my head getting pregnant. Under the façade of my public head, another had begun to grow, a private, more genuine one. The way Pallas Athena, the Greek goddess of wisdom, grew in Zeus's head, my true head had been developing inside my official one. As they fought for space, my head ached.

Have I already defected or not yet? How does one defect, anyway? Most refugees probably ask for political asylum at a police station. And then? I don't know. I could not have visited the Austrian embassy in Prague and casually asked a clerk, "Excuse me, ma'am, what would be the correct procedure for getting asylum in Austria?" The all-knowing experts from the state security would have gladly discussed my interest in defecting with me and then let the information soak in behind bars.

The most important decision of my life and I've been unable to gather any information. After thirty-five years I know exactly what I am running from. But towards what?

"May I bother you for a light?" somebody behind me asked while I was smoking in the corridor.

I struck a match. An unfamiliar cigarette. A warning light flashed in my head.

"I felt like we were being treated like a herd of cattle at the border," he complained.

"It will be faster and more pleasant on the way back," I comforted him.

"Could you tell me the name of the station in Vienna we're coming to? I've forgotten it."

The alarm went off in my head. For a Czech, it is as impossible to forget the name of Emperor Franz Josef the First as for an Englishman to not know Queen Victoria's. If a chance of running into a secret police informer in Prague was one in four, how much greater was it on this train?

"Franz Josef der Erste Bahnhof," I said.

He put on a look of a daydreaming man. "Do you know that Prague Central Station, from which we departed, used to bear the same name? It means we'll arrive where we came from."

"Except we have a seven-decade delay, because our starting point was renamed some seventy years ago," I went along.

He tried to bait me. "Well, if the Empire hadn't disintegrated – no borders, no humiliating checks – you could go to Vienna any time you felt like it."

Guessing by your cigarettes and your shoes, you're there with every second train, I thought, but I said, "It would soon become boring."

"They scared me there," he went on, "with their automatic rifles . . . you can never tell."

"They let decent people be, and those with a clear conscience have nothing to fear," I answered and retired to our compartment. The conversation had strayed dangerously towards being a crime against the party, and possibly even high treason.

My thoughts haunted me. The darkness ahead. I knew next to nothing about Canada, the country we wanted to settle in. Nothing beyond the information found in officially approved books. Only the stories of one man who had actually been there.

More than a year ago, while we were still tormented by the pros and cons of leaving Czechoslovakia, we met a strange old man during a stroll in the Šárka Ravine. He didn't fit, wearing checkered trousers, a wildly coloured shirt, and a baseball cap with a red maple leaf. He didn't have a look of resignation. Bursting with optimistic vitality, he had just returned home after half a year in Canada, where he had been visiting his son. His son's family led a good life, though they were quite average people. He was so full of impressions that he had to share them all. For four hours we soaked in his tales of this different world. Canada seemed to be quiet, kind, orderly, and generous, sharply different from the picture painted by official ideology. He spurted out stories like a volcano: One time he'd encountered a mounted policeman in a park; at first he was scared, but the cop just wanted to know if he was okay, lying there on a bench. Another time he'd picked up a bruised apple from the sidewalk. The home-owner took it away and instead gave him a full basket of sound ones.

All the stories were spiced with refrains – *if I were younger, if I were in your place*. Later, we couldn't tell him that the picture of Canada he had painted had pushed us forward, that the vision of the promised land he had depicted kept us afloat when we were drowning, even when we wondered if his anecdotes were too weak a hook to hang our lives on.

I brood too much. The rational half of my brain, trained to process information, would like to have everything laid out, nice, clean, and clear-cut. My imaginative half supplies me with propaganda-induced, terror-filled visions wherever there's informational twilight or darkness.

Brooding prohibited! Take heart from the story of the old man who devised the most original way of escaping. According to lore, he whitewashed his way to freedom. He didn't give a damn about what was ahead. He had the guts to do what he wanted. He could never get lost in the world if he managed to outsmart the whole system of checks and double-checks the way he did.

After he hatched up his plan of escape, he sold his goat and bought a wheelbarrow, a few cans of paint, and a brush. He began to whitewash all the roadside posts, starting kilometres before the border zone. The locals saw him every day and got used to his presence. By the time he made it to the first border checkpoint, he was already a part of the landscape. The guards had a talk, a smoke, with him, and let him work. He progressed one kilometre a day, painting all the markers, trees, and posts on the right side of the road. The left side he would paint on his way back. By the time he painted his way to the second checkpoint, he was one of them. Nobody bothered to ask him for his ID or for his permit to enter the border zone. He must have one, they reasoned. Somebody must have assigned him this job, somebody must have given him security clearance. He had no trouble getting to the barrier itself. Then he had the nerve to turn back and go home because he wouldn't work overtime.

The next morning he had a big breakfast, a shot of rum to steady his knees, and then locked up his house and left. He told the sentry at the barrier that he had to finish painting the remaining two hundred metres to the actual borderline, so that "the tourists wouldn't gossip about us in a bad way." They laughed, let him go, and even phoned the guards in the watchtowers to say that it was all right. He painted everything that there was to paint, all the way to the sign reading Czechoslovak Socialist Republic. Then he walked on to the German customs office, where he applied for political asylum. He had nothing more than his smeared coveralls, some Czech currency, half a can of paint, and a few cigarettes.

We've got a better deal. We have four pieces of luggage, a whole carton of cigarettes, and even seven hundred dollars, most of it in traveller's cheques. And there are two of us to cope. Jana's common sense will stop me from being indecisive or letting my imagination wander.

Besides, the helping hand in landing this *salto mortale* – or, hopefully, *salto vitale* – will be provided by Theo. In two hours I'll see him, my brother by choice. We have gone through so much over the eighteen years of our friendship that the shared experience has welded us together like Siamese twins. At the beginning we promised each other that if either of us started something dangerously foolish, the other would beat the idea out of his head. I almost did that a couple of years ago when he began to think about emigrating because of a pretty German tourist, whom he met and got drunk with in a pub. He declared he was in love and wanted to live with her. If I had restored his common sense with a few slaps then, I wouldn't be riding this train today. But instead of a punishing hand I offered a helping one, becoming the co-architect of his criminal deed. He will pay me back now. He will greet me at the station. When he left, I went to see him off and watched his train disappear into the long, dark tunnel at the end of Prague Central Station. The tunnel suddenly concretized for me the abstract concept of emigration.

That night I worked on the TV script that Theo and I had been writing together until three days earlier. Suddenly my pen stopped, the cone of light around me seemed to dim. I could see Theo clearly, getting off the train in Stuttgart. He didn't look like a future conqueror of Europe but like a lonely figure with one suitcase, lost on a strange station platform, in a strange city, in a strange world. A naked person devoid of the protective shell of home, friends, background. All he had was his head and two hands.

How did he feel? He could never write to me about it. We both knew that any of his letters to me would be screened, and though he was beyond reach of socialist justice, he had to protect me. Not preventing a crime was a crime itself. Denunciation was required and enforced by the law.

Tonight he will tell me. Every detail!

He will not. He won't have to. In two hours I will become that little figure lost in the chilly universe of the hostile, predatory West that waits to devour me.

The West hasn't always been predatory. Even Czechoslovakia used to be the West – between the world wars. Then came the national socialism of Hitler and afterwards the international socialism of Stalin. Czechoslovakia became the East overnight. Mentally it took more time, in spite of the enthusiastic work of thousands of communists, propagandists, secret police, and hangmen. The image of the West, unchanged since 1938, survived in our parents' memories and with that generation has been slowly dying out. To present the East as paradise, the West had to become hell. We believed some of the things they told us, we doubted the rest, but even when we knew the image was false, we still didn't know the truth.

They transformed us from individual humans into a herd. They gave us a cow shed, some pasture, relative security, and milked us moderately. The obedient ones got greener grass and less milking. Life wasn't unbearable. They protected us from the wolves and other beasts of prey circling outside. It was safe and warm in the herd. Those who rejected it and escaped were branded as traitors and always came to a bad end. Occasionally they were shown on TV. Tired, broken, and speaking the clichés of the secret police, they confirmed that life in the herd was better; the wolves outside really were bloodthirsty. Inertia kept us home. Patriotism whispered into our ears that better times had to lie ahead. After all, the land we were grazing on was our land, our motherland. The grass we were chewing had grown from soil bestowed to us by our forefathers who had lived and toiled on it. The land was ours. It didn't belong to those in the pay of the Soviet Union who had erected the electrified barbed-wire fence around it, to those who had turned us into cattle. There were bugaboos outside the fence.

"You'll perish if you abandon the Motherland," they repeated incessantly, twisting a poet's words for their propaganda. They really beat this slogan into our heads. Even if you didn't believe them, you still didn't know the truth. They washed our brains of the ability to be free. But not of the desire for freedom.

I have this desire. But can I behave like a free man when I was born inside the fence and have never experienced any freedom? Reason says that freedom means accepting the responsibility for one's life. I have done this, I believe, within the rules of the game. I've followed the right path when I had to choose between the truth, as I saw it, and a full trough. I was willing to be kicked out of university for being silent about politics instead of actively endorsing them, as was required. I declined an academic career when it was offered to me in exchange for my public denunciation of my father. I didn't cry uncle when I found I could publish neither my research papers nor my literary writings. I've lived in the slow lane, looking for a non-political opening into the fast one. I've indulged in the luxury of having character in a society that rewards spinelessness. I've kept silent. I couldn't do more. If I had fought, it would have been on their turf, with their rules, their referee. A bullfight. A form of suicide. A man vanishes, and the memories of his integrity fade away.

The countryside the train was speeding through was lovely, but I hardly noticed.

"Daddy, let's play." My son arranged the pieces for a game of checkers.

"Watch out, I'm going to jump you one," I warned him.

"Jump, and I'll jump you two!"

Instead, I jump back six years, to the time he was born. A tiny, pink, helpless bundle in his cradle, a continuation of me and Jana, the best of us both. We supported him in his struggles to roll and to sit, in his fight with gravity when he learned to walk, and his duel with a spoon when he learned to eat by himself. We protected him inside our secure family world. Till today he hasn't known they lie in waiting out there, yet their tentacles are already reaching to his little throat. If we had stayed, one day he would have been held responsible for our behaviour. He has no idea that he's been held hostage in exchange for our civic obedience, the same way I was a hostage for my father's. I was punished because he had integrity, because he didn't succumb to their blackmail.

Do I have the right, the moral right, to allow my integrity to destroy the life of my child? Is integrity that precious? Does it exist at all? They say that it distinguishes man from beast. But is it that important not to be a beast when all others are? Do I have the right to pull the carpet from under my little fighter before his real fight starts? These questions gnawed on me. Only the most selfish man can resist them.

They know it, the bastards! That's why they came up with their blackmail and don't hesitate to use it. It's their style: They grab you by your genitals and hold. And you know damned well that in their other hand is a straight razor.

"Now I can really hunt you down!" My son interrupted my thoughts. He already had two kings and I was on a desperate flight. Better quit and flee the board entirely.

"I'm going to play the winner," Jana said, because she understood I had to think this out.

I'm enjoying a cigarette on the platform at the end of the train heading for Vienna. I've made it. I've succeeded in zigzagging through their bureaucratic minefield. Jana and I will have to sacrifice a lot, but our son will have a much better life. I am beyond their reach. Unbelievable.

Strange. How come I've slipped through? When the authorities allow somebody to travel to the West, they usually keep one family member at home, a hostage, the guarantee of return. Why did they let me go with my whole family? Will my defection provide them with one more stick to beat my parents with? My mom and dad will be desperate when they realize they won't see us again. They are not allowed to get passports, and I cannot ever go back because the authorities would find me guilty and sentence me for "unauthorized staying abroad." They will confiscate my property. Not that there's much of it, just a nice apartment maybe some comrade could use. They are only people, after all.

Do they know something I don't? Is Canada not accepting immigrants? Will Austria deny me asylum and return me straight to a Czech jail?

Or do they know that I'll fail? Do they know me better than I know myself? They have plenty of information in their dossier on me, and they command teams of psychologists, sociologists, all experts at breaking people down. Have they calculated that likely I will break myself down? Are they gambling that their indoctrination will be stronger than my reason and my resolve? That my sub-conscious mind will steam-roller me and I will humbly crawl back and let them parade me on TV? They've always arranged things so they can't lose.

Until now, our defection has been a conditional clause hinging on one word, "if." If they allow me to travel, if they allocate me hard-currency money, if they grant me an exit visa. "If" has made the whole project non-binding. Until now, the irrevocable decision lay in the future. I could have used the excuse that I wanted to emi-grate, but they prevented me. I wouldn't ever discover that I'm a weakling. At least I could be pissed off.

I light another cigarette.

They've outsmarted me. They've opened the door to the jungle, as if saying, "Help yourself! You are completely free to assume responsibility for your life – if you have the guts. A much worse jungle is in your head, we've made sure of that. You are a puppet in our hands. We've manipulated you since birth, and you've seen what happens to those who have tried to cut their strings. They collapsed. Go ahead, you self-opinionated fool! We're still holding your genitals, but now it's you who has the razor. We know you'll cut yourself free, sooner or later – if you don't slit your throat right away."

I have committed adultery with ideas forbidden by the church of socialism. Like a sinner in the Middle Ages I've been nailed to the pillory log through my offending member. It's the way they used to punish adulterers. Within reach of the condemned man they put a sharp knife. He has the freedom to choose. About the way he dies. Of hunger, or blood poisoning, or of bleeding to death after he cuts himself free. I'm nailed to the log. They've given me the blade.

Will I manage to carry out the third solution? To chip away at the log, pull out the nail, and remain relatively unharmed? After all, one can live with a nail hole.

I am both the sinner pinned to their log and a puppet they are still manipulating. Perhaps I can use the blade as a sword and cut the strings they have fixed to my head. Luckily, they are fixed to the outside head, not to the one that aches but is mine alone. Will the aching, underdeveloped head have enough presence of mind to carry me over, to assume control of my body, and to revitalize my wooden arms and legs so that I can stand upright on them?

If not, I can vegetate as well here as there, with you . . . the herd.

I'm watching the rails converging far behind the train. And I'm struck by the thought that they denied us the knowledge of perspective, tried to fool us into believing that the rails join on the horizon, making passage impossible. I passed that horizon a few minutes ago; the rails parted and let me through. In reality, parallel lines meet and cross each other in infinity. I'm rushing towards that point. Within the next two weeks the moment will inescapably come when I, Jana, and Ivo are in the middle of infinity, on the intersection of our past and future lives. I will have to die to be reborn. I will be alone.

I, the nail, the blade.

2

WITH THEO

DURING THE NIGHT the hot city sloughed off its haze. On the tin windowsill there were a few drops of dew. The fresh cool air and blue sky promised the most summery of summer days. Soon, we would go for a walk.

Theo and his girlfriend, Uli, met us at the station, and as soon as they smuggled us into their small hotel under cover of darkness, the floodgates of speech opened. Theo, just in his shorts, happy as a Buddha, presided over a table littered with bread, salami, cheese, brandy, Coca-Cola, and overflowing ashtrays. Words gushed from him as if from a shipwrecked sailor rescued from a desert island after two years. He reconnected the thread of speech his departure had snapped. At long last he could, with a gourmet's gluttony, spout out what he had read, heard, seen, and experienced – and all in Czech. He was the same person we used to know: a robust conqueror of life; smart, witty, playfully juggling words and images, capable of seeing tragedy through the eyeglass of comedy; sending his listeners into fits of laughter through his flamboyant language and imagination. His psyche didn't seem to be damaged in any way by the hardships of emigration: life in a foreign country, the struggle to master the German language, insulation from friends, life on welfare, and his dependency on Uli, with whom he's been living in West Berlin. Most likely he has hidden such hardships in the depths of his mind and has sealed the door. He will break the seal the day he sits down to write about it.

We decided to spend the day exploring both Vienna and Theo's experience with emigration. Our fate is postponed. We hopped along the sidewalk like kids on a trip near the end of the school year. We were on the main street of this neighbourhood – Thaliastrasse. At the corner we gaped at posters in a big shop window: Visit Jamaica! Dream Holidays in Tahiti! East African Safari! The Canadian Rockies Are Waiting for You! Only $2,400, on sale here, at Thalia Travel.

"Nice lures," I chuckled. "People come, check the prices, and then buy a week in a cheap country inn eighty kilometres from here, or an even cheaper week at Balaton Lake in Hungary."

"Some surely do," said Theo, "but some buy two weeks in Tahiti or in the Rockies. It's not as expensive as it looks to you. People really do travel there."

I shake my head. "Do you expect me to believe that? The seven hundred dollars I brought with me is almost my whole year's salary. Any of those trips would cost me my income for three and a half years."

"Yours, because there they ripped you off on both salary and exchange rate. For somebody working here, even Tahiti is affordable."

"Bank presidents, big businessmen, sports stars or pop musicians . . ."

"Nonsense! That's ideological crap. I mean ordinary people living in the apartments around here. Not every year, but occasionally. The West is not the East."

"Look, Mom, pears! Bananas!" A small greengrocer's shop was so full of fruit and vegetables they overflowed onto the sidewalk. Shallow baskets brimmed with cherries, apples, strawberries, pineapples, peaches. Nobody guarded these treasures except from behind the counter inside the dark shop. Ivo carefully chose a peach, two pears, and a banana. I bought them, along with some tomatoes and a green pepper. Why not pretend we're on holiday – in the West.

We boarded a streetcar that ran down a canyon of five- and six-storey apartment buildings. A street that could easily fit in some older quarter of Prague, except here there were more shops; almost all the ground floors were occupied by them.

"Look, this greengrocer's shop is owned by Mr. Radish," laughed Theo. "The owner must like what he sells."

"It would be a pleasure to shop there. It is not any anonymous 'Fruits and Vegetables, retail outlet #746,'" I agreed.

"When Mr. Schumacher repairs the heel of your shoe, you know he knows what he's doing because his great-great-great-grandfather was master of the craft when the names were given out." Theo developed the idea.

"He also gets free advertising." I took it one step further.

"It depends. I once saw a Mr. Blacksmith who was a dentist."

We were pushing foolishness into absurdity. The good old days were back.

Yellow and brown ceramic tiles at a corner shop spelled out Julius Meinl, Delikatessen. He used to do business in Prague, too. The shops remain, but the name has disappeared. The signs were torn down when they expropriated his chain. Perhaps one of the former first ladies had her jewelled fingers in it. She used to be a salesgirl in his firm before she married a locksmith who later, through abetting a few judicial murders, made it to party general secretary and president. But the people of Prague remember the name Meinl. Our grandmas used to buy coffee, tea, vanilla there. In those days they called it colonial merchandise. At home we had an old cocoa tin with an oval label showing a head of a black man with a red fez, the same sign they have above the shop entrance here. Are we in the times of our grandmothers?

Vienna resembles Prague. No wonder, she was the capital of the Empire in which Prague was a provincial centre. Both cities grew wildly at the end of the last century. But the atmosphere is different – Vienna is cleaner, tidier, more colourful, more relaxed. Perhaps the architecture is not the main thing.

With a merry chiming the streetcar entered an avenue called the Ring: six lanes of traffic, alleys of chestnut and lime trees, wide sidewalks – a boulevard in the grand style. It encircles the heart of the former Empire: the Imperial castle, ministerial and aristocratic palaces, the university. These are stately, expansive edifices commanding respect, but no more beautiful than their counterparts in Prague.

We got off at the Opera and walked down the sidewalk that once bore Haydn, Mozart, Beethoven, and all the others who turned Vienna into the musical capital of the world. Even today the air seemed filled with their melodies, and Mozart seduced our feet to a few dance steps. The world is ours, or at least Vienna is. We walked with eyes and ears wide open, alert, as befitting tourists. A fiacre, drawn by two white horses, passed by. The coachman looked as if he had the honour of serving the Emperor himself. His customers sat stiffly. They didn't point, didn't exclaim in amazement about what they saw, didn't even smile.

Across the Ring from the Opera was the Air Canada office. In the window was a mosaic of colourful posters: Lake Superior, Vancouver, a Newfoundland outport, Toronto. The touch of a distant dream.

"How about dropping in for a few booklets?" Uli suggested.

"You can't do that," I protested. "They only give them to people who buy tickets. I know the way it works in Prague. One bored clerk is doing her manicure because there are seldom any clients. They always say they have no booklets."

"Let's see." Uli motioned Jana and Ivo inside.

"Here they do give away booklets," Theo said. "They are here for you and not you for them. After all, you do intend to go to Canada, don't you?"

"Yes, but we don't know how to get there even if we are permitted to go. How can we afford the fare?"

"I couldn't find out. At the consulate in West Berlin, they refused to tell us anything. 'A genuine refugee doesn't care and flees because he has to,' the consulate clerk said. 'Everything will be revealed at the appropriate time to those who are accepted.' They have a distorted image of refugees running for their lives. From the movies, I suppose."

"How many people from the East can scrabble enough money together to pay for the tickets?"

"It must work somehow. I've never heard of refugees being stripped to their underwear and ordered to swim across the Atlantic. Now and then somebody would drown and the newspapers would have a field day."

"On the other hand, Canadians would have a guarantee they got only healthy and persevering people."

"Somebody would get around the rule, anyway. You know people are a swindling lot. The rich ones would buy a rowboat and even take some luggage with them."

"Can you be serious for a moment?" I pleaded.

"If you have to buy the tickets, you've got some money already and you'll work for the rest."

"How big a pile of dirty dishes does one ticket represent?"

"Smaller than you would expect. A ticket to Canada costs about four hundred dollars, so you need to make up five hundred dollars."

"If we need that much, I'll make it somehow. But what's the procedure once we get there?"

"I'm in complete darkness. I couldn't find out anything."

"About half of all Canadians are not born in Canada. There has to be some way to settle them, doesn't there?"

"Sure. You can't just let them step off the plane and send everybody into a new life with a mighty kick in the butt."

"Why not? That's what I expect, more or less."

"Human rights, you know."

"Never heard of them. From my experience, I expect the swimming and the kick in the butt."

Jana and Uli came back with Ivo, who was carrying an armful of booklets and flyers about Canada. Surprise!

The corner of Opera Ring and Mariahilferstrasse was occupied by the Lorenz Büchner bookstore. Who could resist this writer's and reader's paradise? Not me or Theo. There were thousands of books here for leafing through or reading. Most of the authors were unknown to me. But wait – Orwell's *1984*. High treason! Back home they would lock you up for owning or selling this book, while here you could buy a copy without special clearance! Kundera, Mňačko, Gruša – here were all the authors officially eradicated from the history of Czech literature because they fled the country. A complete edition of *Gulag*, with photographs! And, no! Marx. How could he be among the decent people? His theories justified some of the greatest massacres of this century. I would ban him at once!

"There's one trouble with bans," Theo reminded me. "To have Orwell on display here, you have to have Lenin, too. Solzhenitsyn's *Gulag* next to Stalin, who sent him there. This is freedom of expression. If you don't accept it, you'll end up with one wall filled with Marx and the remaining shelves full of those who sing his praises."

"If I were a millionaire I would buy up all the Marxes and throw them into a sewer."

"It wouldn't help. They would print more and even make money on you. Look here." Theo picked up a volume of *Das Kapital*. "Printed in Czechoslovakia. A contribution of the Ministry of the Interior to the export of the revolution. You wouldn't eliminate the disease. You would help to finance the subversion of the West. You just have to hope nobody reads it."

"Just like back home."

One whole section was dedicated to Emperor Franz Joseph. For Vienna he's the embodiment of a great past when she was one of the premier capitals of Europe, in the same league as London and Paris.

"Look at those kind, forget-me-not-coloured eyes." Theo opened a sumptuously illustrated biography. "You screwed up colossally, Your Highness." Insulting Franz Josef is deep-rooted in Czechs. Our grandparents fought him for independence or at least a confederation. But the Emperor's personality wasn't strong enough to spark hatred. Instead, he became the subject of slander and jokes.

"If he hadn't been so hopelessly mediocre in his later years, the history and the boundaries of Europe would look different, and we wouldn't be in the situation we're in now."

"Do you know what I've learned?" Theo roared with laughter. "In the census before the 1907 election, His Imperial Majesty stated as his 'occupation': civil servant, first class. Not a statesman, not even a politician, just a civil servant. Not the head of the Empire, but the head of the bureaucracy. No wonder Austria collapsed."

On our way out of the shop, I saw a rack of postcards. "How about sending some?" I wondered aloud.

"Save your money," Theo said. "By the way, I suggest you give nobody your address. Keep quiet until emotions at home subside and reason takes over. Reproach is the last thing you need."

So many stores! Their magnetic forces caused constant rearrangements of our small group. Jana and Ivo falling behind to look in a pet store; Uli showing Jana some lingerie; Theo and I buying two cigars to celebrate our reunion; Theo and Ivo checking out the window display of a postage-stamp dealer, while Uli took me and Jana into a florist to admire the orchids on sale.

There were stores with endless rows of clothing racks. Shoes by the hundreds. How many styles can man come up with to fit a single foot? Leather goods. Genuine oriental rugs, long extinct in Prague. Electronics everywhere. Stereos that would drive any audio fan crazy. Things I'd only heard of, such as computer games. Pocket calculators that cost a month's salary in Prague here cost peanuts.

A crucified Christ above a church entrance looked across the street at a big sizzling poster of a semi-nude beauty luring customers to a porn cinema.

We passed a half-empty café where people quietly sipped coffee or beer and read newspapers clipped to bamboo frames.

"There's so much of everything! But the stores are almost empty. People aren't buying. They don't have any money to spend," I said.

"Viennese are deliberate folks, and Mariahilferstrasse is one of the best-known shopping streets in Vienna and as such is relatively expensive. People have money, but there are so many stores that people don't have to crowd. You don't have to earn the right to your purchase by waiting in a line or fighting for it. If there were lines, another store would open next door. Law of supply and demand, you know?"

"Just theoretically, from school."

A newsstand with dozens of magazines shining with vivid colours. I was hit! Right between the eyes! At least twenty per cent of the magazines had naked or semi-naked girls on the covers. Not only men's magazines, but those about gardening and cars as well. It shocked me to see a beautiful girl showing her bare breasts to the traffic on the street, but the other pedestrians weren't crashing into lampposts, cars didn't swerve onto the sidewalk, streetcars remained on their rails. It was a visual refreshment in the boredom of everyday. Definitely a more pleasing image than one of a half-naked combine operator behind the wheel of his machine, urging you to meet the planned harvest quotas. Which of these two is more abnormal?

The similarity with Prague was obvious. Still, Vienna was a different world.

"This is how Prague might look if it wasn't for the dead-end street of socialism," I said.

"Don't be silly. Prague would be far more advanced – she was before the Second World War. Austria is a poor relative of the West.

The day before yesterday, when we came here from Berlin, I had the terrifying feeling I was back in Prague. Compared with Germany, everything was so small, poor, slovenly. I was soaked in sweat, afraid that I would never be able to sneak out again."

"How a city looks all depends on where you come from. Russian soldiers in Prague in 1968 thought they were in the West."

"Even small cities in Germany are more affluent than Vienna. And Germany is said to be a poor relative of the U.S.A. and Canada."

"You call this poor?" I spread my arms to include the shops crammed with goods. "I wonder what the rich ones look like."

"Multiply what you see by ten and you'll be close."

"My imagination fails me."

"Look there! McDonald's."

"What do they sell?"

"Fast food. Hamburgers, French fries, that kind of stuff. Good. Clean. Inexpensive. Ivo, how about a hot-fudge sundae?"

Instead of answering, Ivo rushed inside. We followed him, our bellies loudly reminding us it was time for lunch, though I felt uneasy about how much it would cost. A Czech tourist, travelling on a meagre government allowance, is not used to eating in restaurants.

We feasted from polystyrene boxes and drank Coca-Cola. Were we really in the West, or what?

"You're going to enjoy this everyday here."

"Look, it's not that I don't like Vienna, but wouldn't it be better to move to West Berlin with you?" I asked, motivated mainly by the prospect of having his support for a longer time.

"Forget Berlin. It would be a hell of a lot of fun to go through emigration together because we would turn it into a comedy, but it would be against your best interests. You want Canada, don't you?"

"Europe only as a last resort."

Theo took his time lighting a cigarette before he continued.

"Canada has quotas for immigration by states, not by nationalities. The Austrian quota is much higher than the German. It means you have a better chance from here, and that you'll get there quicker. For most emigrants, poor Austria is a transit state. Well-to-do Germany attracts everybody from Antarctica to the Chukotskiy Peninsula. And they want to stay there. Germany's got more than enough of us. Crowds of people have abused its asylum laws. The government can't stop the flood, so they make getting refugee status as hard as they can to discourage applicants. For almost a year before I was granted asylum, my permission to stay had to be renewed weekly. Every Wednesday I spent six to eight hours in the waiting line. Sometimes they closed right before your nose. I saw a guy stick his head in the window to claim his right, the window slid down on his neck and almost guillotined him. He had a huge laceration for three weeks afterwards. The next day you had to bring your renewed permit to another line, which took the whole day, to get financial assistance. This line was merrier though, because the whole family had to be present. Kids were running around screaming, pregnant women fainting, men cursing. I could have compiled a comparative thesaurus of cursing. What a pity I couldn't understand a single word. It would have been a beauty."

"So there's no easy way out for us," I said. "We've got to hit the bottom and drown alone."

"You won't drown. And you are not alone in the way that you were when you were concealing that you wanted to defect. Here the authorities won't proclaim you insane when you say you want to live in Canada. On the contrary; you'll find that gears shift, levers move, coils spring up, everything rattles and shakes. A machine catches you, pushes, pulls, shoves, and drives, and in the end spits you out in Toronto or Sydney. Just go along. They really try hard to help every honest person live his life the way he imagines. Perhaps it's one of the manifestations of freedom."

"Is Canada accepting any immigrants at all?"

"We should know more this evening. Uli is going to call Traiskirchen."

"What's that?"

"The door to that machine. It's the central refugee camp, the focal point of all those who flee here with their bag of hope. It's run by the Austrian government and connected to the whole world. Besides, there is a number of assisting organizations that won't let you drown. Before all the action runs its course though, you'll be on vacation, enjoying Vienna and McDonald's," he said cheerfully, finishing his coffee.

"I can imagine myself looking at the restaurant from the outside. And, if I'm really lucky, I might be doing some job in the back."

What a feast for Jana's eyes! Furs, the real and rare ones. Piles of shoes overflowing from boxes on sale. A hardware store. A jewellery shop glittering with real gold and diamonds. More clothing stores so full that their racks spilled out onto the sidewalk. People were digging through them as if the dresses were old rags. The prices, even for us, were very low. One season out of fashion turns elegance into junk.

The Herzmansky department store had six floors so thickly loaded with merchandise that they had barely managed to fit escalators in. The toy department had a huge pile of Lego, where three children were playing, supervised by a salesgirl.

"Leave me here," Ivo pleaded. "I'll build a rocket for you like this one." Before we could answer he was elbow-deep in the pile surrounding a six-foot-high rocket that a team of clerks must have spent a whole week making.

"You can do your shopping," the salesgirl assured us. "Just tell me his name and I'll call you on the PA system if necessary."

We wandered off to browse through the incredible plenty, the gluttony of consumer society. The crisis came towards the end of our tour, among pyramids of glass and china. For a while Jana just swallowed and winked hard, but then she collapsed at the corner of the display of Zwiebelmuster china and cried. Had the tension of the last days finally found an outlet? Could be. We crouched down, trying to comfort her. In vain. She was unreachable, enveloped in a waterfall of tears so unstoppable it seemed as if it would flow through the soaked handkerchief, down her skirt to the floor, then cascade down the escalator to the ground floor and out onto the street.

"Why can they have all this and we can't?" she sobbed. "What did we do to deserve it? Most of it is made in Czechoslovakia, the best quality. We had nothing, or only second or third quality. Why did they force us to live third-quality lives?"

Watch out! A man in a uniform! For a moment I was afraid we'd end up at a police station. Tear damage to the escalator, wet floors, unauthorized outburst of emotion in a public place.

Uli explained something to him in German and he escorted us to . . . the cafeteria. In a moment he was back with a glass of ice water and a cup of coffee for Jana.

"Are you sure it's nothing serious? Medical care is available, if you need it. Just ask any clerk," he said. He paused. "Despite this, I hope you like our department store."

We bought coffee for the rest of us and a shot of brandy to get Jana back on her feet. She slowly calmed down. So did I. Is this the way they behave in the predatory West?

Our son was busy in the toy department. He wasn't worrying about us at all. We rested.

"It's all right, darlings, it's all part of the process," Theo assured us. "I had it, too. Those weren't tears. Those were nerves. But after you have defected you will feel lightness, you will float, fly. One suitcase of property cannot hold you down. Suspense will play *pizzicato* on your nerves like old Paganini, but it's due to the cold draft of insecurity. Then one security after another will arrive: Here's the bed I can sleep in and even make love on. Sorry, that was a diversion. Here's a chair I can sit on, here's a table for my work. Here I have the possibility, even the right, to get a meal, and there I can go to a washroom. In time the security will grow and then you'll have some property, which in turn will bring more security. Just be patient."

"Twenty years?"

"Absolutely not. Three, four years. If you have a job it'll be faster. And you will no longer live a life of third quality. What you deserve, you get. It's up to you and no one else. You have already escaped from serfdom. You are free!"

"It hasn't yet made it through to my mind. I thought that guy was going to lock us up."

"Don't you feel it? Freedom is sitting here, in Vienna, sipping coffee with me, a national outcast. It's incredible! Isn't it beautiful to start from scratch again? To set your limits yourself instead of having them imposed on you by some politburo of slyboots? The way you make your bed is how you'll sleep. There's nobody here to force you into a cot for midgets because of the political sins of your forefathers or relatives. There's nobody to order you to sleep on a fakir's bed, unless you want to, of course. Your standard of living is up to you. Should you really hit rock bottom – if you can't stand any more, if you're hungry, or your cheeks are puffed up with the mumps – there is a safety net that won't let you die."

"In Germany. But in Canada?"

"It's pretty much the same throughout the West. Once they take you in, you're their man and they won't let you perish."

"Once they take me in." I finished my coffee with a deep sigh. "If they take me in."

"Have you ever been in a porn shop?" Theo had a twinkle in his eye.

"Don't ask such a stupid question. They haven't opened them in Prague since you left. You know that the comrades have always been strict guardians of our morals."

"Let's go then. You've got to experience this facet of freedom as well."

"I'm not in the right frame of mind. As for freedom, right now it weighs so much it's pulling me down like a backpack full of bricks."

"You've got to train for freedom."

"In lieu of thanking you for the advice, I'll tell you a nice story I heard in Prague about a training session that took place behind closed doors. They somehow got a few movies, rented a projector, and for a screen they hung a bedsheet over a curtain rail. Before they finished there was quite a crowd with sore necks down in the street, including two cops on the beat. When the show was over the cops came to the third floor, confiscated the movies and the projector, and took the organizer into custody. They charged him with causing an unauthorized gathering of people and gross indecency."

"I wonder if it was a movie produced by the Ministry of the Interior?"

"You must be kidding!"

"Far from it. You will learn lots of things here that you would never have guessed. The general decay in Czechoslovakia has gone much, much deeper than you can imagine. The truth is that our secret police have been one of the bigger producers of pornographic materials in Europe. They've been making more money from sex than from all the cultural exports combined. To get money for spying and financing subversion. The ends justifies the means, *n'est-ce-pas*? Why not support the feminist movement by selling pornography?"

"The same way they pay for the peace movement by exporting weapons."

"On that subject – watch out, brother. Russians occupied half of Austria ten years after the war and their, and our, secret services are well entrenched here. Not only in respectable businesses, but also in the underworld, in strip joints, illegal brothels, and so on. Keep your eyes wide open!"

★

We were sitting on a bench in a small park on the Gürtel in front of Westbahnhof. We couldn't take in any more. We were flooded. Our minds weren't registering what our eyes saw.

"I'm sorry we couldn't show you the West at its best – Germany – to make you understand the full advantages of living here," Theo said sadly.

"It was enough to turn our heads into a beehive. We should go home."

We picked the shortest route back through this city of plenty. Even though I had seen too much already, I still paused at the poster of Banff National Park in the window of Thalia Travel. I wished I could make a quick reconnaissance trip to Canada, just for a few days. To go with somebody to his work, see what his home looked like, talk with him. To get at least a glimpse of the country we have chosen as our new homeland. But I couldn't. Our emigration would be blind – irrevocable and scary.

"Do you recall who Thalia was?"

"One of the Muses, but I forget of what."

"Comedy, brother, comedy. I see it as the symbol of your journey. Put yourself under her protection and she will assure that you will see everything through the eyes of comedy."

"I can't wait for those side-splitting laughs," I sighed, as if my soul were leaving me.

Theo threw his short-sleeved shirt on the bed and made himself comfortable at the table. His eyes followed me and Jana, pacing in opposite directions between the door and the window, as if this large room were a jail cell. Ivo looked at the pictures in the Air Canada booklets.

"So, tomorrow to Traiskirchen?" Theo suggested tentatively.

No, not yet, two more days, one more day, I wanted to groan.

"Uli and I are running out of money. We must go back to Berlin tomorrow. You have to apply for asylum. The more you protract this agony, the more you will ruin yourself mentally and financially."

"Where is Uli?"

"Gone to make a phone call to Traiskirchen, to get detailed information."

"Are you crazy? Talking about defection over a public phone?"

"Relax, you're here and not there. Sit down and have a drink," Theo ordered. "There's a couple of inches left in the bottle. At least it will prevent you from drumming on the windowpane."

His fingers were playing with his glass when suddenly he turned serious, as if he was caving into himself. For the first time that day he took off the mask of a laughing tourist and spoke with slow deliberateness.

"It *is* shitty business. It definitely is! When I was standing at the gate of the asylum office, I had the feeling that I had just crossed a wooden bridge that I had soaked with gasoline. I had matches in my hand. If I stepped in that building, I would never be able to go back. Never. It was a tough moment, even though I had Uli to support me. The match weighed a ton and the matchbox at least ten. But a year of thinking and making preparations gave me momentum and it pushed me up the stairs. I struck the match and threw it over my shoulder. I haven't ever looked back at the burned bridge."

The door clicked. Uli was back. She was met with one attentive face and two imploring.

I wrote the information down on a piece of paper, clutching at the straw of habit from my work. Sort out, evaluate, process the information, and then make a qualified decision.

We can apply for political asylum at any police station and be transferred to Traiskirchen or go straight there.

Until the decision about asylum is made, the Austrian government will assume responsibility for our housing, food, other essentials, and medical care. It will assist in the emigration process. It will give us a small financial allowance.

Canada is accepting political refugees and their families according to criteria that are not available. Other countries currently accepting immigrants are the U.S.A., Australia, South Africa, and, in a negligible number, New Zealand.

It will be six to eight weeks before our asylum application is decided. The whole immigration process takes four to six months.

Was that it? Was there nothing more? My pen wandered on the paper. All I knew for sure was that for the immediate future we would be taken care of. But what if we were not granted asylum? Would it influence the Canadians? Would the Austrians give us work permits? Was it possible to find a job without one? What is their definition of a political refugee? Someone who has done time in jail for politics? Someone who has been tortured? Crumbs of information. I still knew nothing.

A quick exchange in German rattled between Uli and Theo. I detected some apprehension in their voices.

"I told you it's madness to speak about defection publicly!" I exploded.

"It has nothing to do with defection. But the phone is next to the hotel kitchen, and now they know you are stowed away here. They can kick you out or demand that you pay."

"Or call the police right away. We've already spent one night here."

"In this case you could apply for asylum right here," Theo burst into laughter.

"Goddamn it! Shut up, you stupid bastard! Take your so-called humour and shove it!" The pressure that had been building up in me since the morning erupted. "Pour me a brandy. No, give me the bottle!" Everybody was silent for a while.

"Sorry. I know you mean well. If you were not counterbalancing us, there would be nothing else to do but jump from this third-floor window."

"How about dinner?" Uli suggested, and she and Jana started to cut bread, tomatoes, cheese, and salami.

Theo and I leaned against the windowsill, watching the falling dusk.

"What is the West really like?"

"You've kept pressing me the whole day for the formula of the West in one sentence. There is none. It doesn't exist. Man lives here, works, is happy and unhappy like always and anywhere else. The huge difference lies in the fact that here he is free; he lives in a more normal world. What he does with this normality is entirely up to him."

"Do I have a chance here?"

"I can't guarantee you success. Nobody can. It's up to you and only you."

"I feel like a madman," I sighed.

"That's a good sign. Reasonable citizens back at home are already farting in their beds after a day wasted away by waiting in lines, reading lying newspapers, and voting unanimously at meetings. Now they are resting before the next day of waiting in lines, voting unanimously, and so on."

"Just before we left I heard they are preparing a new bill. Those who are unable to appreciate the advantages of socialism under single-party rule should be deprived of their legal rights. Failure to understand such an obvious thing would be sufficient indication of feeble-mindedness."

"What more do you need to convince yourself?"

"It's not a matter of reason. I'm scared. The unknown."

"That's just because you're undergoing it for the first time. Emigration creates terrible tension. You are naked in the world. You face a permanent IQ test in which you must prove you're able to come out on top in any totally unfamiliar situation. To do this you must dig from within yourself qualities you had no idea you possessed."

"I only hope little Ivo can cope better and easier than we."

"You bet. His home is where you are. In the long run you're preparing him for an incomparably better life than he would have there."

"Should I or should I not defect?"

"I can stand next to you, even hold your hand if you wish, but only you and Jana can and must make the decision. It's the first prerequisite of freedom. You must have the guts to take your life into your hands. That's the price for your right to become free."

"Afterwards, there's no other way but up, is there?"

"The worst is behind you, though you don't think so. You have already won the battle with inertia, momentum, and fear. You have crawled out from that latrine there."

"For how long will all that shit remain within us?"

"For a long time. Maybe for life. During our thirty-five years we've been soaked with it thoroughly. But its hold on your mind is bound to diminish. There's different air around here."

Eleven p.m. Uli sleeps quietly. Theo snores lightly. Ivo has finally fallen asleep, too. Jana is leaning against the headboard, her eyes closed, but I can tell by her breathing she's not sleeping. I am sitting in the window, trying to penetrate the darkness that hugs Vienna. The darkness that separates us from dawn.

Two a.m. The chimes in a nearby church are striking the hour. Jana sleeps fitfully. The darkness. The silence. The cold. The cigarette butts on the sidewalk under the window.

Suddenly, from that darkness a rope begins to materialize, the kind of rope high-wire artists use. It starts at this window and disappears in the night, but I know it continues above the rooftops and chimneys of Vienna, above the fields and vineyards beyond the city, high above the wild cliffs and rocky peaks of the Alps, across Germany and the lowlands of Netherlands, across the whole stormy Atlantic, the blackest darkness above it and the bottomless abyss underneath, and then it begins to descend towards Newfoundland, the frontier of the promised land. I know that though I've never walked on one before I have to step on this vibrating tightrope. My child in one hand, my wife in the other. Despite my doubts, despite vertigo, despite storms, gusts of wind, lightning, and darkness, I have to walk across those breathtaking depths, never doubting that, before my energy runs out and I fall, I will reach solid ground on the other side.

Foolish thoughts. I'd better crawl into my sleeping bag on the floor and try to get some rest. Mornings are wiser than evenings, as the folk proverb claims.

But . . . is wisdom what we need?

3

THE DECISION

I WOKE UP feeling as though somebody was driving a six-inch nail through my head. A migraine headache. The sky was dirty white, but it wasn't raining. If it were, it would have rained skimmed milk.

Had I slept at all? It didn't feel like it. A cold shower cleared my mind a bit.

While Theo and Uli ate their breakfast in the hotel dining room, we packed all our earthly possessions. When they came back they brought a tray with buns, butter, jam, cheese, and a pot of coffee.

"They've sent you all this stuff from the kitchen. They overheard Uli's talk with Traiskirchen yesterday and wish you good luck."

Jana and I exchanged glances. This couldn't be true.

"You see," Theo poured a cup of coffee for me because my hands were too shaky, "you're not alone, even now. Eat! You have to, even though you've got a lump in your throat."

The whole of Vienna was without contrasts, without shadows. Ashy. The Banff poster at Thalia Travel had lost its colourful appeal under this grey blanket. The yellow awnings of Mr. Radish's store were not pulled out. Every street was soaked in grey, even the chestnut trees on the Ring. Pedestrians didn't have the spark they had yesterday. The magazine stand irritated me. Cover your breasts, you shameless woman! How can anybody think of lust?

The motor train to Traiskirchen pulled out before we could make it across the busy intersection. But Uli found a bus waiting just behind a corner. It would take us there, too, even faster. On hearing our destination, the driver offered us a free ride. He gave us tickets, though, in case an inspector got on. Uli stayed with our luggage at the front and we collapsed in our seats. Theo began to tell Ivo a fairy tale. "Once upon a time, over nine seas and nine mountain ranges . . ."

Buildings, streets, cars, billboards, trees slid past the bus windows. An attractive part of the city, but we'd lost our tourists' eyes.

"The valiant prince on his quest for happiness sailed across the Atlantic Ocean to the kingdom named Canada. . . ." I could over-hear Theo. He was mentally preparing Ivo! Thanks. I still didn't know how we were going to tell Ivo that our vacation might have to be postponed. What lay ahead of us was as far from a vacation as I was from optimism. My fears were buzzing in my head like feverish hornets:

We're ground between two millstones. We're the children of parents whom we are hurting badly, but also parents of our son whose future we're responsible for. We'll be throwing away every-thing to get – what? Hope. But at whose expense?

Will they allow our nieces and nephews to enrol in university after we're branded as traitors? Should I instead throw in the towel and accept the blackmail? Why not flow with the current? Will I see my parents ever again? Will my dad's heart, weakened by two attacks, survive the terrible news? And Mom? Shut up, for heaven's sake, or you'll get a heart attack right here, right now.

"The prince was given his first task: overnight he had to produce a huge block of maple sugar."

Does a fairy exist somewhere who can advise me how to climb a diamond mountain and cross the Atlantic on a spider's thread?

Why do I have reason? And emotions that refuse to obey it? Have those bastards chipped away so much of my self-confidence that, when I have to lean on it, it will crack and I'll collapse? How much will I have to pay for what I call integrity? And why does integrity so often mean pissing against the wind? How come it was always the fools, their togas and trousers stained with urine, who pushed civilization forward?

We were leaving the city now, and as the horizon widened, the weight of the dark, ever-lowering clouds seemed to stifle the whole landscape.

My thoughts pressed harder and harder.

Suppose I do defect – that's the easy part – then what? So far I've lived my life in the lee of the family, school, job. I've always had the safety net of friends, acquaintances, my and my family's connections. I have gone through moral crises before, but never through the crisis of existence. What truth will I discover about myself when I'm under real pressure, in the fire and the frying pan, between the rock and the hard place, all at the same time?

Jana will support me, though right now she doesn't look like she can. She's had a harder life, she's more used to it, she's proved she can make it. Never under this kind of pressure though. We'll have no other source of strength but each other. Either the upcoming horrors will divide us or fuse us inseparably. To share the good and bad till death do us part.

Freedom is a comprehended necessity, they say. But now I reject the necessity for freedom. Defection is a felony. Only criminals desire freedom.

My headache is pounding. My stomach is dissolving into ulcers. A single letter separates defection from defecation.

How long can seven hundred dollars sustain us? Do I have within me the fierceness that will enable me to survive and protect our place in the sun? Not to protect it, to fight for it. I don't think I do.

"As a second task, the prince had to cut down the trees and build a marvellous log castle."

I wish Traiskirchen were over nine rivers and nine mountain ranges. *Stop time!*

How can these shaking hands carry my bags – let alone our fate? How can I rely on my reason when it's being ravaged by earthquakes, typhoons, and atomic blasts that blind me with their flashes so that, at times, I can't see even the neck of the passenger in front of me, much less the future?

There are acres of vineyards along the highway. Three bottles of their wine might solve my problems now.

Half past ten. Fourteenth of July, 1983. Some two hundred years ago this day, the people of Paris stormed the Bastille, giving rise to a new era, a modern concept of a citizen. *Liberté, egalité, fraternité.* They were a different breed of toughies then; they burst in and attacked their oppressors, while I am sneaking out to escape more beating. Is defection an act of courage or of cowardice?

Jana was immersed in silence, burrowed deep within herself. Now and then a solitary tear rolled down her cheek.

"Should we do it?"

"I don't know." Her fingernails tore at a handkerchief. "I'm blank. You must decide."

I must decide.

When I do, she'll clench her teeth and will get things rolling. Her helplessness is temporary. Her common sense has always counterbalanced my flights into barren theorizing.

"When the prince completed his third task, his horse said to him, 'Take your sword and with one mighty swing cut off my head.'"

Is our life in Czechoslovakia so unbearable we should throw it overboard? Is the vision of freedom stronger than the anchor to our past? If I abandon my country, will I perish? Is it possible to replant a thirty-five-year-old tree? Will our health betray me or Jana?

Too many question marks. My whole life has been a reaction to some question mark or other. It calls for an exclamation mark. *Action!*

We will be crossing the Atlantic on a tightrope. Darkness. Storm. Night. Abyss underneath. Is the tightrope even anchored on the

Canadian side? We'll find out when we're halfway across. Some do make it to the other side, but the bones of others lie scattered on the ocean floor. And if we cross over, we'll have to start from scratch and depend on strangers.

I have two hands and a head. Jana, too. Nothing more, but they will do. They will have to do. They are six cornerstones we can build on. I'll manage to marshal whatever we need for survival, won't I?

"The weeping prince cut off his horse's head, and his faithful beast was transformed into the most beautiful princess anyone had ever seen. A princess with a golden maple leaf on her forehead."

Uli got up and motioned us off the bus. The driver winked an encouragement. Good luck, folks.

We walked slowly across the few hundred metres to infinity. Behind a wrought-iron fence there were lawns, gravel paths, a playground, big chestnut trees, some large and some small buildings. It looked like a boarding school or a recreational centre. Children were playing noisily, adults seated on benches were talking or reading newspapers. Uli led us around a corner.

The gate is wide open in a welcoming gesture, except for a white and red striped bar across the driveway. Next to the gate there's a booth with two uniformed men. The sign with the crest of the Austrian republic on the masonry gate column reads *Flüchtlingslager Traiskirchen*. Theo doesn't have to tell me that it means "refugee camp."

Ivo sits on Theo's shoulders and presses his cheek against his hair. Theo is now the only one who can give him a sense of security. I wish I could. We drag our feet back and forth in the gate. My eyes search the others' for the tiniest bit of support. Theo's eyes, Uli's, Jana's, my son's. All of them are tense. Slowly, each movement followed by four pairs of eyes, I reach into my shoulderbag for our passports.

Two green booklets with the gold imprint of the Czechoslovak Republic coat of arms on the cover. The emblem features a lion, for a millennium the symbol of the Kingdom of Bohemia. He was all right. I neither want to nor can part with him, he's part of me. But above his head, where for centuries a crown shone as the sign of an independent kingdom, there is now heraldic nonsense. The five-pointed star of socialism. They stole the lion's crown of independence and replaced it with the star of vassalage to the Soviet Union. This star has driven me here.

"I can interpret for you," Theo offers.

"I will . . . myself," I whisper inaudibly, but I know he understands.

The two passports are growing heavy in my hand, as if they are thick autobiographies. First shriek in a maternity ward in Prague, first steps, first words, the sandbox in Kinsky's gardens, skipping rope in Grébovka, my first walk to school, vacations with my grandma in Chotouň, listening to my grandpa in a beehive shed, eating the cherries at the top of a tree, first kiss, exams, graduation, wedding, never-ending strolls through the streets of Prague with Jana, with Theo, friends and a handful of loved ones, our first tiny apartment, three thousand books, a literary and non-literary career, the conception and birth of our son, the graves of our forefathers, the love of Jana's sisters and my parents . . . and the whole enveloped with the fabric of the mother tongue we speak, think, and feel with.

Those passports are more than a symbol of the state, more than a symbol of the nation. I can feel roots sprouting from them, the roots of our lives, our beings. They tickle my palm. I grasp them instinctively. I should hold them fast and never let them go.

Am I to give all this to a cop? For hope?

I can see nobody. I am alone. The heart of infinity. The open razor. Time has stopped.

"I apply for asylum as a refugee."

4

IN THE CORRIDOR

I WOKE UP. The rising sun was shining straight on my bed. A quarter past six. Almost twelve hours of deep, uninterrupted, dreamless sleep. My mind was clear and bright. I knew where I was; why I was there. I rolled over in bed, and our roommate, a Romanian doctor, put his finger to his lips. The others were still sleeping. I gathered my clothing and a toilet bag and followed him into the corridor.

"The more they sleep, the better for them. In the meantime we'll bring breakfast."

The washrooms were still empty and acceptably clean. I washed my face, brushed my teeth, and put on my jeans and a T-shirt. The doctor was waiting at the door, holding two jugs, one big, one small. At the end of the corridor a group of sleepy people gathered. The representatives of each room. They'd pick up breakfast for the whole dormitory so that the others could sleep longer. A smiling cop emerged from his office. He read the room numbers aloud, making sure that every one had a representative present so that nobody would miss the meal. Then he unlocked the door and led us to the basement. Another cop followed the group.

"They don't want us to mix with the others. There's all sorts of people around here, including some riffraff, and we have to get some rest first and round up our wits," the doctor explained.

I recalled what he told me yesterday: Our corridor was locked because it was the special wing for newcomers, but the rest of the building was a regular refugee camp. In it lived the people waiting to go overseas and also those who had already gone, but had failed and had come back, or those whom all countries had rejected. Some of them had been wasting away in Traiskirchen for five, six years. They lived at the expense of the Austrian government, and more often than not they were drunks. Sometimes they stole, sometimes they fought. A few days before, they pushed somebody out of a fourth-floor window.

The mess for refugees in the basement was spacious, clean, and well lit by large windows close to the ceiling. Long rows of tables and chairs were empty. For the regulars, who ate in this room, breakfast began at seven. As we moved along the serving counter, the cop called out the number of people in each dormitory, and in a big brown paper bag we got buns, bread, salami, cheese, yogurt, and either oranges or peaches; the big jug was filled with tea, the small one with milk.

"Don't be surprised by the peaches," the doctor smiled, "I know they are scarce, in my country even more than in yours, but you'll see for yourself the sorry state that many people come here in. To prevent their collapse they need nutritious food and lots of vitamins, at least for the first few days. That's why we get special rations."

We climbed the stairs and I felt like I was back in kindergarten. One cop in front led, the other one followed, both keeping a sharp eye on us so that we wouldn't get lost, trip and scratch our knees, or fight for the peaches. Not until the door to the corridor was safely locked again did they disappear into their office and we dispersed to our rooms. My family was still sleeping, and the doctor decided to have a short nap as well. I loitered in the sun-lit corridor, reliving what had happened yesterday.

The cop at the gate took my passports as if they were bus tickets and went away with them. We waited for half an hour. When he came back he escorted us to an office. First a short form had to be filled in. In a few minutes we confirmed our decision with our signatures. We waited some more in a hallway with a grey-faced Hungarian for whom they had to get an interpreter.

The arrival of a big cop meant we had to say goodbye to Theo and Uli. They had to hitchhike back to Germany and then take a plane to West Berlin. Berlin lay in East German territory, and if Theo was caught there, he'd be locked up and extradited to Czechoslovakia.

"Thanks, brother, you gave us a hand in the worst moments."

"Keep your spirits up and keep us posted. Don't lose your cheer when the shitty side turns up. Just remember Thalia and laugh it off. See you . . . somewhere in this world."

The cop grabbed our two big suitcases and gestured to us to follow. We picked up our remaining luggage and trailed after him through the back door, across a small park, down the asphalt road, then down the gravel path towards the main building. A U-shaped structure, five storeys, with the unmistakable look of a military barracks. Up the wide stairway. Ivo couldn't take his eyes off the big six-shooter hanging at the cop's hip. On the upper floor the cop unlocked a door, let us pass, and locked it again. Then he motioned us through another door.

It was a police office like any other. Worn-out wooden tables and chairs, typewriters, filing cabinets, a closet full of forms and papers. Two policemen with fatherly looks. If it hadn't been for their grey uniforms and guns, each could have passed for a small-town postmaster or stationmaster. They apologized for having to submit us to a few procedures.

Jana had revived. The decision had driven away her apathy and she had found new energy from God knows where. She took over, interpreting for me because only she spoke German.

Each of them took one of us. Ivo was given crayons and paper to keep him busy while we were questioned.

It was how it must be when they arrest somebody. A detailed description: Height – 190 cm, weight – 86 kg, build – medium, oval face, blue eyes, brown, slightly thinning hair, no distinguishing marks except an appendectomy scar. Dental history, and about a hundred and fifty other bits of physical description. The "postmaster" had a worse time with me than his colleague did with Jana. The few hundred German words and basic grammar I crammed into my head shortly before our departure didn't provide for fluent communication. Most of the time we used sign language. If I had been in a different frame of mind, I might have enjoyed it. It was like a silent Chaplin movie. But these two cops handled dozens of people of different nationalities and languages every day, and their pantomime had been honed to perfection. Within an hour everything was done, including fingerprints. Perhaps I should have felt uneasy when they registered me as if I were a criminal, but, oddly enough, I was satisfied. I felt I belonged here and I understood and even appreciated the care they took to weed out potential and real criminals and troublemakers.

"That was smooth." The "stationmaster" rubbed his hands with satisfaction. "What's your situation regarding clothing, toilet supplies, and female hygiene?"

"We have all we need."

"Good. Should you lack anything just pound at our door. We've got plenty of everything in the stockroom. Don't be shy."

"Thank you very much, officer."

"Now, it's almost three o'clock. Aren't you hungry?"

"We can cope, but perhaps something for our son." In the corner of the office there was a small stove top crammed with big pots. They ladled out three huge servings of beef with mushrooms and rice and handed us a jug of tea.

"Follow me," said the big cop, who had just brought in another newcomer. He led us down the long corridor. Small groups of people gathered here and there followed us with curious eyes. The cop stopped at door number eighty-two. An oblong room with plank flooring, a big wooden table with several chairs, five military bunk beds, and a tall window above a radiator.

A young man sprang up from the table and helped us with our luggage. He shook our hands cheerfully again and again, as if he were happy, as if he were congratulating himself that he had us for company.

"Don't worry, sergeant, I'll take care of them. I'll show them around."

"See you later." The friendly giant nodded.

We took the two bunk beds next to the window. Luggage on one upper bed, Jana on the lower, Ivo on the other lower, and I above him. Then we ate our meal. I hadn't enjoyed a meal so much for a long time. For a moment I thought they must have a wonderful cook. On second thought, maybe the cook's skills weren't the most important ingredient.

"May we offer you a cup of coffee? We brought some with us," I asked our roommate, who was at the table, busy with some papers; his wife leaned against the headboard of her bed, reading a book and chain-smoking.

"With pleasure! What a treat! We ran out of it yesterday morning." He pushed his papers aside to make room for the cups.

"French, English, German, or, if the worse comes to the worst, Russian," he offered in German.

I chose French. I took it at high school and then at university. I hadn't used it for years, but I hadn't forgotten everything.

Our roommates were Romanians, both physicians. They'd already spent four days here. They also wanted to go to Canada.

"How did you manage to get out? I heard that Romania is almost sealed air-tight."

"Because of an error by our beloved Securitate," he laughed. "I attended a pediatric conference in Salzburg in Austria. The day it closed, my wife was on her way to a surgeons' gathering in Trieste. She just went through Italy and we met here, at the gate. The all-powerful secret police overlooked the fact that for a day we would be in the West simultaneously." His wife nodded, managed a hint of a smile, but her eyes were turned inward, to some point in the past.

"I wonder if you could help me." He pushed an application for a Canadian immigration visa in front of me. It was filled in in pencil, many times erased and rewritten. "Wouldn't it be better if I put —"

"For heaven's sake, you have a son's name in here. Where is he?"

He, too, caved into himself.

"At his grandma's," he whispered.

"Will you be able to get him out?" From Czechoslovakia that feat would be next to impossible.

"I hope so. In some perverted sense, our Securitate plays fair. It's true that escaping is nothing short of a miracle, but once you've succeeded they let the rest of the family go. The paperwork takes about a year, but we can't apply until we're in Canada."

A rough deal if there ever was one! And I thought we had it hard.

"There's nothing we can do about it now," he sighed. "The poor boy will have to tough it out for a year and a half. That's the price for a better life for him."

"I wish he didn't have to pay it at the age of four," I sighed, too.

We attacked the questionnaires and applications. Not only for Canada, but for the U.S.A., Australia, and New Zealand as well. The doctor cheered up a bit. He talked and talked, neither expecting nor demanding an answer. I listened because I understood he had to talk the whole evening, talk all the time till he flew to Canada; that he had to fill in the applications again and again, even for countries he never intended to go to, that he had to keep himself frantically busy to avoid thinking, to keep one step ahead of his desperation.

"Today's bedtime story, children, was written for you by Ivo Moravec, and it is called 'Shaggy Fluffy,' " said the announcer over our transistor radio.

"Listen well, Terry, that's about us," my son said to his teddy bear, hugging him and leaning against me.

Of course it was about them. It was one of the few literary works of mine that ever made it public. The peak of my writing career so far: a series of four fairy tales on national radio. And of all the days they choose to begin broadcasting them, they've chosen today! The words of the story I created reach me as if from a previous life that had ended. And yet, it hadn't quite ended, its reverberations reached all the way to the camp as a message from my dead self to my living one. From my position at the absolute bottom I enjoyed my summit, my good fortune. They didn't know I was here yet, they hadn't banned my stories yet. For four days I could send messages to myself, words of encouragement, proof I wasn't a nobody, that I had succeeded, that I knew something.

"Good night, children." The announcer closed the broadcast.

After breakfast we sat down with the doctor once again.

"I apologize, but I remember almost nothing from yesterday's conversation. I didn't really take it in," I admitted.

"I noticed that when you mixed up French and English, but it happens to all of us here. Everyone comes as if he were hungover after a two-week drinking spree. It's just the reaction to extremely high levels of adrenalin. In a few days you'll be all right, just like us."

Still, I could see that he, too, had some distance to cover to get back to normal. His wife had been staring at her closed book for the last two hours.

"What's ahead of us?" I asked.

"You're going to be here for five, maybe six days. You'll get some rest, they will question you about your asylum claim, then they will transfer you. Either somewhere else in this camp, but I don't think so, or to one of the lodges they have subcontracted all over Austria. That's where they usually send families with children. A holiday in the Alps till the Canadians invite you for an interview, and then there again till departure."

"How many refugees does Canada accept? How picky are they?"

"Relatively large numbers. They use some kind of point system: language proficiency, occupation, family circumstances. They prefer complete families and decent people."

"What professions do they favour?"

"None. We're disadvantaged, my friend. They don't seem to care about higher education too much. If you were a tradesman, carpenter, welder, locksmith, plumber, technician, perhaps the door would be open wider. It's tougher with a university degree in Canada."

"I thought that every nation jumps at educated people it can get for free."

"So did I. But it looks like it's not always the case. Don't ask me why. I don't know their criteria exactly though. I just heard this. When I'm out of here I'll go to the WCC to ask them."

"What's that?"

"A support organization, the World Council of Churches. Check them out, too. They'll give you advice on how to handle the interview. They have an office in Vienna. I must have the address somewhere –" He began to search his papers.

"Do you think they might tell me about their criteria at the Canadian embassy?"

"They're tight-lipped. Still, you might drop in for some newspapers, you know, English-language training."

"And if they reject you?"

"No appeal. The embassy's got the final word."

Between seven and nine a.m. the corridor was almost empty. Now and then some figure with a towel and toilet bag, or just with a toothbrush and toothpaste, headed for the washroom. But at nine a.m. it came to life. It was a wide, spacious hallway paved with large yellow ceramic tiles, whitewashed walls painted light brown to eight feet. On one side were the doors to the dormitories, on the other side, except for two rooms and washrooms, were high windows that let in the morning sunshine. People were strolling its length, children running around or playing in its corners. But, most important, small groups were forming according to nationalities or language abilities, gathering in semi-circles around radiators on which empty cans served as ashtrays. The corridor was a kind of a debating club, buzzing with talk the whole day. Everything that anybody felt impelled to share was discussed. A great many victories were told and retold, plenty of *laesa crimen majestas* were committed, seas of suppressed injustices found their outlet for the first time. Beyond the reach of their oppressors, people had the urge to talk about everything that had driven them to defect. The corridor was one huge fifty-metre-long and five-metre-wide confessional.

Two Czech families with children came yesterday, not too long after us.

"So, what mountains did you have to trek over?" asked somebody who had taken this route.

"Never left the road. We came through Yugoslavia all the way here," they answered.

"Then you must have green passports." Besides the regular green passports valid for all countries of the world, Czechoslovakia issued special ones, grey ones, valid only for Yugoslavia and nowhere else.

"How could we get them? We made it through with the grey ones." The storyteller paused to increase tension, sipping tea from a china mug with a broken handle.

"Don't tell me the Yugoslav guards let you pass! You'd be the first ones I've heard of." The speaker scratched his head in disbelief.

"We didn't ask them," the two men laughed. "We made sure we wouldn't have to beg." Finally, they were getting into their story.

"Two weeks ago some friends came back from Yugoslavia. They had made it all the way to the border, but the guards wouldn't let them pass. They locked them up overnight and told them if they tried once more they would confiscate their passports and report them to the Czech authorities."

"That's true," one listener confirmed. "They threatened us with the same thing."

"Our friends came back. They didn't have the nerve to cross the mountains with a baby. But they told us what that border crossing looked like. My pal Joe," he motioned to his stocky friend with his thumb, "is an artistic blacksmith and he can do anything with iron. We hatched our plan together. I fetched the material and he welded a special roof-rack. Inside it he hid some black-market money we had, jewellery, and the kind of things we couldn't risk taking in the open. Really nice work, nobody could detect anything."

"We reached the border just after midnight. Less traffic at that time. We put the suitcases inside the car and lowered the roof-rack so it covered the windshield. That was our plan. Have you noticed the bars at the borders are always high enough to smash off your head?"

"At least your teeth, if you're lucky," we agreed.

"The only thing we didn't know – was the bar made of wood or metal? It was about four inches in diameter."

"Lucky bastards. At the Rozvadov crossing to West Germany, the bar is made of a steel I-beam, filled with concrete. Three feet by three feet! Two electrical motors are needed to open it. My uncle has seen it!" another listener contributed. "They say it can stop a tank at full speed!"

"We waited for some time until there was no traffic. Then we started. The children lay down on their mothers' laps in the back to have some protection; Joe and I were in the front. At first I drove defensively, but after the last turn, when I could see that nothing and nobody was in my way, I stepped on it. When I got to the bar I was doing well over a hundred."

"I closed my eyes," Joe confessed.

"The bar bent the Mercedes star and then slid up the hood. Splinters and pieces of wood flew everywhere, and I had to slam on the brakes because the Austrians were only three hundred metres down the road. Even before I stopped, Joe was springing from the car and running to customs. Gentlemen, gangster movie revisited."

"It must have driven the Yugoslavs crazy!"

"I could see one of them in my rearview mirror. He ran after us loading his AK-47. But he reached us too late. Joe had already given our passports to an Austrian officer. The Yugoslav guard yelled at us till his mouth was foamy, as if he had rabies. He wanted to drag us out of the car, but the Austrian explained that we had already applied for asylum and thus were under the protection of Austria. He couldn't let him take us because there are certain rules. The guard was half out of his mind; he wanted to shoot us, or himself, or the Austrian. In the end he just kicked the car door and went back to his post, still shouting curses over his shoulder."

"I've never heard of a shooting at that border. It's probably prohibited. But how you can tell for sure?" said the man who had made it across the mountains.

"The Austrian checked out our roof-rack with admiration and then said, 'It wasn't your escape that worked him up so much. It's that you were the third to smash their bar this week alone. Though nobody did it with such style.'"

"Everything ended well, I see. Nobody got hurt? How about the children?"

"They got a kick out of it. That Mercedes, though old, is a tank. We've lost only these china mugs, they broke in the trunk." He pointed at his handle-less mug.

"It's worth it, isn't it?"

"When we left the border half an hour later, we could see the Yugoslavs bringing in a new bar. It had already been painted."

In our room the doctor was frantically gathering his papers. Their names had been called over the PA system. Their stay here was over.

"I left some tobacco and papers for you. I got them from my predecessor. Everybody who smokes runs out because nobody assumes he'll be locked up."

"Where will they send you?"

"I don't know yet."

"Thanks for all the information."

"Just pass it on to someone else."

"I'll miss you. We've known each other only twenty hours, yet I feel we've been pals since kindergarten."

"Maybe we'll meet some day. Maybe in Canada."

For half an hour we'd been leafing through the Air Canada brochures with Ivo.

"What would you say if we made a trip to Canada?" Jana asked him, risking a direct question.

"I'd like that. Will we go fishing, just like on this picture?" Ivo pointed at a photo showing a camper on a riverbank somewhere in the Rockies, and a father with two children fishing for trout.

"Sure we'll go fishing, but it will take some time. We've been thinking, we might move to Canada for good." I waited for his reaction.

"We think we might like it better there than in Prague," Jana added.

"Will we sail in a big ship across the Atlantic?"

"Something even better." I warmed up, encouraged by his positive response. "We'll fly in a huge airplane and we'll see the ocean from above."

"Will I have a seat by the window?"

"I think it can be arranged."

"And will Grandma and Grandpa come to see us there?"

"Sure they will, but it will take some time, too. We'll have to check it out first to know what to show them and where the best fishing is."

"That's fine. It's going to be a big holiday."

"A big holiday, Ivo. A holiday for a lifetime."

★

Before evening another newcomer arrived. He wore only a shabby T-shirt and jeans, freshly ripped in several places.

"Somebody must have mugged you in Vienna," we welcomed him.

"No time for that. I've never been to Vienna. They brought me straight here from Heidenreichstein."

"There's no crossing there. How did you get through?"

"From my cottage. Over the wires."

Silence. Our jaws dropped. An escape from Czechoslovakia over the wires was generally considered impossible.

"Yes, over the wires," he repeated, enjoying his celebrity, how he left us breathless.

"Well, in that case, you've got to tell us everything to the last detail," one man said, rubbing his hands in anticipation of an exotic story.

"My brother fled in 1968. He's in Australia. That's why they wouldn't let me go anywhere in the West, not even to Yugoslavia, in case I defected, too. When I realized the legal ways were closed, I applied for permission to buy a cottage inside the restricted border zone. Two years later the permission came and I bought a place not far from the border. It was a ramshackle hut, so I spent a few years repairing it. But I always found time to wander in the woods, picking wild mushrooms. I walked, looking not so much for mushrooms as for the location of their cameras, booby traps, tripwires, and other devices that send up a signal rocket or set off an alarm in the barracks. They caught me quite often, but I always flashed my permit and they had to release me.

"I came to know the bush like the back of my hand. The guards got to know me, too, from the woods and from the local pub. After a few beers they would tell me a lot of things. I learned the trails and the schedules of the patrols and how much time they needed to get to any spot if they detected an intruder. I discovered that the border line was a few hundred metres behind the wires, and that a road beyond and parallel to the wires enabled them to react really fast if somebody succeeded in getting over.

"I waited for five years. Twenty-two times I was locked up overnight, and I was arrested at least a hundred times. This morning, I made my move. Ideal weather for mushroom picking, with patches of mist just above the ground. It was now or never. I went like this, with nothing but a basket and a mushroom knife, strong enough to cut the wires. I snuck my way through the booby traps and I was lucky, none went off. I picked mushrooms all the way. In one area the forest stretches almost to the wires, then there is some thirty metres of tall grass. The sentries in the watchtowers had half an hour till the end of their shift, so everybody was thinking more of bed than of watching. I crawled on my belly all the way to the wires. There's one spot with a small depression where the wires run a little above the ground. Just as I was trained to do it in the military, I squeezed underneath. Then I sprang up and sprinted forward, literally for my life. Of course they saw me, but I was counting on the fact that a beer-drinking buddy would feel uneasy shooting at me. I was about a hundred and fifty metres beyond the wires when they opened fire, more for an alibi than to kill me, I suspect. The bullets hit the dirt at least ten metres behind my heels. I flew over the road, through a small forest, some meadows, another thicket. I ran and ran because I couldn't be sure I was in Austria. I feared they still might come for me if I wasn't far enough away. In the end my legs gave out and I collapsed into a ditch. Damned cigarettes, I thought my lungs would burst. After two hours I had recuperated a little and I stumbled to the nearest village. I found a cop to give me asylum. He told me my cross-country sprint had been over four kilometres long."

"What a story! I'd never believe it possible." The blacksmith who had fashioned the roof-rack shook his head.

"They gave me something to eat and plenty to drink and let me sit in jail a few hours. Boy, I was looking forward to seeing my brother in Australia. I left my basket of mushrooms at the wires. The *corpus delicti*, I suppose, when they put me on trial. By the way, could somebody lend me a pen and a piece of paper so I could write to my brother? And how about a smoke?"

The next morning, the washrooms and toilets weren't too crowded. Somebody was washing his socks in a basin, someone else, invisible behind a plastic curtain, was whistling loudly in the shower. I checked all sixteen cubicles. Eleven were in working condition, five clogged. I had seen worse. I picked the cleanest one and sat down. The sheet-metal walls, painted khaki, were covered with graffiti, as anywhere in the world. But in the minds of the men at Traiskirchen there was no sex, only politics.

In the light smell there floated cries of human souls that for the first time in their lives could express themselves freely about the horrors they had just escaped. Some of the graffiti were mathematically exact. The name of a politician or a dictator, an equals sign, and a picture of an animal, a part of the human anatomy, or the gallows. Others used language, sometimes a single noun, but in most cases the noun was embellished by a string of adjectives. I was sorry that swearing is in idiom and rarely uses international words. I might have learned something. Most of all I wished I could have deciphered the terrible oath of some poetic soul who, judging by structure and rhyming scheme, had expressed himself in the form of a sonnet. The poem, written by a passionate hand, offered an opinion about Hungary, socialism, and the Soviet Union. What a pity I could not understand it all; the Hungarian language is renowned for the richness and foulness of its swearing. It must have been a beauty; sonnets are not written by barbarians.

For me these cubicles, these confessionals, these wailing walls, revealed more about the contemporary world than all the media combined. If I had the money, I would buy all sixteen cubicles, including the clogged bowls and the faint stench, just for the graffiti. I would buy them and donate them where they belong – to the Museum of Man.

I stared at the ceiling. I lay motionless on my bed, but I was boiling. I didn't feel right. I felt cheated. An hour earlier, we had come back from asking about our asylum claim. I wasn't given a chance to present my case the way I had intended to.

They stopped me, politely but firmly, whenever I wanted to get into some detail or other. Stick to the questions, please. Present facts only. Facts are a nice thing, gentlemen, one can put them in a few lines. But it's their consequences that for almost fifteen years have soured my life with desperation and hopelessness.

Let me speak.

Granted, you know about the persecution of well-known dissidents. But how much do you know about the gradual stifling of an ordinary man? The whole repressive machine is very well hidden these days. I suppose you also know how they blackmail citizens by punishing their children. But do you know that avoiding politics is impossible? *Everything* is politics. Active participation in party politics is demanded. Have you ever been, gentlemen, in the situation where you could not agree and must not disagree? My steering clear of politics was a strong political statement.

My father was a politician. Very high level. One of those who triggered the Prague Spring of 1968, one of its major players. One of the first to be expelled from the party, fired from his job, marked for revenge. The only work they let him do was in construction. He didn't break, he didn't recant. On the contrary, he became a dissident. He attracted new waves of revenge.

I was not interested in politics. I experienced it at too close range to be attracted to it. I witnessed the murderous power of socialist politics. I didn't fight against it.

All the same, I was a victim of its revenge.

Proof? There is none, except, perhaps, in the archives of the secret police. The comrades played their dirty game from behind the scenes so they couldn't be caught with filthy hands.

Persecution? Interrogation? Jail? Torture? Gentlemen, advanced socialism rarely uses overt violence. It tarnishes the image at home and abroad.

Invisible violence – that's another story. Violence to minds, integrity, souls. No one has ever proved torture marks on the soul. Perfectly invisible. Perfectly lethal. Killing from the inside, killing the reasons for living.

Interrogation at police headquarters? No need. They knew what they wanted from their informants around me. They learned more from their regular political screening and evaluation at my work, and the rest – most likely – from bugging my apartment. My father used to live there, before me, and they surely bugged him. During his interrogations it was plain they were well informed about my activities.

Was I ever jailed in a concentration camp? The whole of Czechoslovakia is rounded with barbed wire, you know that. In a jail cell? I had my own custom-made cell. Portable, invisible, with moving walls that gradually shrank my breathing space. I was like a mouse in a cybernetic maze. It starts running and a secret police "researcher" puts an invisible wall in its way. The mouse bloodies its snout. Through the process it discovers, step by step, where its limits are.

More specifics? Here they come:

For two and a half years I studied at university with a sword hanging over my head, not knowing the day or hour they would kick me out, despite my excellent academic record. Finally, I passed the state exams and defended my thesis. At last, a few days of rest before graduation.

My student scientific work made it through the university and national rounds into the international one. One of the fifteen best theses in economics in Czechoslovakia that year, gentlemen.

There was a party to honour the winners. Music, dance, wine, women, singing, as the saying goes. Finally, some fun after years of tension and anguish. Till a drunk comrade professor told me at a urinal, "Don't cheer too much, and keep your mouth shut. At the party committee we have still not decided if we should let you graduate or not!" I confess, gentlemen, to wanting to stick his head in a toilet bowl and flush. He was saved by my guess that since he had warned me, he might also put in a good word on my behalf when my graduation came up for the vote. His indiscretion was the first open indication I had that I was the object of the authorities' particular attention.

One month later, besides the routine interview, I had to undergo a special investigation at the economics research institute where I had applied for a job. The party committee questioned me for two hours about my political opinions. I made it through without compromising myself. Very exhausting.

They hired me anyway. Presumably because that research institute was somehow off the fast track where power, prestige, and careers were made, so it had softer standards of political correctness. But they denied me access to the secret data. In Czechoslovakia, as you may know, most economic statistics are secret. What possibility of serious work had I been left with, then?

Neither having written the best thesis on the faculty nor my award-winning scientific work as a student was sufficient for the comrades to approve my application for PhD studies. They closed the door on my academic career.

When I met my thesis tutor I learned that I would not be allowed to participate in university research. I knew he had a high opinion of my abilities and I considered him a relatively decent man. He told me they might consider my application for a position with a university research team if I publicly denounced my father and applied for party membership. I could not. I was deeply offended.

I had bloodied my nose hitting two invisible walls. A scientific career prohibited, a working one restricted.

After a year at work I was drafted for compulsory military service. I was banned from command though I had been trained for it as a non-commissioned officer. I admit, I wasn't angry about that; a military career never had any appeal for me. I mention it just as further proof of politically motivated discrimination.

The fourth wall I hit unexpectedly. Forty-eight hours before my departure to a four-day meeting in Poland, the Ministry of the Interior refused to issue me a passport. Never mind that my employer had designated me for the trip and that I had prepared the whole agenda for the meeting. The denial of a passport is, gentlemen, reserved almost solely for political offenders. I was to be deprived of the informational benefits of travel and tourism abroad. Why, then, should I go on studying foreign languages? Why go on with anything?

The rejection of my second application for PhD studies drove me, after some six months of brooding, to the edge of the decision to write off economics as the cornerstone of my professional life.

I gave them yet another chance. I spent a year creating and testing a hypothesis and writing a research paper on it. On my own initiative, beyond my research program, at home, at nights, at the expense of my family. They didn't even let me defend it, never mind publish it. Stirred waters showed me more invisible walls: I could not become even a lowest level manager; I could not lead a research team, nor become an independent researcher. My name must not appear on research reports unless hidden among those of others who "co-operated."

How would you feel, gentlemen, at thirty, knowing the work you love and are good at is not wanted? Why spend years studying just to be sentenced by an anonymous somebody at the Ministry of the Interior or the party to spend the rest of your life as a clerk, crunching numbers for the reports of your less able but more politically correct peers who were rewarded by being elevated up the rungs of their careers? How would you react to the realization that your profession was reduced to a means of feeding your family? Half of your life goes down the drain. Wouldn't you raise your voice?

I switched my attention. I focused on writing. Perhaps literature would be more palatable to them. I spent three years learning the craft of writing song lyrics. Some singers and composers wrote songs with me. Then the insiders among them who controlled access to recording suddenly showed me a cold shoulder and avoided me. Their association with me could damage their careers.

I tried writing for the theatre. There's less money in it, maybe the controls would be softer, I reasoned. I also wrote my fairy tales.

Finally, a breakthrough. Radio bought my stories and asked for more. But when I delivered the manuscript they were very uneasy. In a dark corner of a hallway they told me in a whisper that they had run into problems with their superiors. They managed to salvage the ones they had already bought, but any future co-operation with me was "highly undesirable."

I'm in a rather tight cell, am I not, gentlemen? Over fifteen years I'd built two parallel careers, both were blocked. The only direction to go was downward. My cell didn't have a bottom.

Should I wait for my theatre play and TV script to get rejected?

I gave them one last opportunity. For the third time I put in an application to study for a PhD, a few weeks before I came here. It was my last attempt to live a worthwhile life in Prague. You don't have to be Einsteins, gentlemen, to figure out what they did with my application.

At the beginning, I was slow to catch on, but then I realized that to live in misery I needed at least the hope that things would turn for the better. In the end, I knew that even hope was denied me. I left the republic without saying goodbye to my unknown personal handler at the secret police.

One last thing, gentlemen. Just in case this tale isn't enough. Defecting and applying for asylum is a crime under Czechoslovak law. If you send me back, I'll go to jail.

This, gentlemen, is what I would have told you had you been willing to listen.

★

A rather shy newcomer joined our debating club in the corridor.

"Can you hear the silence?" The young man asking the question was freshly shaved and looked well rested. He alternated between moments of happiness and moments when he drew his head between his shoulders as if he expected a blow. In a nervous twitch now and then, he checked the space behind him. We all fell silent after his question so we could agree with him.

"What a beauty! Finally. After six years I could sleep until I woke up by myself."

"Did you work in a blacksmith shop?" the blacksmith asked with interest.

"I was a streetcar driver," said the man, "but that wasn't the trouble. Talking to passengers, honking, name-calling, it was a sweet music. I love streetcars." He blushed. "Home was the trouble spot."

"Did you live next to a quarry where they blasted rocks every hour around the clock?" asked another listener.

"That would have been angels' singing." The newcomer settled into his story. "You know about the terrible shortage of apartments in Prague. When we got married, six years ago, we had to move in to my mother-in-law's place. And my mother-in-law . . . I wish you could meet her." The young man began to tremble just at the thought. "If she had pursued a military career, today she would be a general. What a voice! What decisiveness! A field marshal. *Generalissimo!*"

"It's over now. She's behind the wires," we consoled him, curious about what a mother-in-law had to do with emigration.

"The first year was passable. She tested the battlefield. Then she staged a frontal attack. We could do nothing, we had no other place to live. She counted on that and interfered with our private lives. Well, 'interfered' . . . She bellowed commands! When to wake up, when to go to bed, what clothes to wear, what to have for dinner, how come we had sex again! After two years I was half crazy, after four I hit the bottle. I did what I could to find another dwelling, but she was a big shot in the party and always managed to abort any solution through her connections. You see, if we had moved out, she would have lost her favourite entertainment. Six months ago they told me I was so low on the list I might get a new apartment in twenty-eight years. I said, 'Enough! We're moving out of Prague, even if it means leaving the streetcars. Anywhere, under a bridge, if necessary.' My only other options were to get divorced or drink myself to death, or both. Then I realized Czechoslovakia was too small; she would find us. That voice of hers would reach us anywhere. I had to put an ocean between us, or even two. At last we tricked her into using her connections to secure for us a hard-currency allowance and exit visas. We're emigrating to Australia."

"You're a political refugee because of your mother-in-law?" somebody asked. "Do you think the Austrians will swallow this?"

"They have to. A mother-in-law is not politics, but a mother-in-law in the party who abuses her power is! And the fact that, thanks to the socialist planning of residential construction, I've got no place to live for the next twenty-eight years is politics!"

"To play it safe, I think you should throw in something more political."

"Sure, there were other things, too. It's just that the old bag was so aggressively close. That hag was socialism incarnate!"

Hearing that, we all shuddered.

Late that night the corridor was almost empty. Two men were still circling, as they had the whole day. Nobody understood their language, so they were on their own. But somehow it was known they both came from the same place – Iranian Kurdistan. One of them was a Kurd who had participated in the latest uprising for Kurdish autonomy, the other was an Iranian commanded by the Ayatollah to wring the Kurds' necks. They both came here the same day and discovered they had faced each other on the same section of the front. Maybe they had glimpsed each other's face along the sights of their rifles. But because they hadn't been able to kill each other, because they didn't enjoy the shooting at all, they deserted from their respective units and, across Turkey and the Balkans, somehow made it to Vienna. Their distaste for shooting people drew them together. They became an inseparable twosome, strolling in the corridor or sitting on a windowsill. They had plenty to tell each other. They slapped each other's back, laughed like crazy, and celebrated the fact that they had failed to kill each other.

The corridor began to appear to me in a new light. All of us who spent our days here looked like we had just recovered from a bout of serious illness. Our eyes shone, but our bodies were somehow slowed down. Looking at us, strolling in slippers or barefoot, reminded me of a health spa promenade. Only the little mugs of healing waters were missing. No, they weren't. They were replaced by talk, by a geyser of words that healed us all. After a year or two of not being able to talk about our plans, or share our fears, we suddenly found ourselves among our own kind, among initiates who could appreciate sophisticated tricks as well as straightforward courage. We were like convalescents who had battled the same illness and could analyse in detail its course.

Then it occurred to me, it might not have been an illness. I had seen this mixture of crushed bodies and shining eyes before. In the maternity ward, when my son was born. I began to realize this corridor was a maternity ward of a kind. Each of us, man or woman, was at the same moment a woman in labour and an infant being born. We were delivering ourselves into a new life. Here our new selves separated from the old ones, here they made their first steps. The corridor was a delivery room to a new life in freedom, run by kind cops with guns on their hips.

The newest additions to our small group took straight to bed and stayed there for two days. Now and then the door of their room rattled with a thunderous sneeze. Then the first one joined us. He wore a thick sweater and had a red, puffy nose.

"Judging by your looks, you must have taken the North Pole route."

He spread his arms as if even this road wouldn't surprise him. "It wasn't far from that."

"Tell us, make it funny, exaggerate," we begged for another story. He cleared his nose deliberately.

"We were stupid!" he opened. "We thought we could talk or bribe the Yugoslav border guards into letting us through. But they detained us and escorted us fifty kilometres inland. They warned us, 'Once more and . . .' You know, denunciation to Prague.

"We decided to take the chance, but somewhere far from this crossing, in another zone of the border. We consulted the map and picked a very remote area where, perhaps, bears still thrive. Very high, rugged mountains. There was a road on the map that ended not too far below the crest that was the boundary line. We drove as far as we could and set up camp. The next morning, six of us, with our kids, set out as if for a hike. We took just the bare necessities, leaving everything else in the tents. If they had caught us, we would have used the tents as an alibi and claimed we intended to return to camp.

"We walked through forests, avoiding the meadows. Two hours later we had to piggyback the kids, they were so tired. Nice way to climb a steep slope, I can assure you. Luckily, it was a mature forest, with very few bushes and undergrowth. Thin air though, over three thousand metres above sea level, hard breathing. Around four in the afternoon we made it to the tree line. There were just six, seven hundred metres of steep meadow between us and the crest. An open space. We could be seen, with binoculars or without, from miles afar. We had to wait till dusk. We were lucky, clouds gathered, and soon it was almost dark. At half past seven we began to climb. The children, well rested, were on their own legs again, and our backpacks were light, as we had eaten most of the food. In one hour we reached the crest.

"The other side was the northern slope of the range. No grass there, just boulders, rocks, and rubble. Very steep, too. The tree line seemed to be at least a kilometre below. We couldn't stay sitting on the border. There was still some light, but the wind was fierce. We descended on all fours, passing the children, who were tired again, from one to another. Then came the rain and lightning. The wet stones soon turned slippery. There was darkness all around. In the lightning flashes we could see we were some four hundred metres below the crest. It meant we were in Austria. We found an over-hanging rock and decided to spend the night there. We shoved the kids into the backpacks, using them as sleeping bags, covered them with whatever we could, and waited.

"Have you ever experienced a major storm in mountains? Now I have – and never again! We were soaked to the bone. High winds kept our wet, cold clothes stuck to our skin. Lightning was striking so close we jumped at each blast. The kids were crying; our teeth were chattering with cold; the echoes of thunder were slapping us from all sides. Around us loose stones and boulders kept crashing down. What a night! After midnight the storm receded. At last we could boil some tea on the solid fuel stove we'd brought. The kids finally fell asleep. Stars appeared, and the air had a January chill. We kept our spirits up joking about how warm we would be in Australia.

"The dawn came around four o'clock. Beautiful, breathtaking, I can tell you. Sunrise in the Alps. We were quivering like jelly, but it was beautiful. Imagine all the colours – all the shades of blue, whiffs of pink and then yellow – poetry coming alive. Every tourist waits for that. Not us, though. We couldn't wait for that damned sun to rise high enough to warm us.

"When full light came and we had stretched our cold limbs, we crawled and slid down the rest of the slope to the edge of the forest. There we took off our clothes. We were like a nudist colony, but nobody was around to see. We dried our clothes over a bonfire, jumping around to get warm. Tribal dances pale in comparison. We were just putting our clothes back on when we spotted a soldier up there, on the crest. He watched us through binoculars. Austrians don't patrol their border, so it must have been a Yugoslav. I indulged myself, ladies and gentlemen. I did what I had always wanted to do. I dropped my pants and mooned him and the whole of socialism.

"The rest was a piece of cake. Two hours downhill until we hit a logging road, another two hours through meadows where cows were grazing and ringing their bells. In a small hamlet a man was loading a truck with milk cans. He gave us a lift to the town at the foot of the mountain, where there was a cop. There were none in the hamlet. What kind of state is that – with a hamlet no cop watches over?

"Never in my life have I entered a police station with such enthusiasm. They were great. They sent for food and then we had to show them our route on the map. They hit the ceiling, shouting, 'It's a miracle you're here, scores of people have been killed there. It's an infamous avalanche slope, stone avalanches and slides, you understand?'

"To celebrate our survival they sent for a pitcher of draft beer. They apologized for having to put us in detention cells, but they had no other place we could stay overnight. It wasn't until then that we got goose bumps realizing how close an escape we'd had. But we made it, and never in my life have I been so happy and felt so free as I did in that cell, behind bars.

"A number of locals came to have a look at us because we'd survived that avalanche slope and because almost nobody ever makes the crossing in their area. We were the first ones this year, and it made us celebrities of a kind. Next morning a van picked us up and delivered us here.

"We're sneezing like hell, but what's a runny nose compared to freedom. We'll sweat it out in Australia!"

One of the cops emerged from the corner office. Slowly, with his hands behind him, he made his way down the corridor and back.

He was smiling, answering greetings with a nod. Ostensibly, he was on the beat, but there was nobody to control. The cops made their rounds to see with their own eyes what a useful job they were doing. All of them were middle-aged fatherly figures. They were assigned to this duty for the summer, the high season of defections. They came from small towns all over Austria and they liked it at Traiskirchen. There was a lot of action. Scores of people, hundreds of fates passed through their hands. It was quite a different job from investigating the theft of a chicken or the damage done to a fence by a drunk staggering home from the pub. They never took anything, not even a cigarette, just the feeling they were our support.

Only once did we see the big one show a less than amiable face. Jana was leaving the washrooms when she heard him thundering. At the end of the corridor a group was having a good time, but it was past bedtime. When the giant noticed the panic in Jana's eyes and the soap box rattling in her hand, he stopped in the middle of a word and in a soothing voice said, "Don't worry, ma'am. Good night," and winked. Not until she had disappeared into our room did he finish his word. Once again his thunderous voice rolled down the hallway, causing windows to rattle, doors to jump off their hinges, and sleepers to fall out of their beds.

The cops weren't there to protect the outside world from us. They carried guns to assure us that nobody could break the locked door, grab us, and drag us back from where we had come.

The two guys from the Mercedes were loitering around a radiator.

"Gentlemen, I have a job offer for three. Fatigue duty," I announced.

"How much?"

"I don't know. But the cop said it would be paid. Better a small something than a big nothing."

"Toilets included?"

"The corridor, the washrooms, the toilets. I'll take the toilets."

"Let's go." They came to life. "There's nothing else to do, any-way. What you learn in the military service pays off in emigration." They lifted their bums off the radiator and we went to pick up pails, brooms, mops, brushes, and a hose.

It was a welcome change for us as well as for the others. Something was going on. Even those who rarely appeared in the corridor emerged from their rooms and enjoyed getting in our way.

"Did they order you to do this?"

"How much does it pay?"

"By what patronage did you manage to land this job?"

There were looks – amused, down the nose, indignant – when I headed for the toilets. Looks that, imagining the clogged drains, declared, "No matter what, I wouldn't do that!"

I hummed a song while sweeping and washing, and I laughed over the graffiti. Clearing the drains, I found out that people are all the same. You can't tell Iranian shit from Polish. Seeing the shit in a bowl coexisting quite amiably, I realized that the differences among people can't be biological. They are fruit of mental toil, most likely by those who have never cleaned toilets. Once each toilet was unplugged, the shit whirled harmoniously down the drain. The few hairs left at the basin after shaving were also international, and the dirt in the shower could not be identified as Czech, Hungarian, or Kurdish. It was dust from the roads of the earth, and regardless of religion, race, or nationality, it dissolved under the attack of deter-gent, brush, and effort.

When I re-emerged in the corridor the same people were still standing there, as if they had been watching me through the closed door and walls all that time. Looking at their faces, I could guess which one would succeed in emigration and which one would lose. I might have opened a fortune-telling business, to such a degree cleaning shit had opened my eyes.

Later, over a cup of coffee, next to which a hundred-schilling note was displayed, Jana asked me, "Why?"

"To test myself. I needed to know the answer to the question I wanted to ask myself while leaning over a shitty bowl. How do you feel now, you Master of Arts? The next time it might be for real."

"And?"

"I made the deposit in my memory bank that you can't tell people apart on the basis of their shit, but you can according to their attitude to it."

The more stories I heard, the more dimensions our corridor acquired. A promenade? Yes. A promenade in a maternity ward? Why not? But all the stories conveyed something that to an outsider would appear insane. We could not detect it in others, never mind in ourselves, but we were all a bit deranged. From a statistical point of view, definitely abnormal. This discovery transformed the corridor into a promenade in the maternity ward of an insane asylum, the ward for simple fools. That's why the cops, the nurses, kept us here under lock and key! We all could have been diagnosed as having "a decreased ability for social compliance with the ruling political system." From the point of view of the potentates, of course, we were highly dangerous lunatics, struck with imbecility. We were those who couldn't bear to watch freedom from a distance, over the fence. We had gone mad, and, despite the law of political gravitation, we'd begun to crawl upwards – towards the stars.

Another blink and I could see the corridor as a sandglass, with all of us, silly as we were, streaming the impossible way – from the bottom half up. We were the grains of sand in that narrowest point struggling into the upper funnel of freedom. The corridor represented the bottleneck, the resting point on our crawl upwards, towards freedom and the stars; the safe haven, the place for regaining the strength we needed so that we didn't slip and fall back.

5

MOOD SWINGS

WE DIDN'T WANT to leave. We were comfortably established on our four beds, familiar with the rhythm of a simple life of eating, sleeping, and verbal gluttony in the corridor. The terrifying past of making the decision was behind us, and the jaws of its consequences still safely hidden beyond the locked door. We had temporary security, and thanks to it we felt euphoric.

Then the cop unlocked the door and we had to step out, back to life. He led us to the ground floor, where he put our luggage in a storeroom while we went through the necessary round of bureaucratic dealings ahead of us.

The lower floors revealed a quite different Traiskirchen. Barracks. *Flüchtlingslager.* Walls painted khaki, hallways clean but faded. Through open doors we could see dormitories for fifty or more refugees. A few people we saw had tired, sad eyes. Their walk was lethargic, their backs were slightly hunched. Their posture spoke not of readiness to fight but of resignation.

"They won't put us here, will they?" Jana breathed out, looking at a drunk asleep, sitting against the wall.

"Let's hope not. We have a small child. More likely, we'll be sent to some lodge or another, as the doctor said. They can't expose kids to this, can they?" I tried to resist the anguish that began to wash over me.

We stood for an hour in the hallway of another building, next to the door of an Austrian Ministry of the Interior office. Then we were inside. Four groups of people formed semi-circles around desks, distinguished by language. We gathered with two other Czech families around a no-nonsense but not unlikeable woman who gave us directives in perfect Czech.

"Now you are going to do exactly what I tell you. No protests, no buts. If somebody has already given you information – forget it! If you have applications filled in – throw them away. If you have visa photos – keep them for your family album. Now go to our photographer; his office is just a few blocks away. Here's a sketch showing how to get there. You won't wait for the pictures; he'll deliver them to us. You won't pay anything. Hurry up to get there before he leaves for lunch. Then run back, on the double, so we can finish the paperwork and arrange your lodging before evening. Understood?"

"Yes, ma'am," said those of us who had undergone military service.

Maybe because the other families had children smaller than Ivo, we won the cross-town run to the photographer and back and were the first in line.

"I'm going to fill in the application for an immigration visa to Canada for you. Though you might be able to do it yourselves, I know what the Canadians expect, and it's in your interest to be presented in the most attractive light." She smiled and her calm self-confidence began to flow into us. It was good to feel the support of someone experienced. We didn't dare consider what would happen if Canada rejected us because we'd messed up the application.

"I've got your names and dates of births, and I know there's three of you." She smiled at Ivo, who sat in Jana's lap. "Next – your education?"

"University of Economics, Faculty of Industrial Economics," I said.

"University of Chemical Technology, Food Processing and Biochemical Technology," said Jana.

"Where did you work? Your job description?"

"Institute of Machinery Economics. Prognosis of structural changes in the machinery industry due to technical development till the year 2000."

She waved her hand in a gesture of confusion.

"You'd better translate that into a human language. What did you do?" I explained to her what was hidden under this pretentious title. She thought for a moment.

"We'll put in here 'industrial economist.' It's vague enough to make it understandable to anybody. Suggests a wide variety of possible jobs."

There's a whiff of conspiracy. With her support we're going to make it to Canada. She nodded at Jana.

"Complete analysis of water. Chemical and instrumental analysis. Laboratory work."

"You'll have a better chance than your husband of finding a job," she remarked with satisfaction. At least one of us had suitable qualifications.

"Any other jobs?"

"Little bit of everything. You know the way it works in Czechoslovakia. If you want something done, you'd better do it yourself. As a curiosity, perhaps, literary writing. No use in mentioning it there, I guess, because of the language barrier."

"Unless you have certificates, Canadians consider such skills to be hobbies. They don't inquire about them."

"I worked for a year as a streetcar conductor," Jana offered hopefully.

"That's not a trade, I'm afraid. Next, how many foreign languages can you speak and write?"

"French, English, Russian, some German and Italian," I said.

"German, Russian, some English," added Jana.

She nodded with appreciation. "Good. You wouldn't believe how many people emigrate without knowing a single word of a second language. Do you have any money?"

"Seven hundred dollars U.S.," I proclaimed proudly. Almost a year's salary.

She laughed. "It will come in handy for postage stamps, pantyhose, and bus tickets. What the Canadians have in mind is half a million dollars, plus."

"Half a million! My God. Do any refugees have that kind of money?"

"I suppose so, otherwise they wouldn't ask. But I've never met one in my twelve years here."

"I guess they don't need to go through Traiskirchen."

"Do you have any substantial debts in Czechoslovakia?"

"Do they mean half a million, plus?" I dared to joke. "We owe the state about one third of the loan for a washing machine and a sofa."

"Your guarantors will have to repay it for you. From Canada's point of view, it's not your business any more." Clearly, she knew about life in Czechoslovakia. "Do you know anybody in Canada?"

"I wish we did, but unfortunately no."

"Finally, there's a number of supporting organizations involved in the whole emigration process. They provide information, assistance in official dealings, sometimes money to cover the expense of these dealings. They make your stay here easier." She pushed a paper with seven or eight acronyms in front of us. "You have to pick one of them."

The acronyms were unfamiliar. Which of them had the doctor talked about?

"I know nothing about any of them. Perhaps you could advise us which one can really help when you're in a crisis?"

"I'm afraid I'm not allowed to advise you."

I realized we were not alone in the office. But her pencil, running down the column of initials, stopped significantly at the WCC.

"I think we'll try this one," I said in a low voice.

"The very best choice," she approved loudly.

What would we do without her! Our luck hasn't deserted us yet.

"Now sign these blank forms, and I'll have the information you gave me typed in. We'll send them to the embassy. You'll hear from them in four to six weeks."

For a moment I was shocked. Signing blank forms? For the Ministry of the Interior to fill in? Was she crazy? What if they typed in whatever they liked? What if they framed me somehow? I could only hope they wouldn't. Did I have any choice, anyway? She looked like a decent person. And it was in her interest to get Canada to accept us, as Austria would then be rid of us. We had the same goal, just different motives.

I checked that it was really a Canadian embassy form and signed it. Then Jana added her signature.

"That was easy. Now go to the upper floor, where there's a branch office of the WCC. After that, go to the administration building, next to the main gate, where you handed in your passports. They'll arrange your accommodation."

She acknowledged our thanks with a smile. "I hope it works out. You've got a reasonable chance."

In the small office of the WCC, it looked like a chess tournament was being played. At every available surface somebody was scribbling away, filling out a form. Among them the grand masters, refugees like ourselves who worked there, were moving and giving advice.

"Czechs? Where are you headed? Canada? Good, it's a simple form. I'm going there, too. If you need any help, just holler."

We didn't need help, and in a few minutes, clutching a one-time handout of 250 schillings, we were registered under the protective wings of the World Council of Churches.

The ground-floor offices of the administration building were busy. The bustling clerks were trying to process the day's batch before the end of their shift. One of them spoke to us in German.

"It's up to you." I pushed Jana forward. "From now till Canada all official proceedings are your business. I can't understand a word he's saying."

He sent us across the hallway to have our photographs taken. There, the photographer ordered Jana to sit on a stool in front of a strange, suitcase-like apparatus with a Polaroid sign on it. The suitcase flashed and I replaced Jana on the stool. After a second flash, the photographer did something inside the back of the machine and then handed us two cards moulded in plastic. "Go back to the office, please."

The clerk spread in front of us two papers and, assuming we wouldn't understand them, explained, "This is your official permit to stay in Austria until we decide your asylum claim. Keep it in a safe place. Those two cards with your photographs are your ID. We'll keep your passports for now. You're going to be accommodated in Hotel Zoch, in Vienna —"

"Wonderful!" Jana couldn't control her enthusiasm at the prospect of staying in a hotel and in Vienna.

"Wonderful?" he repeated with a sceptical look. "If you think so." He shrugged. "Now go to fetch your luggage and then wait in front of this building. Somebody will pick you up in an hour or so."

We rescued our suitcases and backpacks from the storeroom and joined the others who were also waiting. Unlike in the corridor, at the gate the conversation was faltering. Everybody's attention was already focused on the future. For five days we had been close to each other, but in most cases we didn't even know each other's names. If we met again some day, we'd be strangers. What bound us together in the corridor was not necessarily a liking for each other, but the ordeal we had all gone through. That's why all our talk was about our successful escapes. In the brief time since we had left the corridor our trails had already parted. Everyone would follow his own track to his destiny in Canada, the U.S.A., Australia, or Austria.

Now and then a Volkswagen van pulled in, picked up a family or two, and sped away.

"I can hardly believe their care includes delivering us to the hotel," I said.

"Probably it's simpler than giving people an address and sending them to it alone. Some of them would get lost and the cops would have to search for them all around the country," Jana pointed out.

"Don't tell me that somebody who succeeded in defecting and is determined to make it to the other side of the world couldn't manage to get to Vienna or whatever other place and find his hotel." I was indignant.

"Most emigrants don't speak any German. How many of them have money? All of them are still off balance. You, too!"

"Me? Never felt better."

"Then have a look at your ID photo."

I pulled the plastic card from my pocket. "Is this supposed to be me? No way. That photographer is a swindler! He did it on purpose. How could I feel so great and at the same time look like a cornered animal? Show me yours! Very nice, too, indeed. How can we look so run-down after five days of rest? It means that a photo like this one will be on our visa application! God help us. If they don't reject us it will be out of pure charity."

"It's a good thing nobody will ever know what we looked like when we came here, when we really hit the bottom."

"Not even we will. Luckily. We might weep. Tell me, aren't we darlings of fortune? Born under lucky stars?"

"So far it hasn't looked too much like it."

"Hasn't it? Everything's running smoothly. All we face now is more waiting – for the interview and then for departure to Canada. In the meantime we'll enjoy Vienna. If I wanted to brag, I'd say everything is following my plan, but, unfortunately, you know I

had no plan so I can't impress you with how ingenious my whole
project –"

"It looks like you are back to your old self," Jana said contentedly,
leaning her head against my shoulder. "Keep talking. When you
fool around like this I feel safe."

Ivo climbed onto her lap. Sitting on our suitcases, we looked like
the Holy family in a Renaissance painting. After all, they had their
experience with exile, too.

The gate through which we had staggered 120 hours before, we
now drove through in great style. Just the three of us in a
chauffeured eight-seat van. In a few minutes we had left the town
of Traiskirchen and were speeding through countryside that resem-
bled a kitsch painting. The late afternoon in summer; an avenue of
ripe cherries along the road; golden wheat fields alternating with
deep-green vineyards; blue sky with white popcorn clouds. A
warm wind blew through the open windows and we all grinned
from ear to ear.

"Do you speak German?" asked the young man behind the
wheel.

"A little bit," Jana admitted. It was enough for him. He began to
talk, explaining with wide sweeping gestures this and that along the
road. All we could understand through the hum of the engine were
local names – Baden, Gumpoldskirchen, Mödling. To our left, we
saw a range of vineyard-covered hills, among them a freeway
wound towards the Semering Pass. The tone of his talk was
affirmative; had it changed to a question he would have discovered
he was speaking to the wind. When he reached the freeway he
stopped gesturing, and in the heavier traffic his chatter thinned out.

Hurrah! Vienna! Life was beautiful! What would we do in some
godforsaken hole, even if it was in the most scenic corner of the
Alps? Here we were on our way to a metropolis where all the action
was. Once again, a lucky strike. I started humming. Jana joined in
and then Ivo. The driver winked at us in his rearview mirror and

started a song of his own. We were entering Vienna as if our van didn't just have tires bearing the Goodyear winged sandal, but as if it had itself grown wings. We drifted under white clouds in the darkening blue. We floated even when we waited in a traffic jam or for a green light at intersections. We were gliding towards some beautiful small hotel whose name we had forgotten, but which had to be beautiful because it was in Vienna. We were luck-stricken.

Vienna that evening was charming and gracious, even in the working-class neighbourhoods we were passing through. We could see people returning from work, relaxing on benches in a park, standing with beer mugs on the sidewalk at the door of a local pub. In the distance, behind majestic trees, was the Imperial summer palace – Schönbrunn. Starting tomorrow, starting in a few minutes, I realized, we'd be part of this city. We'd be able to stroll its streets, to become familiar with it, to learn from it, and to enjoy it until we took off for our new home.

We stopped at the end of a quiet street close to a large square. The driver led us across the street, into a carriage entrance with a big sheet-iron gate and up narrow stairs to the second floor. In the corner of a spacious hallway was a small office occupied by a slim woman. Tight-fitting, short leather skirt, shape-enhancing sweater, legs in dark stockings propped on the desk. She might have been fifty. She might have been eighty. Hard to tell because of her heavy makeup. Still, some decades ago she might have turned a few heads. She was talking on the phone with a cigarette in the corner of her mouth and gestured for the driver to put our papers on the desk.

"We had a jolly ride, didn't we?" The driver slapped my back. "Good luck, folks!" The next moment he was gone.

The office looked like the set from a 1930s movie. There was even an old-fashioned phone with high forks and a nickel dial. The woman talked fast while she riffled through our papers.

The hallway, laid with black and white ceramic tiles, was without people but not without life. Somewhere on the upper floor a door banged, and we could hear scraps of talk in a guttural language. A burning cigarette butt flew past a window and crashed, sparking, on the concrete floor of a small inner yard where a pale girl was skipping rope near a garbage container. A light smell enveloped us, too complicated for us to decipher its components. The walls of the hallway were dirty, and the closer to the floor the darker was the hem of dirt. A second door opened upstairs, and we could hear an accelerating clack of heels and then a precipitous vomiting that echoed from the yard back through the open window. A surge of draft brought with it the smell of burned rice. Everything was underlined by the hushed sound of a radio playing an Arabic melody, now and then interrupted by what sounded like a curse.

The sounds and smells brutally invaded me and dissolved my high spirits. The cloud of euphoria that had carried me to the hotel turned darker and darker, heavier and heavier; it no longer had the strength to keep itself afloat, let alone me. I was plummeting in a free fall, down among unfamiliar sounds emanating from behind strange corners. Like rustles in a dark jungle, they made me nervous.

Finally, the woman stubbed out her cigarette, pushing two other butts out of the overflowing ashtray, banged down the receiver of the antique phone, swung her feet down from the desk, and sized us up.

"Welcome to Zoch. Do you speak German? Good." She took a heavy iron key from a nail on the wall and motioned us to follow her. At the end of the hallway she turned right onto a wooden gallery that overlooked the inner courtyard. One more right turn and at the very end she unlocked room number twelve and let us in.

"Drop into the office in half an hour. I'll issue you your things." The clicking of her high heels faded away.

From the door we surveyed our new home. The room was about four by four metres. The walls were a faded blend of yellow, pink, and grey. Next to the door, to the right, there was a high window with frosted glass. Three beds with yawning mattresses stood at odd angles. One wooden and two metal lockers. My mood bottomed out.

"What's this?" I whispered.

"Could be worse." Jana was fighting her disappointment.

"Worse?" I began to gear up, furious that my euphoria had soured. "What did that old Lorelei say?"

"Three ladies were living here. They left for Australia this morning."

"Ladies? They were not ladies! Look at this pigsty! A pig would die in a week. A man couldn't bear it! Ladies! How am I supposed to sleep in this?" I squeamishly picked up a corner of a blanket thrown over the bed.

"We can use our sleeping bags," Jana offered.

"I'd rather pitch a tent. The floor looks like packed soil mixed with oil. The pegs will go in easily." I took out my pocketknife and scratched off some dirt. "There's hardwood underneath!" I exclaimed.

"First thing, open the window and let in some fresh air," said Jana.

The window burst open, seemingly pushed from the outside by the sound of flushing water. I looked out. Just a few metres across the yard were a couple of small windows. Toilets. Somebody was staring into our room from a window on the upper floor.

Ivo, who hadn't been devastated by the contrast between his vision and reality, was exploring the room. In the corner, behind the beds, he found two socks.

"We'll have to clean it up," he stated, carrying them to the locker.

"You bet we will. We'll wash it out like Hercules cleaning the Augean Stables." I was steaming, but Jana's expression was becoming thoughtful.

"It shouldn't be that hard." She sized up the room like a general would a future battlefield.

"There's some animal or something under the bed," Ivo announced.

"Good heavens, no!" Jana exclaimed.

No animal, just two crumpled, filthy rugs.

"At least there's a washbasin with hot and cold running water," Jana offered hopefully, turning on the faucets. "Correction, cold and colder water. That greenish plate around the sink is plastic tiles. The mirror is not as dirty as it looks, just a bit blind along the edges."

Ivo opened one of the backpacks and piece by piece began to carry Jana's clean underwear to the locker. It was the last straw for her.

"Very well done, darling. You're helping me marvellously, but, you know, I'd rather clean it first." She diverted Ivo from his well-meant activity. "And you, don't sit there as if you had both backpacks on your shoulders! It's going to be okay."

"Okay? Sure. Naturally!" I agreed ironically. "Perfect, even though my view is of the toilets, even though somebody is peeping in my room, even though the yard makes every sound resound like we're in a well. Even though sunshine won't come here the year long and, judging by the sounds and smells, I'd better avoid the neighbours."

"What did you expect?" Jana flew at me. "That you'd live in a Hilton? Do you have a roof above your head? You do! A bed? Three of them! Table and chairs?"

"The table is only three-quarters high," I protested feebly, stunned by her sudden strength.

"You can eat on it. Write letters, too. If it doesn't match what you dreamed of, it's your mistake, not theirs. The only thing it needs is a thorough cleaning. For the time being, pack those rugs behind the lockers, then take Ivo with you and get lost!"

"Daddy, look! A little spider." Ivo made another find, this time in the corner below the window. With a sigh I squatted beside him.

"That's good. Little spiders bring good luck, and we need all we can get."

"Will we keep him here?"

"I don't think he would like it now that we're around. We'll move him to some other place he will love."

We caught the spider in a matchbox, took him outside, and released him on the roof of the garbage container.

"He'll get plenty of flies here. You'll see how happy he'll be."

"And we'll have good luck all the time because we will visit him." Ivo approved of this solution.

When we came back we found Jana with a broom, looking like a victorious warrior leaning on his lance. The floor was swept, the beds were in order, the luggage arranged in the corner behind the lockers. On the table were three sets of bed linen, plates and mugs, cutlery, and meal tickets.

"This is what that old Lorelei has issued us. When we leave for Canada we have to return everything."

"Do you think we will ever leave?" I asked morosely. "They can't take our desire to live in Canada seriously, can they? It seems to me like kids' play. We pretend we want to go to Canada, they pretend to help us, and we all have lots of fun."

"Looks to me like they are helping quite substantially," said Jana.

"You know what people say – never oppose a lunatic."

By bedtime we'd done all we could. The worst dirt was out. The beds shone with white linen. Ivo was already asleep, and we were sitting on the windowsill in the darkened room, watching the life in the hotel.

"I'm sorry for this afternoon," I apologized. "The squalor here sent me down fast. I'd been flying too high."

"There's much more to come," Jana pointed out. "Luckily, there's two of us to handle it, and our moods alternate. Like children on a swing, one of us is always up."

"Maybe because each of us is struck down by a different cause."

"Don't worry about the room. Either Old Lorelei will give me or I'll buy a brush and detergent. They can't be too expensive. You won't recognize it here in three days. The only thing I'm not sure about is how to get the sunshine in here."

"I know. It's all right now. I feel better."

"If this is to be our home for the next half a year or so, we'll make it Home."

"You're much better at these things. We'll make it Home."

"As long as it's something tangible, something I can fight with a broom or brush, I'm not afraid. That's my half of the worries."

"What's mine?"

"The worse that will come. The bugaboos. The intangibles. Fear. Anguish. Loneliness. Solitude. Insecurity."

"When we make our Home here, the bugaboos will not enter."

6

HOTEL ZOCH

"IT'S UP TO YOU," said Old Lorelei with a shrug. "Traiskirchen pays for your housing, food, basic hygienic needs, and, if necessary, medical care. If you want to clean up your place, I won't get in your way, but I won't help you either. It's your business both workwise and moneywise." She picked up the phone to indicate our hearing was over.

So we were on our own, and the next move was ours. First we established our co-ordinates. On the city map, despite some searching, it was easy. Square F3.

On a map, Vienna looks chaotic, as does any other European city that has been growing, without an urban plan, for the last two thousand years. Initially, all I noticed was the spiderweb of streets. The major ones run from the centre towards the outskirts, like spokes of a wheel. These are called *strassen*. Connecting them is a dense network of smaller streets, called *gassen*. The two biggest *strassen* are the Ring and the Gürtel. The Ring, circling downtown, was built in place of walls that once protected the heart of the city.

Two or three kilometres farther from downtown were the city's main fortifications. When they began to constrict the city's growth, they were torn down and in their place the Gürtel was built. If the Ring is a showcase boulevard, then the Gürtel is a purely utilitarian street. Cut through endless blocks of old apartment buildings, it is the main traffic throughway circling the city. Three or four lanes in each direction, between them streetcar rails that occasionally dive underground or rise on pillars above the street, according to available space. The busy artery vibrates with heavy traffic from early morning till long past midnight. Unfortunately for the traffic flow, every so often it is interrupted by a *strasse* running out from the Ring, at a busy intersection with traffic lights. To make up for delays at the lights, drivers have developed a pedal-to-the-metal style of driving. The number of tire marks before each intersection attests to the skids when braking or burning rubber on a green light.

In the area where Mariahilferstrasse crosses the Gürtel, there's an elongated square. Drivers, waiting for the green light, might notice its name, Europaplatz, affixed to the traffic-light pole. A driver northbound on the Gürtel who ceases watching the red light for a moment would see that the Gürtel is quite wide here, it even has a small park in the median. On his right, he would see the wall of a hospital complex partly hidden behind stately chestnut trees. On his left, he would notice that the Gürtel is made even wider by the parking lot in front of the glass façade of Westbahnhof, the train station. But even an attentive driver would overlook in the very corner of the square a common grey building with a plaster sign reading Hotel Zoch.

The hotel, like the whole neighbourhood, was built during the construction boom near the end of the century when Vienna spilled over its fortifications into the countryside. One wing of the building faces the square, so that travellers emerging from the station would notice the hotel sign. The other wing and the entrance are on a small, quiet side street off the square.

The hotel never ranked among the posh, but in its day it offered an acceptable standard of comfort to its middle-class customers. It wasn't big, only nine rooms on each of the upper two floors. The rooms were spacious, with high ceilings and plenty of light streaming through large windows. They had hardwood floors, central heating, and washbasins with hot and cold running water. The better rooms, facing the square, even had a small anteroom and double door to keep out noise. All the rooms had windows with a view of the street or the square; the inner circumference of the building consisted of hallways, with a number of windows leading to the small inner yard. As was the custom in those days, the hallways housed three washrooms and a bathroom on each floor. Two sizeable rooms, a restaurant and a café, were on the ground floor. Through the plate-glass windows, patrons could watch the traffic on the square and in front of the railway station. It was a nice, quiet hotel.

Across the inner yard, dwarfed by the main building, was its poor sibling, a two-storey addition. As it was also L-shaped, the annex and the main building together formed a small, square inner yard. On the ground floor of the annex there was a boiler room, coal room, and maintenance workshop. The six second-floor rooms were accessed from a wooden gallery. The doors and also the windows of five of the rooms opened onto the gallery, making them dark and hard to ventilate. The exception was our room. Not only was it larger than others, but its location at the very end of the gallery meant its window opened directly on the yard. At least we got more fresh air if not much more light. The opposite wall was too close and towered too high above our window. Perhaps these used to be service rooms or rooms for staff. In an emergency, some very poor guest might have been lodged here.

This is how the Hotel Zoch used to be, but, gradually, the patrons' growing demands for comfort sent them elsewhere, and the quality of customers declined. There was less money for maintenance. The plaster began to crack and fall off, the window frames shrank and rattled, the ceramic tiles wiggled. Tourists and businessmen were replaced by salesmen of ever lesser order, and, judging by its looks, the hotel might have even experienced a period of being an hourly hotel, because along this section of the Gürtel prostitutes offered their services. The hotel was ripe for the wrecking ball. A modern office building so close to Mariahilferstrasse could make much more money.

And yet, the hotel didn't give up. Not only did it divert the wrecking ball, but it rose once again to the challenge of providing a home away from home for those who were in need. Today its fame is more widespread than ever before because now it is remembered by former guests on four continents.

The wave of refugees who fled to Austria after the imposition of martial law in Poland, the outbreak of civil war in Lebanon, and the Islamic revolution in Iran were so overwhelming that Traiskirchen could not accommodate all who arrived. To cope, it had to subcontract a number of small hotels and lodges all around Austria. Zoch was lucky and got a contract. The building came to life again. The restaurant and café were subdivided, and any cubicle with running water and enough space to cram in a bed and a table was turned into a guest room. The hotel, designed for forty people, suddenly hosted almost a hundred. It became a safe haven for refugees and a gold mine for its owners, who decided it was worth postponing demolition.

But the wrecking ball still hovered above the hotel. That's why its owners allowed the window frames to rot, the plaster to peel off the bricks, the overloaded washrooms to break down. That's why nobody cared about the walls soaking up the smells of dirt, urine, perfume, disinfectant, successful and unsuccessful cooking, old smelly socks, laundry, cigarette smoke, spilled alcohol, detergent, and vomit. Anything was acceptable, as long as the hotel kept buzzing from dawn to night. The walls resounded with a complicated symphony of noises: the background hum of the Gürtel, PA system announcements and the metallic banging of carriages from the railway station, the slamming of doors, talking, heels clicking on the gallery, toilets flushing, radios playing, snoring, children crying, the telephone ringing, shouting in strange languages, singing, and belching.

In the hundred years of its service, the hotel had learned to be tolerant. Behind its closed door it would allow us to create the world we want.

But what of our mental co-ordinates? We were in uncharted land. As ancient Romans used to mark unknown areas: *Hic sunt leones.*

Somewhere in the predatory West, in the twilight dawn, rags of fog wallow on the ground. We can glimpse a shadow of a beast of prey hunting, the wings of a circling vulture, hear a snake's hiss, the splash of a shark. To survive, we must discover and learn the ways of this land. Come hell or high water, we must collect stones and erect a hearth, gather twigs and splinters, and find a way to light a fire to illuminate the place we're in, to keep at arm's length the demons, bugaboos, witches, and devils. We have to succeed with bare hands and almost no money.

We can sense small groups of people in the fog around us. Our competitors. We have to start moving forward. Survival of the fittest. From the multitude only the chosen few will fly overseas.

Watch your step: *Here are lions.*

Cautiously we stepped onto the street for the first time. Our mission: to shop without spending one penny more than absolutely necessary. The street was empty, save for a line of parked cars. Across the way was a small tire-repair shop. A bulky man in clean coveralls leaned against the door frame and when our eyes met he nodded.

Two blocks to the north we emerged on a wider street with streetcar rails down the middle. We turned left. The farther from downtown, the less expensive the stores should be, we reasoned. We were not in Prague, where the prices were the same everywhere.

"You're walking like a hunter," Jana laughed, "with a light step, darting eyes, and your ears up like a hound."

"I'm an explorer. I must be careful. I don't know the city, the language, or the native customs." I didn't add that I had no idea what kind of neighbourhood we were in. The West equals crime, doesn't it? Especially in poor neighbourhoods like this one. There may be gangs of young thugs. There may be prostitutes, pimps, drug dealers, crooks, and pickpockets waiting in dark doorways. No cop in sight. But perhaps there's less danger now, in the morning sunshine. They might still be sleeping off their nighttime evil deeds.

There were more shops along the main street. We looked in the shop windows, trying to work out the prices. They didn't seem too expensive for the items on sale, but for us everything cost too much. Every schilling spent made Canada more distant and less accessible.

A group of women on the corner put their shopping bags on the sidewalk and indulged in excited gossip. The street was lined with three- and four-storey apartment buildings, in front of some of their windows there were a few flowerpots, in another window a matron with her elbows on the sill was carefully registering the activity in the street to feed more gossip. Besides the stores, the ground floors were occupied by small repair shops and workshops. We heard a hammer hitting metal, a saw cutting through wood, a plane smoothing a plank, merry whistling and singing. In a small park a grandma watched her toddler trying to walk around the stroller. From an open window the smell of fried pork floated to our nostrils. Perhaps it was not that dangerous around here, after all. Working people are not criminals.

Meinl's Delikatessen was on the corner. A reputable business. Little danger of a rip-off there. We bought a big bottle of juice concentrate and a pound of coffee. Jana even managed to communicate to the willing girl behind the counter that we would like it ground as finely as her grinder allowed. This small victory, together with the keen aroma of coffee, lifted our spirits. Perhaps we were on holiday, despite everything. We continued to check shop windows and said hi to everybody who looked at us. If Vienna were like Prague, then everyone knew each other in the neighbourhood and we should make a good first impression.

The street ended at a massive red-brick church. A small open-air market lay in its shade. Canvas stands with fruit, vegetables, flowers, kitchen utensils. Very clean, very attractive, cheaper than the stores. The prices were written in marker on brown paper bags. I counted out fifteen schillings and bought a bunch of bananas for Ivo.

In the middle of the market there was a brick booth with counters on three sides. The prices? We couldn't believe our eyes.

"Damaged merchandise, if I understand it correctly." Jana pointed to the sign hanging on two chains from the ceiling. "It's guaranteed to function properly. The flaws are minor."

We scrutinized every piece with six eyes. Wow!

In twenty minutes we were hopping home armed with everything we needed to fight dirt. The most conspicuous was a plastic pail, expelled from the company of decent pails by the fact that its colour wasn't homogenous. It had smudges and spots ranging from crimson to light pink. But it had a handle and wouldn't leak. In it rested a brush with two bundles of bristles missing, and a damaged box of detergent wrapped in a plastic bag. Ivo carried a new broom, just the right size for him because its handle had been broken and was only two feet long. As well, we had several just-a-little-rusty bits of steel wool and a dustpan with a heat-deformed handle.

We were the luckiest people under the sun. We had struck gold!

Who could help me? The bug of helplessness was gnawing at my mind. This time something worse than the filth in our room was looming.

In two days we had scored a decisive victory over the dirt. The floor was hardwood again; our clothing was neatly arranged in clean lockers; mattresses had been beaten dustless with a stick Ivo found in a park; the draperies were a few shades closer to their original white; the washbasin and mirror were shining. Casualties on our side were negligible. Brush bristles worn to half their length, steel wool and detergent used up, and Jana's hands covered with calluses.

Seen through a clean window, even the hotel didn't look as terrible as it had on first impression.

"Shouldn't we cash a cheque?" Jana suggested after breakfast.

My heart stopped. This seemingly simple task was impossible. How could I cash a cheque without documents? Damn it, who could give me advice? Old Lorelei? None of her business, she would say. Traiskirchen? No way! They might disown us if they knew we had money. I knew nobody in the hotel. All we'd exchanged with our neighbours was an occasional nod, smile, or hello. A rather insignificant basis to discuss financial matters. Somebody might be tempted to break into our room and steal.

If we lost our $650 in traveller's cheques, we'd be done for in Vienna and the flight to Canada would be far, far away. Who did I know here? Nobody. Who knew me? Nobody. I scanned my memory for people I'd met during the last week. The doctor! But who knew where he might be now. The WCC! I jumped up so suddenly I knocked over my cup of coffee. The WCC was our supporting organization. They should know. They must know! If not – there went all our money.

I found the address in my notebook and located Dr. Karl Lueger Ring on the map we had tacked on the wall next to the door. We could take a long but somewhat familiar route or a shorter one through unexplored parts. A streetcar ride for three would be too expensive. Why spend money when the day's like a dream? The shorter route. Did I have anything left that could be stolen from me?

The streets we walked showed all the copycat and mongrel styles from the end of the century: neo-Gothic, neo-Renaissance, neo-Baroque, Art Nouveau. The closer to downtown, the bigger and more decorated the buildings were. More traffic in the streets, fewer workshops, more stores and offices.

I walk faster than I want, a few steps ahead of Jana and Ivo. I'm not tense, I'm a stick of dynamite. Without seeing, I gaze into shop windows when I have to wait for Jana and Ivo to catch up. I discover an American bookstore and don't even enter it.

For the first time we will have to deal with an office in a foreign country using a foreign language. Will I be able to explain what our problem is? I search my memory for the English words I will need. I can't imagine what solution the WCC might advise, I just hope they will come up with one.

Along this section of the Ring there's a large, castlelike park. Marvellous flower beds in full bloom, cut grass, on the right, two majestic edifices of museums. People are strolling around, relaxing on the benches, even tanning themselves on the grass.

What a way to start our emigration! Penniless! Why didn't I cash the cheques before going to Traiskirchen? But I couldn't think of everything. It was my first emigration; I was allowed to make a mistake, wasn't I? Rather an expensive mistake. You're a stupid jackass, man, admit it.

"What beautiful offices must be here!" Jana points to a modern seven-storey building, shining with steel and glass.

"So what? The WCC should be still farther down the street."

"The Canadian embassy!" Jana shouts and excitedly pulls me over to the polished brass sign next to the door. "Sixth and seventh floor. What a lucky chance. How about you drop in for some brochures or a newspaper, you know, English training?"

No no no, I want to shout, they'll kick me out. They'll give me nothing. I've never been in any embassy. I'm a shy person! But I don't say anything and enter the lobby. Let them kick me out if they want, but I must not hesitate. To be shy and indecisive is a luxury we can ill afford. Any show of insecurity would disquiet Jana. I must look self-confident and sure about myself. It gives her security. In the elevator I recall Theo saying, "They are here for you." It helps me to subdue the fear of a common Czech man who has to deal with high-level officials. I rehearse in English what I am going to say.

I tiptoe into the embassy lobby, as if the thick carpet was larded with land mines.

"Good morning, sir. How may I help you?" The pleasant voice of a woman sitting behind a counter with a sliding window stops me in my tracks.

"I'm sorry to bother you, ma'am, but you know, we've applied for immigration to Canada and I wanted to ask you if you might have, by any chance, some publications about Canada, to learn a little bit. English language, too, you know?"

"Sure." She pulls out something from a filing cabinet and hands it to me. It's a book titled *Canada Handbook*. Good paper, quality printing, plenty of colour photos, four hundred pages – it must cost a fortune. "I'm sorry it's not the newest edition, but I believe it will serve your purpose quite well, sir." She smiles.

"How . . . How much . . . does it cost?"

She looks at me very closely, as if she wants to see all the way to the bottom of my pocket, then nods and smiles.

"For a future Canadian it's free, sir."

I stagger to the elevator; I can't find the ground-floor button. "Sir!" If she had me kicked out as an impudent intruder, I wouldn't have been surprised. If she had sold me that paperback for a pile of dollars, I would have considered it a great favour. "Sir!" Canada must be a marvellous country if they address even a hobo like me as "sir." After all those years of being called "comrade" in offices, how wonderful it is to be called "sir," isn't it, sir?

That "sir" boosted my courage. At the WCC it would be tougher and much more would be at stake. On the other hand, we would be among our kind, so to speak. A blue and white sign in the entrance spelled out clearly in German and English: World Council of Churches, Services for Refugees, seventh floor.

The antique elevator ran on schillings, so we climbed the wide stairs. We had just one more flight to go when the rattling grandfather of elevators passed us. A woman emerged and joined two other people on a bench. Somebody was talking behind a yellow painted door and I stepped forward to read the sign on it. Suddenly the door opened and a stout man with a thick walking cane burst out. What kind of place is this if they welcome clients with a cane? flashed through my mind. But he passed me, leaned over the railing, and used the cane to push a catch behind the elevator's ornate grill. With a jerk it began its dignified descent. Then the man lectured us about pushing the button to send the elevator back down before we stepped out of it, but he spoke German, so only Jana understood him.

After a long wait we were admitted. A glass wall separated a small hallway from an office where the man with the cane was busy typing. At the end of the hall were two doors to the other rooms of this apartment-turned-office.

A small, slim woman stood in one doorway. In her early fifties, with short blonde hair streaked with grey, a light smile, eyes behind glasses shining with intelligence and energy.

"What can we do for you?" she asked in German. When I answered she switched without any problem to fluent English. I gave her our names.

"I'm sorry to bother you, but we're registered with the WCC –"

"I know, your papers are here," she interrupted me. "Get to the point."

"We have $650 in traveller's cheques. When we applied for asylum we had to surrender our passports. So we have no identification documents, and without them we can't cash the cheques. What should we do?"

"In no case ask for your passports back. It would mean you're cancelling your asylum application. You'll get them back after your asylum decision is made or before your departure to Canada. Can you postpone cashing the cheques?"

"Probably not. As soon as they learn in Czechoslovakia that we have defected, they'll confiscate all our property. They might cancel the cheques."

"What if you lose the money?"

"We have already lost more than this. We would go on without it," I shrugged, "but I'd feel more secure if I had its backing."

"Correct," she nodded thoughtfully. "Do you have any other ID?"

"Passes from Traiskirchen." I fished in my shirt pocket.

"Don't show them in public, not even as a joke," she said seriously. "How about a driver's licence?"

"I have it. With photo and address. But without ID, it's not enough."

"Give it a try. Make up some reason why you don't have your passport. Go to a smaller bank. Don't try to cash all the cheques at once. One, two at a time, so that they don't feel they're risking too much."

She spoke fast but with excellent pronunciation and with full concentration on the problem.

"You've saved us!" I cheered.

"Let's hope so," she laughed. "Drop in anytime, now you know where to find us."

As a writer I had little difficulty in coming up with a number of reasons why I didn't have my passport. In three branches of the same organization – the Austrian Tourism Office – they settled for my driver's licence and cashed my cheques. I had a slight bout of guilt, as if I were cheating, though I had bought the cheques legally with my hard-earned money. But the guilt was quickly washed aside by a wave of satisfaction that I had managed to solve our first problem in this strange land and strange language.

My new head had passed its baptism by fire with flying colours. It may have been even better than the old one. It seemed to possess one precious additional property – a kind of sixth sense, an unbelievably keen sensitivity for communication. It could guess correctly the meaning of a sentence on the basis of only two or three familiar words, intonation, body language, and facial expressions. It didn't let me get lost in this city I'd never been in before. Some kind of instinct, working beyond reason, had been brought to life by our extreme circumstances.

"Look at that!" Jana whispered, peering out of our window into the yard. From the tone of her voice I thought she had seen a brick of gold or an attaché case full of hundred-dollar bills. I looked.

"What about it? An old TV set. Garbage. I'm sure it doesn't work."

"Could you haul it here?"

I dragged the TV upstairs and placed it on the table.

"It's really old," Jana rejoiced. "It has an old-fashioned wooden cabinet!" I began to realize her idea was magnificent.

"We've got no tools, except for table knives and forks and my pocketknife with a small screwdriver."

"It will have to do."

Disassembling a TV set with a knife takes time. But after I'd thrown the entrails back in the garbage, we had a supply of screws, nuts, bolts, wires, and, most important, a solid cabinet made of polished walnut.

"Our first piece of furniture!" Jana rubbed her sore fingers happily. "A cupboard for shoes or books or toys. We could use a couple more."

Near the hotel there were two buildings covered with scaffold.

"Son, how about a contest? Who can find more nails, okay?"

He won. Though the sidewalk was swept clean, he found five and I only three. Three of them were more or less bent, five were brand new. As a bonus, we found a mortar-covered plank two feet long. When we cleaned it at home we discovered it was planed smooth.

"I could use it as a shelf under the mirror," Jana suggested. "We need a place to put our toothbrushes, combs, and makeup. But how are we going to attach it to the wall?"

After a few minutes we found the solution.

"We can hammer in two nails, fix loops of wire on them, and let the shelf rest in them."

Easy to say. The brick wall was very hard. We had no hammer, so I tried to substitute a knife handle, a padlock, and a shoe heel, which didn't work either because it was made of rubber.

"You must use something hard," Ivo advised me, "as hard as a stone." In ten minutes I was back from a nearby park with a rock. The rest wasn't too complicated.

"A little bit closer to Home," Jana beamed. "Never mind we had to reach all the way back to the Stone Age."

The room is dark except for a small cone of light from the table lamp that falls on a mess of papers, covered with wild scribbles. Ivo has been sleeping for three hours. Jana fell asleep an hour ago to escape the irritated mood I'd been spreading the whole day and to avoid yet another quarrel over some stupidity or other.

The letter. Since the beginning of the week I've known I can't evade it. As long as I could postpone writing it, I was all right. But now, Friday night, I've run out of delays. I have no room to retreat. I am in a deep hole, once again, because I'm going to hurt my mom and dad badly, to cut them to the bone, to cause them a great deal of pain for a long time.

The message I have to write is simple: We have decided not to return from our holiday and, instead, to emigrate to Canada. But, its brutal consequences scare me. For them it will be a sentence. As if they received a death notice about their only son, daughter-in-law, and grandson.

My headache begins to throb. How can I deliver such a blow? It is said that paper can withstand anything. But I cannot and they cannot. The lines I have to write will suddenly push our actions, in which we have risked only our own hides, into a broader context. I know our decision will wreck our loved ones. It will arrive out of the blue. For their and our safety, we couldn't prepare them for it, to talk about it beforehand. They will be shocked, unable to understand. They won't be able to comprehend that fast. It took us two years to reach the decision and build up determination. When they realize this, they will feel cheated and betrayed. They won't be able to imagine our future, but they will see theirs clearly – a lonely old age without us, our support, denied the pleasure of having a grandson, faced with the possibility they will never see us again. Because they love us, they will be worried. To them we're still small children who have set out into the Big World, unknown but undoubtedly ruthless, hard, heartless and evil, with lions lurking behind every corner.

How can I soften this blow? With an explanation? A detailed description of the reasons that pushed us over the edge? Should I enumerate the abuses of socialism that led me to the conclusion I couldn't live under it? Should I tell them it was because they had brought me up to have certain moral values? That they taught me to search for truth and tell it regardless of the ideology of the day? That this is why I couldn't live under a system based on lies and had to leave it. I lost all hope that its moral degeneration is reversible within my lifetime. But this explanation would require a book, and I'm not able to write one now. Our decision has narrowed my thinking to solving practical problems. How to drive in a nail without a hammer? How to take a bath in a washbasin? I am now thinking in specific terms of survival, not of political philosophy.

Or I could descend to name-calling and shout out every grudge I hold against socialism, in any order. But here's the delicate catch I have to bypass somehow, at least for the time being. They, the whole generation of our parents, sacrificed their lives to build for us a better, socialist future. We, the generation of children, experiencing what they built for us and realizing that working socialism can never be built, run helter-skelter for cover to the opposite side of the Earth.

I sit hunched over the three-quarter table. The pile of wasted paper attests to the fact that, though I call myself a writer, I can't put together a few sentences for my parents. Perhaps I am blocked because I am used to thinking things through to their consequences.

I will write it all down for them, some day, when emotions have calmed down and reason has taken over.

Emotions! They're boiling in me, but I must keep them under a lid. Deny them. I cannot allow them to boil over, to get hold of me. If there's anything that can get us across our tightrope, it's cold reason. Fear, anxiety, insecurity, apprehension. Each of these is capable of paralysing me just when I must keep my balance. I can't share my emotions with my mom and dad; not with anybody. I cannot talk about them even with Jana. Even I have to divert my own attention from them when they threaten to blow off the lid.

To the contrary. I have to keep up the image of a self-confident, calm man who knows what he's doing and has events under control. I have to be a man for whom tightrope-walking across half the globe is routine.

Another thing I shouldn't forget. They will have to surrender this letter to the police, and it will be used as evidence when they put us on trial for defection. The secret police will analyse every word, and whatever I write will be used against us and against my parents. The long fingers of the secret police reach even to the darkened room of a refugee hotel in Vienna.

I'm beginning to feel dull. Common sense says I must write simple, sober, impersonal lines. Just the major reasons. One page must do. In the end it can all be written in a single sentence, as sharp as a razor: We're not going to return.

I write something and seal the envelope without reading the letter. No return address. I couldn't cope with a reply. Within five minutes the letter is in a mailbox at Westbahnhof. The throbbing of my headache begins to subside. I wipe dew from a bench with my palm and cool my forehead. I sit down and breathe deeply. Dawn is slowly taking over the dark skies.

★

The cosier we made our Home, the more of an eyesore the table became. Its surface, painted diarrhea brown, was scratched and gouged. An empty sardine can served as an ashtray.

"Just look at it! It devalues all the work I've done," Jana winced. "We're going to spend a half a year here and we've got some money."

I should have expected it. Cashing the cheques created the illusion we had plenty of money. I thought of buying a map and drawing on it how far our money would carry us. Then, every day, we could erase whatever we spent to see how far from Canada we were. But, still, Jana deserved a reward for her great job on the room.

On Saturday, just before noon, the market under the church was slowly closing. We bought a brown-and-white checkered tablecloth with slightly irregular squares and a smoked-glass ashtray with a few bubbles in the bottom. One cigarette slot had a chipped corner, but it could be smoothed with a piece of quartz from the local park.

Jana returned three times to a stall offering a set of two earthenware cups and saucers. They must have been made on a foot-propelled wheel because they were not quite circular and the thickness of their walls was not uniform. I put on a very inaccessible look.

"What's wrong with you? You never cared about money before." Jana sensed my attitude.

"Now money provides me with a small security, the proverbial straw for the drowning man."

"My security rests in a decent household," Jana countered. "These cups take half the coffee of those big mugs we were issued. That means half a pack of coffee instead of one. After we buy two packs we'll be saving money."

Wonderful. Saving money through spending. How ingenious women can be if they really want something. No discussion is possible. I didn't need to hear the trump.

"And we can use them in Canada, too."

We bought the cups. A few minutes later I stopped walking to watch a flower girl who was packing up her cart.

"Let's go. Time for lunch." Jana pulled my sleeve.

"Over the weekend the flowers will wilt. We might be able to buy them cheap," I mumbled as a vague idea came into focus.

"You've just explained to me that spending money on a coffee cup is a sign of decadence. I can do fine without flowers."

"Old Lorelei . . . How long do you think it has been since somebody gave her flowers?"

"A few centuries or so."

"Wouldn't it be a good investment if she got some from us now? A gesture of appreciation for taking care of us. And for continuing to do so, but we don't have to add that."

A bouquet of dark-red roses, though not too large, looked imposing enough to throw Old Lorelei off balance. In Hotel Zoch nobody thought of flowers, definitely not in connection with this life-battered, cynical, aging madam.

Sunday afternoon I spent with Ivo in the Technical Museum. There was free admission every Sunday. We strolled home leisurely. When I opened our door I was slapped in the face by a wet dress hanging from the door frame. Jana, relaxed and exhausted, was leaning against the headboard of her bed, cooling her hands by waving them slowly in the air.

"Now I've done it!" She greeted us triumphantly. "What a fight!"

We checked the room but couldn't see any substantial improvement. I must have looked stupid.

"Those two rugs that used to be under the bed. I washed them. They are drying in the yard."

I looked out of the window. Both rugs were shining with bright colours nobody would have expected them to have.

"How on earth did you manage that?"

"The hard way. They are not woven rugs; they are knitted from cloth scraps. I figured they should be washable. I cleaned the smaller one here, in the sink, in cold water, but the drain got clogged twice and I had to clear it with a wire from the TV. It was obvious I couldn't handle the big one here. The bathroom was out of the question, it would only get even dirtier in there. But opposite the kitchen door is a small passage and I found a trough there. Presumably it's for dish-washing. There's hot water, even when it runs out in the rest of the hotel. I shouldn't have thrown the rug in there. Look at it – it's at least three by ten feet. You wouldn't believe how heavy it was when it was soaked with water. I kept washing it, again and again, because I couldn't lift it out of the trough. I had hoped you'd come and help me. Then people began to return from their Sunday trips, and I'd have felt embarrassed if they had caught me washing the rug there instead of dishes. So I wrung and squeezed it as much as I could and somehow dragged it into the yard. Have you ever wrestled a python? I did when I tried to hang it over the rack. Three Iranian guys, coming home from the beach at the Danube, finally saved me. After that I just cleaned the trough, mopped up the passage and the hallway to the yard, and finished it all up by washing my dress. Now I'm pooped out."

I kissed her swollen, detergent-sore hands. "Take a nap. We will sit in the window and keep an eye on the rugs. They look so beautiful now, they might tempt somebody."

When I brought them up later that night they were still damp. But the whole room suddenly became brighter and much more cosy. A great victory – now we had a real Home and the bugaboos wouldn't come.

Yellowish light drizzles from a tin street lamp through drops of mist and smog. I'm flat against a wet wall in a niche of a building. Its high walls dissolve in fog and darkness.

I'm in an unfamiliar town in Czechoslovakia. My wife looks out of a window and my son runs in front of the hotel to check if I'm coming. Christ alive! I have already escaped! How come I'm back? How will I manage to get out again? They now know I'm a would-be defector. Faster and faster I search all my pockets. I have no passport. I have no documents at all.

I'm in the middle of a circle of large office desks. Behind each of them towers a brutal bureaucrat with a rubber stamp either in the form of a brass knuckle or at the end of a nightstick. "I'll stamp your document only if he does." One bureaucrat points to his colleague on the left, who points to the next, all the way around to the first one. Their menacing impatience increases.

"I have my documents out there, behind the wall," I say. "Allow me to bring them and you can rubber-stamp your approval."

"To bring the documents you first have to be rubber-stamped and to get rubber-stamped you must have documents." They beat on the desks with their nightsticks ever more impatiently.

On a street again. It's darker and deeper. At both ends the shapes of cops materialize in the fog.

I'm in the cellar of a forger. A naked light bulb swings on a wire, casting feral shadows on slimy walls. I must get a passport. I must make it back to my family. From the walls human ears begin to grow, looming closer and closer to me. The forger changes into a comrade and his quill grows into an executioner's axe. Iron bars fall with a deafening bang from the ceiling, locking me inside.

Breathless and with a wildly beating heart I'm climbing through the darkness of a house where a friend lives. In the light from a match I can see that the door has been broken in by the kick of a police boot. The sharp splinters are fresh, the door swings on one hinge. The apartment is empty. No furniture, just terrifying, weird echoes. I leave the building. I'm in a telephone booth. I don't know a single name in the phone book. The cops are getting closer in the canyon of the street. My wife and son will perish without me.

I'm on a flat roof. I can hear boot steps below in the street. I want to make a passport myself, but I can't get a piece of paper anywhere. I forget what colour the passport is. I can't recall what information is supposed to be in it. I must get it now. Hurry! I can hear the boots climbing stone steps towards me.

I slide down six storeys, hugging the downspout; I'm inside the spout, spiralling faster and faster downward.

Pitch darkness. I'm in the woods. I can smell moss and spruce needles. I sense that dogs are closing in on me. I'm running. There's a swamp under my feet, but it carries me, I'm still on the surface. I must not make a wrong step. Elongated shadows of German shepherds with glowing eyes glide above the ground. I'm running for my life. I'm out of breath. Somewhere ahead is the boundary wall. I collapse. I can't breathe.

Blinding searchlights light up the plain in front of me. In the distance is a huge masonry wall with watchtowers. Behind it my wife waits. She lifts my son onto her shoulders to look for me. I'm surrounded by the German shepherds with fluorescent eyes and fangs. I hear their quickening breath. There, under the wall, two dogs are tearing apart the carcass of a man. I hear my son call – *Daddy!* I'm sprinting towards the wall. A dog hangs from my back, another is jumping at my throat. . . .

I'm breathless, soaked in sweat, hands on my throat. The light has gone. The dogs have disappeared. Where am I? Our room in the hotel. Have I succeeded in escaping again?

Dream! It was a nightmare! My heartbeat slowed down. Jana was breathing evenly next to me, Ivo was sleeping quietly. It was just a nightmare. I dried myself with a towel, drew my pants over my pyjamas, and slipped out onto the gallery.

It took two cigarettes to blunt the vivid images in my mind. I sat on the floor in the corner of the gallery because my legs were too wobbly to carry me. Four-fifteen in the morning. One hour till dawn, two till full light.

Bugaboos! Assholes! They were afraid to attack me in broad daylight, so they ambushed me in my sleep. Why? I had to let off steam. There had been too much pressure during the past year. How to get rid of bugaboos? Sigmund Freud, patron saint of Vienna, help me analyse this one! An interpreted bugaboo is an enfeebled bugaboo.

I was reliving the terror of not being allowed to travel. That would be symbolized by the bureaucrats. The anxiety that my plans might leak out somehow – the ears and cops. The dogs? If they had known what I was after, it would have been my end. And they sniff out everything, sooner or later. Helplessness? There were floods of it. There was nothing we could have done if they had denied us passports. But why did I want out? Mentally, I was better off there; I should want in and not out. It's Hotel Zoch and Vienna and the future that should be haunting me. Why now? Ah! At midnight our exit visa expired, the last possible time, though theoretical, of return without punishment. The last beams and planks of the bridge back have burned up and collapsed into the abyss. I hadn't even noticed, and my subconscious took its revenge.

I felt relieved. Half past six. Almost full daylight. In an hour my family will wake up and everything will be fine once more. But why on earth did I want out instead of in?

Jana once had a period of such terrible nightmares that only Freudian psychoanalytic interpretation got her out of the hole. Since then, she's been an expert at interpreting dreams.

"The fact you mustn't go back only triggered the dream. You don't relive the past, it's over and non-threatening, you relive the present. The past only supplies you with the symbols and images to express your present fears," she began her explanation over the morning coffee.

"The whole nightmare reflects the anxiety that you can't go back. 'Back' doesn't mean 'here' or 'there,' generally it means back in time. You made a step that can't be reversed.

"Darkness, fog, you can't see the sky – it's the expression of your having lost all certainty, even the most basic ones, such as having the sky overhead."

"That's what I had come up with, too."

"The bureaucrats in the arena are a classic catch-22. It stems from the feeling that somebody elsewhere is making decisions about your life and you can do nothing about it, you're relegated to passivity. You have no say in the asylum matter or in getting the interview at the Canadian embassy.

"The forger, executioner, and iron bars are signals that you know there's no illegal way you are willing to take."

"I think you don't have to explain the empty apartment or the phone book —"

"Sure, it's clear enough. You don't know a living soul in your new life, not a single name, nobody to lean on. You have to carry the burden alone. You feel the environment as hostile, menacing — it's the tightening noose of the cops and the dogs.

"The passport you're unable to make —" Jana thought for a moment, then continued, "it might have two meanings. You don't have a passport; it means you belong to nowhere — not to Austria, not yet to Canada, not any more to Czechoslovakia. You don't have any identification document, you're unsure about your identity. You don't know who you are. You don't know the language. That's why you can't remember what to write in the passport. In a broader sense, a passport opens the borders, and you have no idea what the new society will require, what you are supposed to be, what identity you should have.

"The swamp in the dark is a clear symbol that you're moving on the insecure surface of the unknown. You can't see the shaky ground you run on, but you must not make a false step or you'll fall through and drown. Anxiety about a predatory capitalist society that can swallow you — it's the swamp, too. An ideologically implanted fear of capitalism." Jana reached for the cigarette I had just lit.

"The wall ahead is obvious. It's the interview, a terrible obstacle we know nothing about, but which we must overcome."

"Our son represents your anxiety over your responsibility for the family. It's the uneasy feeling you can't take care of him as you would like to, because you're too busy coping with more than enough fears. You banish them from your mind during daytime, and no wonder. That future of ours is a larger-than-life calamity. You prefer to laugh and make light of it. Well, at night your sub-conscious got even. You had accumulated too much denial. Now you feel like you had a good shit after a long constipation. You should be all right for a few days."

A sound of a flushed toilet floated in through the open window, as if on cue. We both burst into laughter.

"Herr Moravec!" Old Lorelei yelled in the yard. Her yell was the hotel's intercom. Any time she needed somebody, she went to the yard and shouted the name. There was always somebody in the hall-way who heard it, banged on the appropriate door, and soon enough the required person would hustle down the stairs to the kitchen.

"The roses have worked!" I looked at Jana with triumph, but she wasn't following me. "She shouted 'Herr,' didn't she? She usually never bothers. She just shouts the name." We looked out the window.

"Mailman's here. Come down to sign for your parcels," she urged when she saw our faces.

There were two of them. The smaller one looked familiar. I had picked out its contents myself from my library in Prague and, according to our prearranged plan, sent it to Theo in West Berlin, ostensibly to enable him to study English. Now the dictionaries, grammar books, and textbooks have reached the right recipient. Hurrah! I can start studying in earnest.

The second parcel was a large box held together with string. From whom? Nobody had our address. We hauled it upstairs. It was postmarked West Germany. It was from Helga. We had met her a few months earlier when she came on an Easter trip to Prague with Uli and they had stayed with us. Impatiently but carefully we untied the knots. We could use the string.

Though it was July we'd received a box from Santa Claus. Inside were sweaters, shirts, children's clothing, woollen socks, some toys, and even two coats. The letter explained that as soon as Helga had got word about our successful defection she organized a collection among her friends. This parcel was their message – *Hold on!* She even put in two luxury items: soap and bubble bath of a rather expensive brand, in beautiful yellow-and-green boxes.

"Oh my." Jana clasped her hands. "What a gift! The only thing I don't know what to do with is the bubble bath. I can't use it in that slime cave of a bathroom we've got here. She's overestimated our standard of housing."

"We can keep it to celebrate our arrival in Canada," I suggested, "but that's not the point."

The initial euphoria was quickly replaced by much deeper emotion. People who had never seen us, and most likely never would, sent us this gift just because they heard we were in need. They didn't only send us the message to hang on, but also the message, much more precious, that nowhere in the world is a person in need utterly alone.

After we received the textbooks our daily routine stabilized. In the mornings Jana stayed with her *Essential English* at home and I went with Ivo to a small, quiet local park. It was only three blocks from our hotel and had a large sandbox and a playground. For my work it offered me the choice of several picnic tables shaded by massive maple and chestnut trees. The summer was gorgeous, and I could have happily spent all my mornings and afternoons there.

I was working on our biographies and résumés. I wanted to be able to present our family to the Canadian consul in a more favourable light at the interview than I had been able to on the austere official application. Surrounded by my grammar books and dictionaries, I was struggling through the translation when I noticed a lanky man with dark hair. He had been delivered to the hotel three days earlier from Traiskirchen. Now he was carefully checking the park, looking over his shoulder and up into the trees, as if he wanted to make sure nobody was hiding in the bushes or in the branches.

"Good morning," he greeted me as he passed my table for the third time. In Czech. He probably deduced my nationality from my books. "I'm Josef." He shook my hand several times. "Aren't you afraid to sit here all alone?"

"Afraid of what? It's a poor neighbourhood here, but decent." He looked puzzled, so I added, "Perhaps you've met a few Turks who are guest-workers in Vienna. I can assure you a Turkish child plays just like yours, and his mom, though covered with a black veil, is just as caring as any other."

"I didn't mean that." He nervously looked over his shoulder and leaned across the table. "What about Them?" He made a gesture as if he were revealing the inside of his jacket lapel. The Austro-Hungarian plainclothes police used to wear their badges there. Whenever they showed it to somebody with that gesture, they usually followed up with an arrest.

He had the normal high-strung and tired look of a fresh defector. His eyes were very tense.

"You know that in Czechoslovakia we develop a sixth sense to detect them. I met the last one on the train," I said.

His relief was visible. God knows what he had had to go through to keep secret his intention to defect.

"How long have you lived here?" he enquired.

"Three weeks in the hotel, plus one week in Traiskirchen."

"What's the way to survive these days?" he asked. Then, to soften the impression of being at a loss, implied by his tone of voice, he offered an explanation. "I'm a construction engineer and I like to see things clear-cut, logically interconnected, so to speak. That's a foundation I can build on." After a short pause he added apologetically, "I have the strong impression I've fallen into chaos and it makes me nervous. Very nervous."

"With time you'll get used to the feeling that nothing is certain except that you have a place to sleep and food to eat," I said.

"I'd like to put together a plan and timetable for getting my life organized."

"It would be a waste of energy," I warned him. "I met a Romanian guy here; he flew to Australia the other day. He made it from Romania by swimming across the Danube to Yugoslavia. Twenty of them plunged into the water one night. Only four of them made it to the other side. The others were shot by border guards or run down by their speedboats. He was completely shattered. We never saw him smile. He was a computer systems analyst, so he tried to put some order into the ruins of his life, glue the smithereens together with a system. Just like you. He spent days and nights sketching diagrams. He wanted to find the solid structure, the model of his present and future. And then one evening he burst out of his room, with an armful of papers, grinning from ear to ear."

"Shouting 'Eureka' because he had discovered a system for his life," Josef rejoiced.

"He didn't shout anything, he was just laughing like crazy."

Josef leaned across the table so anxiously he was half standing.

"'No model exists,' the Romanian told us as he ran to throw his papers in the garbage. 'In emigration there's nothing but conditional variables. Not one constant! Not a single independent variable.' He was laughing not only because he had faced the truth and survived it, but also because he realized his obsession had kept him afloat until he received his first real constant – his plane ticket to Sydney."

Josef collapsed as if I had hit him in the nose.

"How can I plan for contingencies without knowing what's predictable?"

"You don't plan. You deal with the calamities as they come. You live from hour to hour, from one insecurity to the next."

"But this must drive a rational person crazy." His blue eyes were nearly popping out.

"Not necessarily. Keep yourself busy so you don't have time to brood about it. Like the girl at the end of your hallway. She spends whole days sitting in her window, peeping into other people's rooms and shouting at them. Or the old chap living next door to me. He'll offer to repair your alarm clock, if you happen to have one. He repairs clocks all the time, even though he's no good at it because he's a bricklayer. He's still trying to reassemble one he took apart a long time ago. He spends most of the day on his knees looking for springs and little gears that keep shooting away from his clumsy fingers. Every evening he joyfully curses his bad luck; he's happy that he couldn't repair it and has to start again in the morning.

"You may even do something useful. You'll run into a guy in a yellow T-shirt – a Palestinian, I think. For a while, he wouldn't go anywhere without a piece of paper that had German words and sentences on it. He was always reciting aloud that 'there are nine steps leading to our university' and similar gems indispensable to everyday life. Everybody in the hotel knew the sentences by heart, only he always screwed them up somehow, though he kept studying, even in the washroom. In the end he learned them and we all congratulated him, happy that we wouldn't have to hear it again. He will ask you to test him. Don't be afraid to refuse. You couldn't read his Arabic scribble, anyway."

Josef's hands trembled slightly, then he forced himself into calmness. "All right. I accept that no planning is possible. But what's in store for us?"

"It's hard to put in words. You'll be on such a roller coaster of feelings you won't be able to make head or tail of anything. At times you'll feel like you're on holiday. You're abroad, there's no work to go to, you have plenty of time to enjoy your family. You'll have surges of determination and energy and then, for no obvious reason, plummet into complete paralysis. Your emotions will oscillate between extreme extremes. Waiting at the door of an occupied washroom or some dismal meal will send you into a slough of desperation worse than you have ever experienced before. Then somebody's smile or the aroma of coffee will raise you to the skies. This will happen four, five times a day, easily. Then the emigration nightmares will come. There's nothing you can do about them but suffer and rejoice in the morning that you weren't back there for real. And, all the time, you must keep the hope that everything will end well. About practical matters, you can always drop into somebody's room with your problems and find out if others have already solved the same ones. By the way, one of the securities you do have is a safe refuge in the hotel."

"Refuge!" His voice skipped to a high pitch. "Never in my life have I seen anything so terrible." He wiped his face with his palm as if he wanted to erase images of squalor. "I hope I get used to it. The people there scare me. They're not the kind of people I used to associate with."

"It will be good for you. You'll expand your horizons. You have to accept that you relinquished your old life along with your passport and start again from scratch, like everyone else here. Your education and position shielded you from too many things, just like me. There is a whole world we have been barely aware of. Here you're going to get life direct and unmitigated – survival reduced to the basic elements: food, sleep, health, family, hope, friendship. It will purge you of many illusions and stereotypes. You'll discover the basics that count in life."

He thought it over. He stood up, walked around the table, scratched his head. "I don't know," he concluded.

"You'll meet people here in such extreme situations that it'll drive the message home. Maybe you've already noticed one Arabic-looking guy. He's always first in the food line. An Albanian. As soon as he gets his plate filled, he starts to wolf it down and does so all the way up the stairs. Everybody steps out of his way because he sees nothing but his chunk of meat.

"Your old self would say, 'What a greedy gut, what a pig!' Your new self will understand as soon as you learn that he spent five days and six nights digging an underground escape from Albania. He had nothing with him but a spade and bottle of water. He was so hungry he can't get his fill now, even though the cooks give him as much as they can."

"You speak Albanian?" he asked.

"No, but these stories are known around the hotel. What's your story? How did you manage to get out?"

"Through Yugoslavia, crossing the mountains. I couldn't bear it any more at home. As a construction chief supervisor I raised hell because of material pilfering. Some big shots were involved in it. I began to receive threats in the mail, phone calls, saying that I'd be fired."

That's why he was so nervous about spies and everything. Paranoia.

"Are there any other Czechs in the hotel?" he asked.

"I know two. A guy called Honza. He's been in Austria for a year and has a part-time job as a waiter. Funny escape. He used to be a bus driver, and he came to Vienna with a charter. When it came time to drive back, he found out that everybody had defected, except for the five security men who were supposed to watch over them. He told them he had to buy some smokes and defected, too. I think he's applied to go to Canada. The second person is some-body named Jarda. He's got a job and very rarely sleeps in the hotel. I haven't met him yet."

"Is that it?" He sounded disappointed.

"You don't have to limit yourself to Czechs. There are interest-ing people from the four corners of the world here."

"I can hardly speak any English or German," he apologized.

"It doesn't matter. Use whatever you've got, at least you'll get some practice. The other day three Kurdish fellows invited us for tea. They live a couple of doors down from us. They escaped the Ayatollah's troops and walked who knows how many hundreds of miles before they reached a railway. They intend to study in Vienna, but they will not start German-language courses until September. So far between them they know about four hundred words. We spent a nice hour there. Once every five minutes they said something, five minutes later we did. It should have been embarrassing, but it wasn't at all. We felt wonderful. We somehow communicated without words."

Ivo hobbled over to me, complaining that something was hurting his foot. I took off his shoe and shook out the grit that had got in while he was digging a tunnel in the sandbox. When Ivo ran off to the swings, Josef continued.

"If I'm not annoying you, I have more questions. For instance, why is the hotel so filthy? Our room is not that bad, but the hallways and the washrooms? The kitchenette? I wouldn't heat up water there to wash my feet! There are stalagtites of grease hanging from the ceiling, the floor is covered by an inch of greasy dirt, the same with the countertop and stove. And how do you turn on the stove? It has no controls."

"With a coin. Insert it into the cut in the control axle and you can turn on the gas. An Iranian guy showed me."

"But where do you bathe? The bathroom is even worse than the kitchenette. Except the stalagtites there are slimy. The mould on the floor is even more slippery than grease. If it didn't smell so bad they could show it off as an ice cave."

"Nobody has solved the bathroom problem yet," I sighed. "Like a hundred years ago, I guess, a washbasin must do. The hot water usually runs out at around eleven in the morning."

"But why all the dirt?"

"Madam manager obviously couldn't care less, and she picked a real rarity to do the cleaning. He used to be an army captain in one of the brotherly armies that invaded Czechoslovakia with the Russians in 1968. He's been in Austria for three years. He spent seven months in the U.S.A. but came back.

"He's one in a special category of about ten individuals. Steer clear of them, they try to discourage you and undermine your hope. They are wrecks. Either no country has accepted them or they tried it overseas, failed, and returned to Austria because it offers better welfare. This army captain does fatigue duty in a military style – what is wet is clean."

"Is he the guy I almost tripped over on the stairs when I went for breakfast? He pushed a mop between my legs and mumbled something about cholera."

"He always washes the stairs in the morning when it's most heavily used. Everybody has to avoid him, he curses and tries to wet their shoes with the mop."

"Even he must realize that's the most stupid time to clean them. Why does he do it?"

"I have three related theories. First, he wants to be seen working when nobody can see the results of his work. Second, he's a military man and, in the military, fatigues are done in the morning. He hasn't been ordered yet to change the hour. Third, the morning is the only time he's sober. The rest of the day he's tipsy. You can tell he's been drinking because he gives orders to himself before he makes a right turn on the gallery or stops at the washroom door. But when he's drunk, he's not aggressive. Maybe that's why he failed in the U.S.A. Or, perhaps, because after years in the army he doesn't know how to be free. Maybe he feels lost without anyone giving him orders."

"A nice collection, true to God." Josef managed to laugh. "I've jumped from an orderly household into a madhouse. Yesterday my wife ran into a man wearing nothing but his boxer shorts! In the hallway! Doesn't he have enough decency to dress when he's in a hotel?"

"It was a hot day, so he made himself comfortable. In a week you'll be doing it, too." I paused to give him time to get over his indignation, then continued, "I realized only the day before yesterday that the reason is not a lack of decency or upbringing. For all of us, Zoch is our home. That's why people behave as if they were at home and not like at a hotel. There's too many of us crowded in and inevitably many private doings become half public."

"My next question is rather delicate," he began, trying to find the right words. "Is there any stealing in the hotel? Is it a safe place? I barricaded my door last night and I still couldn't sleep."

"I've been here for three weeks and haven't experienced a single big quarrel, not to mention a fist fight. There's no theft. Judge for yourself – everyone has just a few pieces of clothing and hangs their washing to dry in the yard for the whole day without worrying."

"Maybe, when somebody escapes to be free," he said after a thoughtful pause, "he doesn't steal some stupid underwear."

"Nail on the head! You're being over-anxious, you know. When you get under the surface you'll discover this spooky hotel is your security, your home," I said.

"This house where ladies promenade in hair rollers, even in their underwear, where every second chap looks like he's going to punch me in the face, and all this goes on under the supervision of a woman who looks like a bordello madam? Is this supposed to become my home?"

"When you find what's underneath it."

"What else am I trying to do by this whole damn conversation? And you're feeding me funny stories and no substance." He has pegged his survival on a rational comprehension of the hotel. "What is the fixed point? The common denominator?" Josef pressed on.

"We are human beings and we are refugees. We have all escaped from one totalitarian regime or another. Mostly socialist or Islamic. From intolerance. That's why we're now tolerant. The hotel is the most tolerant spot under the sun! Moreover, look around you – Albanian, Hungarian, Iranian, Pole, Palestinian, army captain, you, me – what do we have in terms of possessions? A big fart. Each and every one of us is living on the bottom. These are the common denominators that tie us all together."

He nodded slowly as he searched for words. "What divides people is always some kind of cranky ideology."

"That's what we all tossed away when we defected. There's nothing left to divide us. Our lot unites us."

He brightened a little. "If only I could read the minds of all those various folks."

"You have to discard the party line that told you they are different. They're not, not in basic human needs and reactions. You'll discover that a Kurd thinks the same way as you do about the stupidity of the army captain and makes the same faces behind his back; that Ahmed, who's fluent in five languages, smiles but still encourages the Palestinian who goofs up his German phrases. You'll find that we all laugh in the same situations and all divert our eyes from the ravenous Albanian. Four weeks ago it would have upset me, but I've discovered that, though we come from completely different backgrounds, I feel better being with a likeable Kurd than with a half-witted Czech. What we've gone through puts us on the same wavelength. Language is superficial. An Iranian in the washroom line-up detects you need to use it urgently and lets you go first. Next time you'll do the same for somebody else. You'll sense exactly who's struggling, and it will be your gesture, smile, offered cigarette, or slap on the back that sends him to the clouds. Without thinking about it, we all try to keep each other's head above the water."

His eyes were calm. He was silent for a long time.

"I feel better." Then he added with his apologetic smile, "Except that that philosophy of yours has made me hungry."

"Just like everyone else at this hour. Let's go for lunch."

On the ground floor, there was a narrow passage that led past the kitchen to the former café. At appointed hours they put tables in the doorway and distributed meals. Now it was two o'clock in the afternoon. Why were people forming a line there?

"Money! It's allowance payday!"

We moved slowly in the cheerful line. Behind two tables in the corner of the empty, dusty room were three clerks from Traiskirchen.

We said our name, one clerk checked the list, the second counted money from an iron box, and the third gave us nothing.

"Just one minor thing to be settled. You have applied for Canada, but you must choose another country as a backup," he told us.

Jana and I looked at each other. We hadn't considered an alternative. We couldn't. We had to believe that Canada would accept us.

"Canada hasn't rejected us yet," I pointed out timidly.

"This is just so we could, if necessary, speed up the whole process," he said pleasantly, but when I hesitated in answering, his voice got sterner and he gestured that we wouldn't get the money. "Sorry, but you have to choose another country."

We knew a little about Australia, quite a lot about the U.S.A., all of it twisted by propaganda.

"Well, if I have to, perhaps, the U.S.A.," I said, looking at Jana, whose expression told me it was all the same to her.

He made a note and gave us 480 schillings.

We were troubled by the incident. Canada had not sent us any letter yet. If they rejected us, then it would be time to consider our next move. What if they made us sign an application to the U.S.A., and Canada rejected us because of it? What if the U.S.A. reacted faster than Canada? We were being forced to sit on two chairs! We should have refused, even if it meant getting no money!

Could we refuse? We were completely dependent on them. They knew that we knew it. They could dictate what we did. They also knew that people from a totalitarian state are not used to refusing the authorities anything, especially not the Ministry of the Interior.

"We were duped by them. It might screw up our lives," Jana lamented.

"I signed nothing more than a receipt for money. If the price for not signing is the allowance, let them keep it. If the price is taking care of us or granting us asylum, then we'll be in big trouble."

The rest of the day we were good for nothing.

★

I was in the middle of a letter to Theo, working in my study in the park, when Ivo ran over from the playground to cool off.

"Do you know, Daddy, what I'd like? To have a bath. Like in our cottage at Chotouň."

"I'd love that, too. If I had enough money . . . Wait. You've hit the jackpot! Jump on my shoulders, darling. We still have time to make it to our market."

When we got home, Ivo distracted Jana by taking her to see how much work the bricklayers had done on the neighbouring building. Meanwhile, I ran to the kitchen passage for six pails of hot water, mixed in a couple of pails of cold, and put out the soap and a towel. I had barely finished when they entered the door.

"Your bath is ready, my lady." I motioned with a royal gesture to the centre of the room. There it was: three feet in diameter and a foot high, a child's inflatable pool, filled with warm water, lightly steaming.

"Oh, boys, that's a stroke of genius!" Jana clasped her hands when she found speech again. "Who got the idea?"

"I did." Ivo rightfully claimed his authorship.

"What a smart boy you are! We've got a bathtub! Now there's nothing more I miss. We have food to eat, a place to sleep, and now even somewhere to take a bath! Is there anything more in life to ask for?"

"You've got a really pleasant room," I remarked to Lorenc Landa when he invited us in for a cup of coffee. It was the first time we had been in one of the bigger rooms on the third floor of the main building. Very spacious, in spite of four beds and a sizeable closet. It had two large windows overlooking the street, full of afternoon sunshine. It was even quite clean.

"We've had better," said Lorenc's wife, Tina.

They had arrived the day before. Thanks to the strategic position of our window, we saw them coming up the stairs with their suitcases and bags. To our joy we discovered that not only were they

Czech, but they had two daughters roughly the same age, six or seven, as Ivo. Finally he would have some friends to play with.

"You can't compare it with what we had," Lorenc continued, looking at the peeling paint on the radiator. "We were in Güssing, in Southern Austria. You've never seen a more beautiful small hotel. Just like the kind you see on a tourist poster. Almost new, carpets everywhere, flowers in each window, sparkling clean."

"We did the cleaning," Tina joined in. "All women, who wanted to, took turns. The proprietor paid us and expected a good job. The same with kitchen help. How does it work here?"

"They don't cook anything in the hotel. The food is brought in from somewhere, they just warm it up here. And as a woman there's no way you'll get work in this kitchen."

"But I've become almost a professional cook during the last year," Tina protested.

"As a *woman* you don't belong in the kitchen," I stressed. "It may have something to do with tight-fitting sweaters and the seductive way madam manager sits on a table, but the three cooks who distribute the food are always young, good-looking, strong guys."

"I see," Tina responded. "But why didn't our girls get any milk for breakfast? And fruit after lunch?"

"We haven't seen any milk in the month we've been here. As for fruit, an apple once a week or so. We have to buy it in a store."

"We were getting everything there, as if we were regular guests. Even cakes or an ice cream came after lunch." Lorenc smacked his lips.

"They might have had a different budget. Or perhaps it's because housing is more expensive in Vienna and less can be allocated for food. Why did they transfer you here, anyway?"

"There's not that many refugees in Austria now. They don't need so many hotels and so they closed the most distant ones and moved people closer to Vienna and Traiskirchen. They save money on transportation."

"It must be a shock to be moved to a place like this."

"If you want to get something, you must lose something else. I couldn't find a steady job in Güssing. It has a population of about three thousand and no industry to speak of. In our year there, I worked for less than six weeks. Construction, harvest work, that's about it. There are plenty of jobs in Vienna, aren't there?" He was really interested in my answer.

"To tell the truth, I don't know. We haven't got asylum yet and the work permit that goes with it, so I haven't looked for a job. But several people from the hotel do work."

"Sounds good." He rubbed his big hands. "A full year of holidays is rather too long. I'd like to start a job so we can settle down in Austria."

"What can you do?"

"Skilled tradesman, lumber machinery. But I can do a lot of other jobs, from plumbing to locksmithing to welding."

"How much German can you speak?"

"A few hundred words we learned here and there."

I was startled. I thought they should know more after a year.

"How do you deal with offices with only that much German?"

"If they want something, it's their business. If I ask for something I can always understand their *ja* or *nein*," Tina laughed.

We sat with them long into the night and drank several cups of coffee. The year they'd spent in Austria had washed away their nervousness, and their quiet common sense soothed us. Ivo was so absorbed in playing with his new friends we couldn't get him to bed.

"I like them very much," he told us before he fell asleep.

"So do we, darling. They seem like honest, decent folks."

On Saturday, on our way to lunch, we met Honza. He was dragging his feet and holding his plate vertically.

"Another of the throw-up meals?" we joked, noticing his empty plate.

"I don't know."

The look on his face scared us. Blank eyes, the expression of a man who has just received a death notice about his only brother.

"My God, what happened to you?"

"They rejected me. The Canadians."

What a blow! This was the fate we had refused even to consider. Though we'd heard from time to time about somebody who had been rejected, Honza was the first one we knew personally.

"For what reasons?"

"They didn't say. They are not interested in continuing with my immigration procedures. They are sorry. That's all."

"What are you going to do?"

"First, I get drunk. Then I'll see."

"But you should eat something."

"I've got only half a bottle, but it should do on an empty stomach." He dragged himself heavily upstairs.

What reason could the Canadians have? Honza was a decent guy, a bus driver and skilled car mechanic. Could it be because he was single? Or was he keeping some secret from us? Did he have a criminal record or something? Or . . . yes, this may be it: He wanted to stay in Austria and didn't apply for Canada until ten months after his defection. That must be the reason. We clutched at that straw of hope. This was what made him different from us, that and his single status.

Our name is on the board announcing incoming mail. Who could it be? Theo wrote the other day and no one else has our address. As Jana queued for our food, I collected an envelope. A yellow one, something official.

"What's wrong?" Jana's voice was alarmed. "You've turned white as a sheet!"

I showed her the letterhead on the envelope. "The Canadian embassy."

When we made it back to our room, Ivo didn't jump at the plate of baked spaghetti, though he loved it. He was stopped by our looks of dismay. He raised his brow in question.

"The letter from the Canadians," I told him and put the envelope on the table.

"They are writing to tell us we will fly there soon!" he cheered.

"Go ahead. Open it," Jana urged me.

"I don't know. I feel uneasy about it. Honza sank my courage. How about you trying it?"

"You've got a luckier hand."

I hesitated between pleasant ignorance and stark truth. Yes or no?

The upstairs window across the yard suddenly burst open. Honza, leaning out, shouted to the skies, "Fuck you, Canada. Fuck you." The next moment his plate shattered on the concrete floor of the yard.

We looked at each other.

"Poor guy. But invitation or rejection, let's find out now!" I reached for the letter. "Where's that envelope?"

"Here!" Ivo victoriously waved the paper he'd dug out from the envelope. "I wanted to speed it up so we could fly there sooner."

Jana and I bent over the letter. German. We skipped the lines looking for familiar words. We shouted almost simultaneously. On the third and fourth lines there were the words "interview" and "September 19."

"Ya ho ho ho. Ya hooo, hurrah! We've got it! We have the interview!" We jumped and danced around the room like two kids, like two lunatics, as if we'd received our airplane tickets and not just the chance to fight for them.

"Darling, you've got the luckiest hand!" I lifted Ivo in a bear hug and spun around with him.

"Give me the letter, I want to read it all." Jana finally sat on a chair.

"For Chrissake!" She jumped up immediately. "The nineteenth! What day is today? The seventeenth. The day after tomorrow, Monday!"

"Let me see it! Right. Shit! There's no time to get ready. It's Saturday noon, the shops are just closing, tomorrow they are closed."

"I've got to buy elasticized panties."

"Quick, we have to do the laundry, prepare your dress and my suit."

"Ivo, run over to the Landas and ask them if they have an iron and hair rollers."

"I haven't typed up our résumés!"

The whole Landa family trooped down with Ivo. He'd told them we were going to Canada on Monday and they were curious.

"No, we're just going for the interview, but we have only two days to get everything ready and washed and . . ."

Tina and Jana began to fuss around the room like two panicking hens, taking Jana's dress out of the suitcase to hang it up, wondering about where to iron it, when Lorenc burst into laughter.

"What are you laughing at, you fool?" Tina flew at him.

But Lorenc laughed on and on. "I don't know, you're the learned ones and you can speak German and I can't, but I understand enough to know what September means and that we are now in the month of August."

Before he finished we all were laughing, our joy exaggerated by our relief.

"Lorenc, you saved the day! Name your reward."

"How about a cup of coffee?"

"Right away. Just one more thing." I leaned out the window and, to neutralize Honza's blasphemous curse, sent up a short prayer: "Bless you, Canada. Bless you!"

7

A GOOD JOB, TOO

THAT EVENING, WE basked in the warm light of the table lamp, enjoying our good news. From time to time we rechecked the letter to keep our happiness going. The words were still there, inviting us to the interview.

Suddenly the noises, sounds, and voices that made up the background of our hotel life changed their rhythm and intensity. Our sixth senses detected nervousness.

I stepped onto the gallery and looked out of the window. In the carriage entrance stood a big man with his legs apart. A second blocked the stairs to our level, and a third was on the upper floor. Police! What the hell were they doing here at eleven at night? Another two cops emerged from one door on the third floor and headed to the next. Nobody was in the hallways. From some doors pale faces peeked out. Had we done something wrong? Seeing police uniforms made us all uneasy.

A long twenty minutes passed till they stomped their way to us. One cop in a uniform remained in the door, a plainclothed one entered the room.

"Good evening. May I see your permit to stay in Austria?"

He rejected the passes from Traiskirchen with a gesture. With unsteady hands I fished out of the drawer the two papers we had never really been able to decipher due to their German bureaucratese.

"Is this what you're asking for?"

He nodded, and the other cop made a note. "Who's in that bed there?" He made a few steps towards the dark corner.

"Our son. Please don't wake him up," Jana pleaded in a soft voice.

All the same, he went to the bed and only after he had seen the sleeping child's face was he satisfied. He checked the rest of the room and under the beds with his flashlight.

"Thank you." Both went noisily onto the gallery to bang on the next door.

Nobody had stolen anything, nobody had been murdered, nobody had hidden drugs or weapons. Nothing had happened at all. It was just a routine check by the local police looking for illegal aliens. For a long time after they had left, the mood in the hotel was at the freezing point. Jana and I weren't the only ones frightened by police uniforms.

"Make some more coffee," Jana suggested. "If we go to bed this depressed, we'll have another emigration nightmare."

We sat in silence.

"It's not their fault that we're all allergic to the police," I opened the conversation at last.

"I know the police are different here, but still, did they have to stomp so much? Did he have to go all the way to the bed? I thought he was going to shine the flashlight in Ivo's face. What kind of manners are those, anyway, to invade us almost at midnight?" Jana was upset.

"They pay for our housing and feeding and it gives them the right to check on us."

Here was the sore spot. It was not pleasant, if not outright humiliating, for a grown man to be so completely dependent on somebody.

"Why don't they grant us asylum and a work permit so we could stand on our own legs?" Jana asked.

"Remember what Theo wrote. A public servant's time is different from human time. A few minutes of our anxious feelings is a week of a bureaucrat's time. Our apprehension-loaded day is their month."

"We have to swallow everything because we couldn't defect directly to Canada. They know that, too, otherwise they wouldn't take care of us, but this reminder is rather humiliating," Jana said.

"I don't exactly consider it a humiliation, because we couldn't do it any other way. We cost them money, yes, but it's not a pittance because they don't give it out of pity. I think they understand that we want something, and that it's not their money, but something much more substantial. We sacrificed everything for it, and now we're struggling to be able to live like free, responsible people. That's why I can accept short-term dependency. I am humble about it, but I don't feel humiliated. They help us so that we can help ourselves, so that we can get back on our feet, like parents help their children. As long as we're doing whatever we can towards this goal, our conscience will be clear and their money won't be wasted. This is the difference between assistance and pittance and between humility and humiliation."

Our permit to stay in Austria was back in the drawer and once again the cone of light fell only on the Canadians' invitation.

Lorenc leaned comfortably against the backrest of his chair and inhaled deeply several times. He gazed with pleasure at the children's pool he had just inflated with his breath. He called Ivo over and gave him a big chocolate bar.

"It's all yours for your magnificent idea on how to take a bath without a bathroom. You're a hell of a guy, I'd take you into my family any time."

Within half a minute all three kids were munching the chocolate.

"Why do you do this?" I asked in a low voice.

"Good ideas must be rewarded and encouraged," he answered. But Tina saw the whole matter from a mother's angle. "They will all have constipation. On that subject, do you have another magnificent idea on how to bypass those terrible washrooms?"

"We do. Very simple," Jana laughed. "A potty. In a bout of clair-voyance we packed one and it has been of immeasurable service. Back there in Trais, we lent it out all the time to people with small kids."

"The girls outgrew theirs ages ago but never mind, it's better than catching some disease," Lorenc decided. "We'll buy one first thing in the morning."

A pounding at the door interrupted him. Before anybody could say come in, Josef burst into the room, his eyes popping out, wildly waving a newspaper.

"Here it is!" he shouted. "I knew it! We're done for!"

"Here's your chair." Lorenc pushed one towards him and poured a cup of coffee. "Sit down, cool off, and then tell us what you've found out."

Josef ignored the coffee. He spread the paper in front of us and his forefinger attacked one headline so violently he almost tore through the page.

"I knew it! The KGB is in Traiskirchen! I can't understand any-thing more, but I'm sure we're in deep shit."

"Give me the paper," Jana demanded.

"You can take it easy, Joe," she said after a minute of reading. "They've locked him up. As far as I can make it out, a high-level officer in the Traiskirchen command was arrested yesterday on charges of spying for the KGB."

"Shouldn't we ask them to move us to some other hotel?" Josef suggested, still visibly upset.

"From the frying pan into the fire," Lorenc said deliberately. "They've arrested one mole, at least five others will remain. I bet the Russians have got more than one guy there. Anyway, you must have been a pretty big shot to be so afraid of them."

"No way. I was a construction supervisor on an apartment complex in Pardubice. But a defection is treason!" His voice trem-bled more than the coffee cup in his hands.

"If they were after you, they wouldn't have let you travel at all or they would have already caught you and delivered you back rolled in a carpet." I tried to calm him down with a rational argument. He didn't take it in. He was obviously in a shock.

"This calls for a more decisive treatment." Lorenc went to the closet and filled up Josef's half-spilled coffee with a good measure of rum.

"Look, Josef," he said when he sat down again, "we've been here for a year and we've heard about only one case of kidnapping and that allegedly happened a few years ago. It was some military colonel who knew too much about missiles."

Josef closed his eyes and drained his cup. "They said, back in Pardubice, that they had kidnapped one person's child to blackmail him into returning," he said when he had finished coughing.

"Sounds like their style," I agreed.

"Listen to your common sense, Joe," Lorenc insisted. "If they went after every small fry who defected, the whole secret service wouldn't have time to do anything else but recapture emigrants, and the real intelligence work would go down the drain. Have you written home?"

"Three times, but I only got two answers."

"So you can be sure they've learned your address without the KGB's help because they screen every letter from abroad."

Josef pushed his cup forward for another dose of rum. "What am I supposed to do?"

"Nothing. Go on as if nothing happened. If it makes you feel safer, don't leave your wife and daughter without supervision. Ignore phone calls inviting you to a midnight rendezvous at the street corner next to the Czechoslovak embassy. Pay special attention if the recognition sign is a copy of the party newspaper and a password is 'with the U.S.S.R. forever.' "

Josef's glare told us that he thought our joking was completely out of place.

"It's impossible to discuss serious matters with you!" he exploded finally and, offended, left swaying slightly, presumably to barricade himself with his wife and daughter in his room.

Lorenc shook his head in amusement. "We should buy at least five bottles of that rum. We're going to have much more fun with him."

Ahmed, a tall, sinewy man, attracted attention first because he was black. The only one in the hotel and one of the very few in Vienna. Second, because he strolled through the streets in his traditional African garment, a kind of yellow, green, and black sari. From it two thin arms stuck out – and two bare feet in blue adidas running shoes. His third distinguishing feature was the fact he spoke five languages well, a quality unheard of among the other emigrants. After passing each other a few times in the hotel, we ran into each other in the park. He went directly to the heart of the matter.

"Did they grant you asylum?"

"Not yet. It takes time, I suppose."

"You bet it does. What were your reasons, if I may ask?"

I told him my story.

"Sounds serious enough for you to say goodbye to asylum," he nodded in sympathy.

My heart fell. Asylum was the cornerstone on which our whole future rested.

"I've never heard about anybody who was denied it. Most of the people had less reason for defecting than I did."

"That's exactly why they got it!" He hit the top of the picnic table so hard with his fist my books jumped. His excited voice was full of bitterness. "They grant you asylum for trifles, but as soon as politics is involved they turn a blind eye."

"You haven't got asylum yet? How long have you been here?"

"Almost a year. I filed a second appeal. It will take another half a year, they say."

"You must have plotted a *coup d'etat* at the very least." I tried to make light of the conversation because his straightforward talk gnawed at my hope.

"Bullshit," he growled. "They tried to set a military tribunal trap for me, with the obvious outcome." His hand suggested a noose around his neck.

He was from East Africa. When the Russians engineered the fall of Haile Selassie in Ethiopia and then called in Cuban "volunteers" to stabilize and expand their power, his country went to war with Ethiopia. He served as a fighter pilot.

"A staff typist let me know what they were preparing for me, so I flew to Kenya and asked for asylum. They put me in jail instead. They returned my jet fighter. I wasn't as stupid as to wait till they returned me, too, to the claws of our colonels. I broke out of jail and escaped the country."

"According to the United Nations definition, political asylum should be granted to any person with well-founded fear of persecution in his home country because of his religious, racial, political –"

"Politics," Ahmed cut into my speech with contempt, "politics in the hands of a bureaucrat is an awfully flexible concept. Tell me how an illiterate peasant, who knows nothing more than his village and his field, can get involved in politics when he doesn't even know what it is? Some time ago I met one fellow like that, from Ethiopia. He couldn't tell the U.S.S.R. from the U.S.A. and had never heard about Cuba.

"One day a couple of soldiers with Kalashnikovs raided his hut and in the name of progress began to loot the little food he had. He could cope with that. But when they raped his wife and his eldest daughter in the name of the revolution, it was too much for him. He hacked them to death with a hoe and ran to a UN mission in Sudan. They questioned him and put him immediately on a plane to Vienna. Within a month he got asylum as a fighter against the Cubans. Today he's somewhere in the U.S.A., where he was accepted on the basis of his fight against Russian expansion in Africa.

"As if I didn't fight them!" He became even more upset and began to unravel his garb. "These two penetration wounds are from a slingshot? Thirty-two fighting missions, two kills of cargo planes, once almost shot down by an Ethiopian MiG-21 that had a Spanish-speaking pilot. This isn't politics, is it? I fought with a jet and not with a hoe and certainly killed more of them than that peasant did. 'It can't be taken into consideration,' they say. 'You were in the air force and it was your job.' Could I tell them, they asked me, why I was supposed to stand court martial. It's all bull-shit!" yelled Ahmed. "If I hadn't escaped twice I would have been twice hanged. Unless you present a bureaucrat with your death sentence, or better, your death certificate, he won't believe you."

I didn't know how to respond. Except for Ethiopia, I had little idea what was going on in East Africa. He was on the run from his own army. Something didn't quite fit. But I might have been just searching for an excuse for not taking him too seriously. I still wanted to believe that our application would be judged without bias.

"You still have hope."

"For half a year," he remarked with bitterness.

He knocked on the wooden pillar between two windows on the gallery as if he were entering a room.

"I heard Czech, so I came to make friends," he said in the singing accent of the Moravian region of Czechoslovakia.

We hadn't seen him around before, or perhaps we had, but without noticing him. He was the type that can be overlooked easily. Medium height, medium built, medium brown hair, incon-spicuous clothes. The only outstanding feature was his dark, intelli-gent eyes.

"Jarda." He offered us his hand. "An old-timer. I've been here for two years, and altogether in Austria for more than three. Originally from Brno."

"How come we haven't run into you yet?"

"I'm almost on my own now. I have a job as a travelling salesman. I just maintain a kind of base here. I drive a small truck for a busi-ness that produces and sells school supplies. Everything from atlases and a cross-section of a four-stroke engine to stuffed owls and plastic skeletons. Now, during the summer, it's our high season, so I'm on the road most of the time. I sleep either in hotels or in my truck to save money. How about coming to my room for a cup of coffee? I'm a rather talkative person and our legs will get sore if we just stand here."

His was the first room on the gallery. It was so narrow that the bed, table, chair, sink, and locker, half full of books, barely fit in. Jana and I made ourselves comfortable on the bed.

He had studied German language and literature, and after graduation he'd been offered a teaching job on the faculty while he studied for his PhD. When the dissident human rights movement published its first proclamation – Charter 77 – he was required to condemn it publicly. He refused. He would sign his name to the condemnation only if they showed him what he was supposed to condemn, the charter. They showed him nothing and kicked him out of his position as associate professor and then from the university entirely. It took him a year to find a job as a driver with a bakery. In 1979 he had defected through Yugoslavia. He'd worked as a salesman for a year and had managed to save enough for a down payment on a condominium. They had just begun to excavate the foundations.

"In a few months I'll be out of the hotel and the whole Traiskirchen system." He rubbed his hands with satisfaction. "How about you?"

Because I hadn't slept decently for a couple of nights I unloaded on him how Ahmed's tale had scared me.

"Nonsense," Jarda concluded. "Ahmed's got more brains than most people in the hotel, but I think he's his own worst enemy. He first spent some time in Italy, but he didn't like it and moved here. That alone is enough to sink his claim. Besides, he might have fought the Russians in Ethiopia, but what he didn't tell you is that his country was also socialist, headed by some dictator. I doubt he would have served in the air force if he hadn't been considered politically reliable. We know how it works, don't we? That must be why the Austrians are having a tough time deciding his case."

"Does that mean we have a good chance for asylum?"

He searched for words and then answered slowly.

"Probably not in the first round, but it has nothing to do with politics. Don't turn so pale, I haven't finished yet. I'm not privy to their rules, but I think I know what's going on: The last few years they granted asylum automatically to everybody who bothered to apply. Now they're paying a heavy price. Every crook and good-for-nothing that no country would accept or who failed there and came back is now hanging from Austria's neck like a millstone. I'm referring to the likes of the permanently drunk army captain and his roommate, my dear neighbours. Asylum gives you all the same rights as Austrians, including the right to collect welfare, which is quite generous and quite easy to get. Over the years, several thousand lazy bums and wrecks have accumulated here. The government has to feed them and can't get rid of them.

"So this year they changed their strategy. Those who want to stay in Austria are granted asylum with no problems. Those who have to use Austria as the transit to overseas are denied asylum in the first round. Long before an appeal gets through the red tape, which takes about six months, everybody is settled somewhere in Australia or America or wherever and, without asylum, Austria has the guarantee that they won't come back."

"Won't the Canadians be influenced if we don't have asylum?"

"Most people leave before their case is decided. But, and this is important, even if they deny you asylum, they take care of you until your departure."

"In other words, they play for time. When I think of the collection of wrecks here, I can understand why."

"Of course. The government must protect the interests of its own citizens whose taxes pay for the refugee support. Can you imagine how much it must have cost this relatively small and poor country over the last twenty years? Now they have found a compromise – the wolf gets his fill and the goat remains intact. They will help you reach the country you want to go to, and at the same time make sure the bunch of parasites doesn't grow."

"We want to go to Canada, so getting asylum is not too important, is it?" I made sure that I understood him correctly.

"I guess not. Even if it is important, there's nothing you can do about it. If they reject your asylum application, I will help you write the appeal. I'll be here more often from now on, so we'll see each other. My estimate, though, is that you'll have been in Vancouver or Toronto a long time before a bureaucrat here sharpens his pencil and reads your appeal."

"And with a deep breath primes his rubber stamp and enjoys the orgasm each bureaucrat experiences when he stamps the file with Case Closed," I joked from relief.

"Why do you travel the country with skeletons and atlases instead of working in some office? Your German must be good enough," Jana asked.

"I couldn't be a bureaucrat and stamp Case Closed on human lives. Selling teaching aids is fun. I've crisscrossed the whole of Austria, even the most remote villages in the Alps. I like it. It's a useful job and it's related to education. In a few years when my accent has improved, I'd like to teach somewhere at a high school."

"So you're establishing connections by selling stuffed birds to biology teachers and pointers to geographers?"

"You bet I am. By now I know half of the teachers in the country."

"And should they still refuse to hire you?"

"For that contingency I've already picked out three ladies to choose from. School principals," he said, winking. "All of them widows. Mature but marvellously well preserved. I court one, recite poems from Goethe, bring roses, invite her for dinner. In the end I'll get her to bed. And when her climax is imminent, I'll stop and refuse to continue until she promises to hire me at least as a substitute teacher." All three of us were laughing.

"How easy life would be if we all had a bit of a crook in ourselves."

Wild pounding at the door woke us up. Half past midnight. I unlocked the door and froze in shock.

Two half-naked figures showed up against white smoke, kerchiefs over their faces. I couldn't tell what was going on. A robbery? Your money or your life? Weren't they the two Kurds from the corner room? Had we misjudged them?

"*Feuer? Feuer?*" they shouted. Their cry was inquiring. I stepped aside and one of them ran into our room. No fire here. They disappeared back into the white fog. Because our window led to the yard, our air was clean. But the gallery was billowing with smoke. I grabbed the flashlight and ran after them. They banged at the next door until the old clock repairer responded. I could understand his language and the Kurd looked to me for an answer. Nothing there, I gesticulated, and we continued our search, followed by the old man's cursing.

A fire would be serious. The gallery was made of wood, it would burn like paper, and there was no other escape route from our part of the hotel.

"Here! Here it is!" A shout came from down the gallery. A third Kurd pointed at the smoke pouring out around the edges of the army captain's door. Luckily the door wasn't locked. The Kurd carefully made his way against the smoke inside to wake up the occupants. He overturned a chair and cursed till he started coughing. Both beds were messy but empty.

There! A circle of orange was glowing in the dark corner next to the door. I focused the flashlight. Smoke was rising from a pan of carbonized grease set on a red hot plate that sat on a smouldering wooden box. The Kurd snatched the handle but jerked back with a painful howl. He looked around for something to use. I pulled off my pyjama top to wrap my hand in it, but he snatched the garment from me and grasped the pan again. The hot plate lifted up, too. The pan must have become welded to it. Finally I found the cord and pulled out the plug. The next moment the hot plate and pan crashed on the cement floor of the yard, followed by the wooden box. In the meantime, Jana opened all the gallery windows.

The burned Kurd let off steam. "Fucking drunkards! They got tight, went for another bottle, and almost set fire to the hotel," or so I imagined his tirade might have gone.

"What do you expect from a soldier?" I said in Czech, and as if he understood the Kurd sent a long spit streaming after the hot plate.

The smoke slowly thinned and we cooled down.

"Let me see your hand." Jana touched the Kurd's arm. Despite his protests we led him and his two compatriots to our room. Jana made him sit and checked his palm. I took a small bottle of rum from the locker. We kept it there for the worst emigration night-mares. Jana poured it slowly on his burned skin. He looked puzzled but held steady. The other two watched with curiosity. I tried to explain to him that evaporating alcohol cools the wound and mildly neutralizes the burns. The treatment seemed to help. He smiled, his friends followed suit, and we joined in as well.

"Waste of rum," he began to assure us.

The alcohol helped a bit. He had hard skin on his palms; it looked as if it wouldn't scar.

There were a couple of inches of rum left in the bottle. I handed it to him and gestured for him to take a sip. I didn't realize he was probably a Muslim and shouldn't touch alcohol, but he took a gulp and then so did the other two. "Now it's your turn," they said, and we finished the little bottle.

"Do you know what's wonderful about it?" Jana said when we slipped back under our sleeping bags. "They could have just grabbed their sacks and packs and run. Instead, they took risks trying to save other people."

I recalled what had flashed through my head when I had opened the door. *Your money or your life!* I felt embarrassed. Once again I had fallen victim to a stereotype. Those marvellous men were just trying to save our lives.

We had to start seriously preparing for the interview, so I went to the WCC. In the carriage entrance of the building where the WCC office was, Josef ran into me. He mumbled something excitedly and gesticulated wildly.

"What the hell happened to you?"

"That woman is a dragon! She's no assistance except to the grave, even though they call her Frau Doktor!" He cut the air as if he were fighting a bad dream. "No use telling you, I'd get a stroke!" Once again he waved his hand to fend off an attack and darted across the street.

I climbed the stairs slowly, wondering if I should still go there? What had happened?

Frau Doktor answered the door. She wasn't upset at all.

"Did you manage to cash your cheques?" She surprised me. I didn't think she would remember me.

"Exactly according to your advice," I thanked her.

"How can we help you now?"

"I wanted to ask you . . . I intended . . . If you don't mind –"

"Don't beat about the bush. I'm not going to bite you."

"I've written our résumés for the embassy and I'd like to type them up, if you could spare a typewriter for a couple of hours."

"Leave it in handwriting. Nobody expects you to defect with a typewriter in your backpack. May I have a look?"

She motioned me into her office and offered me a chair in front of her desk. She carefully read the seven-page document, nodding in agreement.

"Excellent. You know how to put it together. Your English is quite good. We'll let your few mistakes stand. It shows how much you know and adds a touch of authenticity. Very good."

"Wouldn't it look better typed?"

"No. When you are at the interview, speak English. Don't worry about mistakes. English! You will earn points for it. If you run into trouble, an interpreter will be there to help you out."

"What kind of questions might they ask? What should we prepare ourselves for?"

"The questions are not that important. They concern your past and your qualifications. Answer them truthfully, that's all. Just focus on making a good impression. Show them you are reasonable, well-balanced individuals, with a good family life, willing to accept any job. The way you described it here. That's the substance of the interview."

"May I ask a few more questions?"

"That's what we are here for."

"If we're not granted asylum before the interview, or if we're denied it, will it influence the Canadians?"

"No. An application for asylum is sufficient. The Canadians don't pay too much attention to political reasons, more to family stability. They're interested in your future potential rather than in your past."

"Next, the school year is approaching. Should we enrol our son in school? It doesn't make too much sense to let him go for three months to a German-language school and then in Canada switch him to English, does it? It might make a mess of his head. Shouldn't we teach him ourselves?"

"Though it would be the most reasonable solution, don't do it. During the interview most consuls ask about school attendance; it's their pet question, for them it indicates an orderly family. I suggest you enrol him in a Czech school, there is one here in Vienna. I'll give you the address. He can go there for the three weeks before the interview and afterwards, if you think it's harming him, he might be 'sick' occasionally."

She leafed through my papers. I liked her common sense, intelligence, and precise thinking more and more.

"I might have some work for you. After the interview."

"Anything, anytime."

"We'll see. I'll call you. No, drop in on your way back from the interview."

"May I venture one more question?" I asked. She nodded. "What happened to Josef? I met him downstairs. He was completely out of his mind."

"I almost had to use the stick on him," she laughed with mock indignation. "Look out of the window. August, thirty degrees in the shade, and he came to ask me about getting some winter clothes."

"Sounds like him. He always ponders the worst alternatives." I began to enjoy the image of a sweaty Joe asking for parkas.

"I told him that before the cold weather came he would be in Australia, where spring would just be beginning. He wouldn't need winter clothing for a year. He was persistent – what if there was a sudden drop in temperature? What if a snowstorm hit? Is he a little . . . ?" she knocked on her forehead.

"Not really. When he's calm he thinks quite well. When he's under stress, real or imagined, he panics, and then he foresees nothing but catastrophe. When he goes to bed he's afraid it will break. When he eats he expects stomach cramps. The other day he shared with me the calamities that would come if Australia rejected him and for the next two hours the disasters if she accepts him. Sometimes we call him Calamity Joe. But why was he so terribly upset?"

"I told him the same thing I tell everybody when he starts to behave like a fool. Do you have two able arms? You do. Find a job. A man, idle at home, is dangerous. He always comes up with some stupidity or another." She rose to indicate the audience was over.

The mood in the van was as overcast as the sky, grey from horizon to horizon. Several of us were on our way to Traiskirchen to fill out and sign immigration applications to countries where we had no intention of going. We knew that these applications might torpedo our success at the interview for the country we did want.

To make it worse, our hands were tied. If the Austrians made signing these applications the condition of their continuing assistance, we would have no way out. Our helplessness against this manipulation by the government caught us off guard. We were used to it in Czechoslovakia, but we didn't expect it in Austria, not after our first good experience. We resolved to fight for a postponement till after our interview.

At Traiskirchen, they kept us waiting for an hour in a dark corridor for some other families from more distant hotels to join us. In the office was the woman who had helped us so much with the Canadian application. She rose behind her desk and glanced at our frowning faces.

"It's not you I wanted!" She hit the pile of forms with her palm in frustration. "All of you have made it through the first round and have a date for your interviews. Unless you fail the interview, you have no business here!"

We began to brighten up. When she saw our shoulders straighten and heard the poorly concealed sighs of relief, she smiled and offered an explanation.

"No country likes you to sit on two or three chairs. We won't spoil your chances. It always turns out like this," she added with a sigh. "You, the decent ones, come, and those for whom we organize this, who I need to get here, always slip away."

So it was possible to slip away, after all. I would have to ask somebody with know-how on how to do it. Just in case.

"You may go." She motioned to the door. "I'm sorry if we worried you. Good luck at the interview."

We cleared the office with rude speed.

The stone fell from our hearts. Our hands were untied. But we had three hours before the van would come to take us back. Nobody expected such a quick solution. The barracks atmosphere in the camp made it unpleasant to wait there, so we decided to see the town. Within an hour we had walked its every street.

We were cold. We walked faster, but in the end the morose weather drove us into a pub on the outskirts of the town. Plank floor, nine wooden tables with no tablecloths, old-fashioned chairs with bent backrests, benches along the walls. A few locals drinking beer. But it was warm inside. We bought goulash soup for Ivo and coffee for ourselves.

"What a happy ending! What good luck she was so reasonable!" we repeated in variations to release the tension.

"Look at him!" I directed Jana's gaze to a table where a man was sitting. A few moments earlier he had parked his red delivery truck, covered with white Coca-Cola signs, in front of the pub.

"What about him?"

"His plate." I focused her attention. "Three steaks, each of them covers half of the plate and there're no potatoes, no vegetables. Look at the gusto he's eating with."

"Order the same if you're hungry. Even though," she hesitated, "each steak costs the same as one winter boot for any of us."

"I'm not hungry. Honest. Only in a psychological sense. I love the way he wolfed the first steak, slowed down for the second, and now is lingering over the third. I love his appetite."

I really wasn't hungry. But the food in Zoch was, so to speak, a pragmatic matter. We ate not to be hungry. The servings were big enough, but there were only six or seven meals on the week's menu and their mediocre quality had made me forget that a lunch or dinner can be one of the pleasures of life, even for common, poor people.

"Stop staring at him," Jana reprimanded me.

"I'm not looking at his plate but at his face. I don't envy him the steaks, I swear, but the way he enjoys them. People enjoying their life boost my own joy." I tried to specify my feelings.

"Not having to sign up for the U.S.A. is a boost enough for me."

When we were leaving the pub we noticed the truck had left.

"Do you know what I'd like to be when I grow up?" I asked Jana and answered without waiting for her response. "A Coca-Cola driver."

I stood in the middle of our room while Jana searched for an appropriate shirt in the box from Helga.

"Do you think it's worth going there at all?"

"At worst they won't hire you, or they'll hire you and then fire you. If you work one day and get paid, it'll be worth it."

"I have a hunch I've overestimated myself. You know, capitalism is very demanding."

The conversation began two hours earlier. In front of Old Lorelei's office stood an unfamiliar, well-dressed man. He was from an employment agency and was looking for skilled bricklayers. I recalled the hundreds of hours I'd spent rebuilding at the cottage, renovating our apartment, or on odd jobs. I could try to sell the experience, couldn't I? The man looked at Old Lorelei for her opinion. She suppressed her smile and without blinking an eye confirmed that, as far as she knew, I was a skilled bricklayer. The roses had really worked! The man nodded and handed me a piece of paper with the address of his agency. Tomorrow at seven. He also chose the Albanian who had burrowed under the border. Digging foundations would be a piece of cake for him.

I ran out to buy coveralls, and back in our room Jana tried different combinations of clothing on me in an attempt to make me look like a skilled bricklayer.

"How about dragging the coveralls through some dust? They look awfully new. Tear them a bit? Smear them with some food scraps?" Jana suggested.

"You always say I shouldn't get dirty," Ivo protested.

"Appearance is not that important. It's not a question of coveralls, but of having the right knack and tricks." I shadow-practised a swing with a trowel.

"Something's odd about you." Jana walked around me, inspecting me from near and far. "Roll up your sleeves."

"How about a baseball cap?" suggested Ivo.

"Will you let me use the one you got from Theo?" I asked him, and he gave me his yellow cap.

"Good idea. You'll need a cap if you're going to spend the whole day in the sun. But that's not it." I posed in different work positions while Jana taught me some basic words – hired, fired, lunch break, payday.

"We can't do anything about it," she laughed in the end. "What's odd about you is your face. You should erase about half the years you spent at school."

The Albanian and I had no trouble in the agency's tiny office. They didn't ask for any certificates or work permits. They just gave us the address of the construction site and showed us on the map how to get there. In the site office they knew nothing about any hiring but told us to wait at the shed of one of the subcontractors. There was a big padlock on it. We waited in silence because we shared only about five hundred German words. I commanded four hundred and eighty and he the rest. Nobody came. The next day we asked a supervisor. He shrugged. If we wanted we could keep waiting. He knew nothing more. After three days the Albanian gave up. I would have done the same if Daniel hadn't appeared.

"Have you seen them before?" Jana asked, looking out of our window.

"They're just visiting. Nobody around here is so fashionable. Not even on Sundays."

A big, broad-shouldered young man in a white short-sleeved shirt and ironed trousers and a good-looking, carefully groomed woman in her thirties formed part of a debating circle at the top of the stairs. Both looked like they had come here from a fashion magazine to pose for an eccentric photographer who'd come up with the idea of shooting pictures of them against the background of dirty, peeling walls. But when we saw them two hours later disappearing with their lunch into a door at the other end of the hallway, we concluded that they were newcomers, after all.

That evening the well-dressed young man paid us a visit. Daniel, a compatriot. He had heard about the bricklaying job and was interested. He was fresh out of high school. With the beautiful impatience of youth he wanted to plunge into life, expecting to achieve anything to which he directed his will and brains. Wouldn't I try the construction site once more? He would replace the Albanian.

He behaved and spoke with a decisiveness that compensated for an underlying lack of self-assurance. Emigration had thrown him from the classroom straight into the adult world. He had studied German. It would come in handy. Why not? I thought. What was better – sitting in my room or on a pile of bricks?

"What happened?" Jana sprang up from her dinner. "You're dirty, so something must have happened."

"Let me sit down and take off the coveralls."

"How did they like your cap, Daddy?"

"Did they hire you? Or did they see through your bluff?"

"There was a long wait at first. Then at about ten o'clock a big fellow passed by. Dan had the guts to offer him our skills. He needed a special kind of bricklayer experienced in making façades. 'Of course, boss, that's us,' Dan told him. Luckily he wanted to see work, not papers. He led us behind a long building to where four guys were working on a scaffold. He sent me up to help one of them, who would give me on-the-job training. Good guy, very likeable, in his thirties. Probably a supervisor. He spoke some English, so we could communicate."

"What does the job look like?"

"I worked with him for three hours and he taught me what to do. In the afternoon I worked with Daniel alone. The whole building is made of concrete and cement blocks that they are panelling with polystyrene. Then the panels will be covered with a plastic net, coated with a concrete crust, and finally a synthetic coloured plaster will be spread on."

"Stop giving me a lecture. Just tell me what you were doing."

"You take a panel, two by four feet, four inches thick, spread a mixture of mortar and glue on it, and push it onto the wall. The trick is that the panel must be precisely even with the adjacent ones, otherwise the wall won't be level. To check for this you have a water level and a two-metre aluminum bar. When you put its edge against the wall, it must touch along its whole length. If it doesn't, you've screwed up and you have to add to or remove some mortar from under it, or spread it better, or whatever, but the panel must fit perfectly."

"It doesn't sound too complicated."

"It's not, as long as you're working on straight walls. When you get to windows, balconies, roofs, niches, corners, or edges, you have to measure and cut the sheet to fit exactly. Except for hauling the pails with mortar up and down the scaffold, the work demands precision rather than strength."

"How high is the building?" Jana was worried.

"Ground floor plus two more storeys. The scaffold has four levels. It's steady enough. It doesn't shake too much."

"Did he hire you or what? Did he give you a contract?"

"No contract. We're supposed to go again tomorrow though. They work eleven hours a day, eight on Saturdays, five hundred schillings per day. Friday is payday."

"What a dolt you are! What if he pays you nothing on Friday? What will you do?" Jana was upset because in Czechoslovakia this kind of rip-off often happened when you didn't have a written contract.

"Do you think he would hire me if I asked for anything in writing? I'm sure he's hiring people to work for him illegally. He'll pay us half of what he would have to pay Austrians, no taxes, no unemployment, no health insurance, nothing. He'll keep us as long as he needs us. He will make a bundle, that's for sure. But so will I. Without a work permit there's nothing I can do but sit at home and brood. He doesn't look like a swindler. He pays three thousand schillings a week. That's two hundred dollars! In three weeks we should have enough for air tickets. It's worth taking the risk, isn't it?"

"Dust off your good manners. It looks like Dan's mom is coming to check you out," Jana said when she caught a glimpse of Edita through the window.

"I suppose she wants to make sure I'm not going to have a bad influence on her child."

Before coffee was ready Edita had abandoned all pretence of polite conversation and had revealed her vivid interest in our room. Jana showed her around as if we had furnished it with Louis XVI. Instead, we had two TV cabinets, several planks as night tables and shelves. The table lamp stood on a box of soft brown wood printed with bright-red Chinese characters. The calligraphy had turned a small crude crate into a work of art. Most likely it had once contained tea. We had found it on the sidewalk at Meinl's. Cracks in the wall were masked with a yellow Disney poster and our son's drawings. Green-and-yellow cosmetics boxes adorned both sides of the mirror. We even showed her our bathroom pool. She loved it. Then Edita squatted and, with the knack of a professional, examined our rugs.

"It wouldn't be too hard to make," she concluded.

"You know how to make rugs?"

"I graduated from the school of textile design. I worked as a designer of everything from rugs to fabrics to ties."

Here was the reason why both of them were always dressed so meticulously and with impeccable taste.

"That's a good international qualification. It doesn't depend too much on language," I remarked.

"How much did your fridge cost? Would you mind if I asked you to keep butter for me? Temporarily, till those hot days are over."

We both burst out laughing. "It doesn't work. We found it. We keep shoes in it, and other things that get in the way all the time."

Edita was delighted. "You've solved everything!"

"Except one thing. How to do our laundry."

After some thinking Edita lit up. "How did your grandma do hers?"

"In a washtub, with a washboard, I guess." Jana brightened up, too. "Do you think we might buy a washboard somewhere in Vienna?"

"If it's too old-fashioned for Vienna, we'll make a trip to some small town or village. We've got a car. Or at the flea market."

"You have a car? Did you come straight from Czechoslovakia?"

"Through Yugoslavia. I won't tell you how I managed it, but I never surrendered our green passports when they issued us the grey ones. In Zagreb we applied for Austrian transit visas and we had no problem crossing the border."

A very able woman! To travel with both passports was a daring feat, indeed. As she left she held the room in her eyes as if she couldn't get her fill.

"What a pity that our noodle of a room is beyond any hope of ever being cosy. There's no space except for the beds and the closet. Its door opens whenever you pass, hitting you in the nose."

"What kind of beds do you have?"

"Green, iron, quite comfortable, I have to admit."

"May I have a look?"

I had guessed correctly. Their beds were military style, designed for stacking. In three minutes Dan and I had hauled one above the other, creating a bunk bed. The liveable space increased by twenty per cent, two square metres.

In the meantime Jana brought our reserve of TV screws and bolts. When she began to fix the rebellious closet door with our stone hammer, Dan darted outside. In no time he was back with his car tools. They had not only a real hammer but even a screwdriver!

Edita beamed with happiness. "Now we have room for all of us. Tomorrow, the coffee party is on me."

"The Solingers have written," Jana greeted me when I got back from work. "Guess what?"

The Solingers had been good friends of ours since our university days. Zoli was a Hungarian who studied beer-brewing technology in Prague. Besides being a chemist, he was also an excellent musician and composer, and we used to write songs together. After graduation he married Karolina, and both of them moved to Hungary. We saw them whenever they came to Prague, and once we spent our holidays with them. After our defection we sent them a postcard jokingly inviting them to visit us in Vienna before we flew overseas.

"Our defection must have knocked their socks off."

"They are coming! They are coming for two days!" Jana cheered and handed me the postcard. They had written that they could come for a short visit, provided they left their children behind in Hungary as a guarantee of their return. They would arrive the following week.

We were jubilant. We'd be able to have a long talk and refresh ourselves by sharing with them our memories of our old world. Wonderful.

"How's it going?" somebody asked behind me. Rudi, the supervisor. He carefully checked what I had done since morning, nodded with satisfaction, and with a wink he commended my work.

"Real pro. Got a smoke? Have a break, too."

Usually we had no break except for lunch, but he was inviting me, so I couldn't refuse. He was in a good mood. I ventured to ask him a crucial question.

"Do you think the boss will fire me?"

"Why should he?" His bushy eyebrows rose in astonishment.

"I'm the last one of the original six. All the others now are new."

"You're the only one of them who proved you're a bricklayer. The others just tried to make some money and either didn't know how to handle a trowel or were tinkering with their work. Take Dan, he worked carefully but too slowly. The boss gives a chance to anybody, but because he worked part time as bricklayer to pay for his university studies he sees damned fast who's a tradesman. As soon as he found out you could do the work, he trusted you. You see, he assigns you the trickiest jobs. I'm only supervising you to keep my conscience clear. He won't fire you unless you start working sloppily." He stretched his whole body and happily inhaled smoke. "Then you'll go to Canada loaded with money, and we'll fly to the Philippines to our little girls." He smiled with dreamy eyes because he had reached his favourite subject and only hobby.

"The Philippines? Haven't you got enough girls here? The beach at the Danube is full of topless beauties."

"It's more interesting there. Much cheaper living. We sweat our asses for half a year here and then for five months we enjoy life there as kings on holidays. Except for air fare, it costs peanuts. You can rent a beach bungalow for next to nothing. And what beautiful kittens are there!"

He dreamed some more and then began to warm up. "They know how to appreciate a well-developed man over there. I wish you could see their eyes when you stand naked in front of them. They are small, tiny, and when they see your size they almost pass out. Half from fear, half from impatience." He indulged in his vision, smiling silently, then he sprang up. "The sooner we finish here, the sooner we'll be in their tender embrace."

Before Dan was fired, Rudi gave us a ride to and from work in his VW Beetle every day, and I was used to hearing him talk about women. Not in the mornings, though. Then he was sleepy and grumpy. After work he came to life, full of drive for new conquests. He liked to regale us on the details of the previous night. He didn't mind I couldn't understand his German. Dan could. Poor lad. He was too much of an adolescent to be familiar with this kind of male relationship with women. At eighteen years of age he believed only in great, pure love. He suffered and hated Rudi for his cynicism. It might have been the reason the boss fired him after a week, because Dan did good work.

I returned to my pail with mortar. It was a tricky piece of work. Stairs, railing, door, window, all niches and corners. Well, I thought, I must not fail his trust. What an excellent joke. Skilled bricklayer. A pro! His words meant more to me than a medal of honour on my coveralls.

I had become used to the job in just ten days. I learned how to climb the ladders, walk the narrow, shaky scaffold. I discovered the tricks that made the work faster and easier. My body ached, my hands were callused and sore from the chemical mortar, but I was satisfied. I liked the job. I could see the results. Every evening when I looked over the thirty or forty square yards of new white panels I had placed there during the day, I felt good.

I was being useful. We were costing Austria lots of money, but I was paying something back. Thousands of us have passed through Austria, but we've left behind plenty of solid work.

The work transformed me. I learned for myself that "falling" from office to trowel work isn't as bad as people imagine. Panelling the building provided me, in its own way, with more satisfaction than writing so-called research reports nobody ever read, because their only purpose was to prove "scientifically" what ideology dictated. If I returned to Prague now, I would not find a trace of my work there. But should I return to Vienna and visit this building, I'll know that under the plaster there are polystyrene panels bearing my fingerprints, that people live in those apartments in comfort and warmth because I did my job well.

I discovered that I could rely on my hands. They are capable of making me a living and gaining me acceptance anywhere, even in the West, because good work is the one currency that can't be falsified or counterfeited.

When I saw the two ladies entering the hotel, I quickened my pace because I didn't want to miss the show. Carefully clad in travelling two-piece dresses and wearing small straw hats, they looked like two retired schoolteachers on holidays in the metropolis.

The set-up couldn't have been more favourable. Ahmed stood in the hallway at the top of the stairs, dressed in his African garb, barefoot and with a roll of toilet paper in his hand. The ladies gasped and, because no one else was in sight, asked him where the manager or receptionist was. Ahmed could speak German well and did his best.

"My esteemed ladies, the office is over there, but it's locked because madam manager is supervising the distribution of dinner. If I may offer you confidential advice," he leaned to them and softened his voice, "I do not think this establishment is worthy of your presence. Just two blocks from here is a very beautiful hotel that would much more closely meet your demands. Our establishment is, so to speak, exclusive, for members only. It's not a hotel but, if you allow me, a *Flüchtlingslager!*"

Their jaws dropped silently. Their suitcases with a heavy thud. A refugee camp! In their eyes, wide with terror, I could read their frantic thoughts: Would they first be murdered, then raped, and finally robbed or the other way around? They clutched their handbags to their breasts.

"Relax, my dear ladies," Ahmed comforted them in a soothing voice, "when you leave our hotel take a right turn, there's a hotel less than two hundred steps away from here. I can guarantee you upon my honour you won't find a single refugee there."

Their eyes darting around, they grabbed their suitcases and, in panic, descended the stairs, one of them forwards, the other one backwards to cover their retreat. We didn't offer them help with their luggage, we knew what their reaction would be. This kind of encounter happened quite often, thanks to the proximity of the railway station. Only one man had ever managed to keep his composure, replying, "Thank you, sir. I appreciate your advice," tipping his hat.

When the ladies reached the carriage entrance and thought they were beyond earshot, they began to cackle frantically. "*Ein Flüchtlingslager! Um Gotteswillen* ... By the skin of our teeth ... I was sure we'd met our end. *Mein Gott, ein Flüchtlingslager!*"

Our yard amplified their consternation and delivered it to our ears.

"Bullshit," Ahmed remarked with deep satisfaction and walked away, leaving me to wonder why hundreds of thousands of political exiles during the last fifty years hadn't managed to convince the citizens of the free world there is a distinction between a refugee from criminal law and a refugee from totalitarianism. It's decent people who have the most reasons to flee the regimes of crooks.

In the late afternoon the Landas had an unexpected visitor and invited us to join them. Their guest was a big, strong fellow who looked rather hungover.

"We met a few times at Güssing." Lorenc introduced him. "They came to Traiskirchen today, tomorrow they leave for the U.S.A. He had some time on his hands so he came to have a look at Vienna and to say goodbye."

"Lucky folks," I sighed. "We have not had our interview yet. Never mind. What's your destination?"

"Sioux Falls, South Dakota," he said with a happy glint in his eye. "I don't know where it is. We lived in such a small hamlet we couldn't find a good school atlas."

I corrected his Czech pronunciation of both names and sketched on a piece of paper the approximate location of South Dakota.

"I've never thought I would see so much of the world," he rejoiced.

"How long have you been in Austria? How have you coped?" Jana asked.

"Over four months. At first it was like being on holiday. We lived about fifteen kilometres from Güssing. A beautiful small hotel, high in the mountains; a kitsch tourist poster come alive. I spent all my time with the kids. We hiked, gathered wild strawberries; we played together. When the summer came we splashed about in a cold mountain stream. Wonderful holidays.

"But after a month I became restless. I need to do something all the time and now I had no work to lay my hands on. You know, a small village, a hundred and fifty souls or so, they did everything themselves. It's hard to make money there and nobody spends unless he really has to. My idleness was driving me crazy; my hands were itching. I couldn't get my thoughts off of what we had done and what might happen. I was irritated and angry.

"One day, after breakfast, I went for a walk to tire myself out, and at the end of the village I ran into an old man chopping wood. Well, chipping wood, he didn't have much steam left. My palms were burning so badly they pulled me towards him. I tried to talk him into letting me have the axe, I begged him on my knees to let me chop the wood for him. He didn't understand, and I couldn't speak any German. He mumbled something and brought me his wallet to show me he had no money. I couldn't have cared less. It was the axe I needed, like a goat needs a good scratching. The logs smelled so sweet my head was in a spin. In the end I pushed him aside and, man, I was in seventh heaven! I had accumulated so much energy over the last month he couldn't carry the split logs into the shed fast enough. As soon as I picked up the axe I immediately felt calm. And how much I enjoyed my lunch! I worked until there was no wood left to chop. He brought me a can of beer afterwards. We sat on his porch steps, silent, because we couldn't understand each other, and I felt wonderful.

"After that, everything was easy. Every morning, unless it rained, I made my rounds of the village and I always found somebody

mending a fence or a rabbit shed, painting, or weeding his veg-
etable garden. I managed to impose myself on them and they let me
have the hammer or the brush. I never asked for any money; it
wasn't the issue. Sometimes they gave me a pack of cigarettes, a
basket of cherries, or a chocolate bar for the kids. The whole hotel
went nuts because everybody thought I was working for money
and denying it.

"When the word spread through the village that we were
leaving, they threw a big dinner in the local pub for me and my
family. The entire village must have been there. A number of folk
brought us lucky charms – clover leaves and cowbells, candies for
the kids – and I had to have a beer with just about everybody. That's
why I'm so terribly hungover. Man, I've got four horseshoes in my
suitcase to bring me good luck! I couldn't refuse them. I couldn't
explain to them that it's me who owed them. If they hadn't let me
work, I would have wound up in a madhouse."

"I don't think you will need any horseshoes in the U.S.A."

"I'll take them with me, anyway. Just to be on the safe side. They
have horses in that Dakota, don't they?"

"Their visit was the kind you have to neutralize by reading a really
good book." Jana shuddered when, shortly after midnight, we
waved goodbye to the red taillights of the streetcar carrying the
Solingers back to their hotel.

"I enjoyed it. Most of the time, anyway."

"I wish I had your ability not to take people seriously when they
begin to act like idiots."

"Unfortunately, we have no good books. All we can do is to go
for a walk and talk about what went wrong." We strolled down the
Mariahilferstrasse.

"They irritated me. Upset me. Worked me up!" The pressure,
accumulated over the last five hours, had pushed Jana into high
gear. "They rubbed me the wrong way from the first moment I saw
Karolina dressed up for a Sunday outing. How loftily she carried

herself! Then, in the hotel, she didn't know how to climb the stairs without her frippery brushing the dirty wall. She walked down the gallery as if she would soil her soles. In the room she checked the chair seat with her finger before she landed her fashion-dressed ass on it. 'Nice room,' she said. 'Cosy, clean.'"

"It was a compliment for you, wasn't it?"

"But I could see the horror in her eyes, and she didn't hesitate to tell me that she'd think twice about defecting if it meant exposing her children to such squalor. Who the hell does she think she is? This shithole of a hotel is the only secure point in the universe that we have. Nobody has the right to badmouth it but us."

"Don't judge her so harshly. She must have been shocked. You have to admit that at first we thought the hotel was an uncomfortably exotic place."

"The only genuinely exotic thing was the roaring from the kitchenette. For a moment it startled even us. The Solingers were so bewildered they didn't know whether to crawl under the bed or run away."

"Zoli told me he had heard this kind of roaring in a movie; cannibals dancing when they quartered the future roast. He didn't look convinced when we explained it was only the Iranians celebrating the first dinner they'd managed to cook without burning the rice."

"At least it slowed Zoli down for a while. Karolina got over it quite fast and returned to her line. My God, what a litany. A whole evening of variations on a few subjects: meat prices were increased again, taxes on their cottage are up by eighteen per cent, she can't get floor tiles for the kitchen, the repairmen for the washing machine wouldn't come for three weeks, their car is rusting behind the left headlight, there are no good fashions to talk about, they had the measles at the day-care centre, at work they hired a new woman who gossips too much —"

"Stop, I heard it, too. Do you think we are irritated just because we couldn't talk about ourselves — our stresses and pressures?"

"Could be. If only they weren't so hopelessly off the mark."

Jana spread her arms in front of the loaded shop windows of Herzmansky's department store. "You can't imagine what you've got here, Jana," she parodied Karolina's enthusiasm. "Look at those mountains of dresses. What a feast! For only a few schillings that you can afford now that Ivo is working and you don't have to consider the exchange rate. At least five dresses that would drive our town nuts cost only a week's paycheque. You're living in a dream. Shoes – simply insane. I won't even mention underwear. Do you know how much they are asking now for a Western-made bra?"

"So much she has to run around without one, I suppose," I remarked. "But consider Zoli's options as well. My paycheque would buy not only thirty-two brand-name bras but also half of a magnificent Yamaha guitar, one-third of a good stereo, or even one-thirtieth of a vw Golf."

"Are they stupid or what?" Jana was in full blast, waving her arms so vehemently a passing cab slowed down, expecting a customer. "Don't they realize that each paycheque is a step closer to paying for air tickets, buying winter clothes, surviving the first weeks in Canada? Fashion? The best fashion is the one that's the warmest, the most comfortable, and lasts the longest."

"She doesn't have to fly anywhere. Tomorrow she'll be back in Hungary. She's relatively secure. She can afford to see Vienna through the eyes of a fashion addict. Besides, she probably believes the ideological fiction that people in the West are either beggars or millionaires. We don't look like beggars, I have a job, so it follows we're on our way to becoming millionaires. She saw that we use cosmetics she can't afford and we already own a fridge."

"She couldn't have been serious about that, could she?" Jana cut in. "She must have realized it was broken."

"She thought it works because she doesn't really think. She has conditioned reflexes. She doesn't expect a non-working fridge in a room. She sees the door, she expects cooled food behind it, not shoes. Though she keeps talking about emigration and might even be intrigued, she's not really interested in opening the door."

For a while we walked without talking. Our irritation slowly dissipated.

"Were we the way they are?"

"We wouldn't have been friends with them otherwise."

"So why do we communicate with them now like a mute with a blind man?"

"We collided with power, got a bump on the forehead, and something in our thinking started to change. We began to suspect that the concept of fashion, the materialism that they pushed down our throats, was a substitute for something greater, something spiritual, something that wakes in us a desire to get on our knees. In the end we understood that promoting vulgar materialism as a life philosophy is like giving a baby a pacifier instead of mother's breast."

The tempo of our talk became slower and slower.

"In a way, our relinquishing everything we had is a symbol. Like in the Middle Ages when you entered a religious or chivalric order. It's a reminder that material things are not a goal but the means of life." I shouldn't take myself that seriously. "Though, just between you and me, a silver fox coat as a means to keep warm is not quite damnable."

"Eighteen weeks' paycheques," Jana smiled. "The point is moderation."

"The problem is we're familiar with and can understand their world, but they can't comprehend ours. It was as if a divider ran through the table between us and them."

"Sure it did," Jana said. "When we walked through the gate at Traiskirchen, we crossed to the other side. Of things and ourselves. That's why we see different things, and the same things from a different perspective."

"Unless they experience emigration for themselves, we won't be able to understand each other."

We walked the whole block in silence.

"Even if we could legally, we would never be able to get back mentally," Jana remarked.

Every word sounded like a hammer driving nails in the lid of a coffin. They resonated in my mind and I began to recognize the faint musical theme that had accompanied the evening. It was the *largo* from Dvořák's symphony *From the New World*, the musical essence of all burials. That's the way it should be. To earth we commit all our friendships back there, behind the wires. For eternal rest.

But the *largo* must be followed by the *scherzo* and then the *allegro con fuoco*. If we can't go back, we must go forward! I hit the lamppost at the Gürtel intersection with my forehead and my fists. "Must!" I yelled into the empty Mariahilferstrasse. I put plenty of determination into the yell, but the returning echo sounded rather desperate.

8

A CASE OF THE JITTERS

"WHAT A WAY to start the week!" I cursed as we left the gate of the police station at Tannengasse. They had summoned us there to hand us the decision regarding our asylum application. We have the right to file an appeal within two weeks.

We sat on a bench in a nearby park and examined the papers, but we couldn't make heads or tails of the jungle of mimeographed bureaucratic words. In the end we understood as much as at the beginning. The decision was printed in capitals in the middle of the page: NICHT FLÜCHTLING.

"For fifteen years politics has bloodied my nose, but it's not enough to be considered a political refugee. What do they want? Twenty years? Or, as Ahmed claims, a signed death warrant?"

"Don't get upset, don't start shouting! They denied us asylum. We'll appeal and they'll grant it next time. Remember what Jarda said."

"I know, I know damn well. And it really pisses me off – it looks like he was right. Everything suggests it, even the timing. They decided only after they knew we had a date for the interview. They are telling us now, just a week before it, to motivate us to perform our best. If we fail at the interview, we'll still have five days to appeal. If we succeed we'll save them work. What drives me up the wall is the fact that politics come into how they assess a political asylum. Not ours, theirs. I understand why, and I even feel for them, but my sense of morality is rebelling. They judge my past, but their main criteria are my plans for the future. They have one standard for refugees who want to stay in Austria and a different one for the others."

"Don't be angry," Jana tried to console me. "I know that after seven weeks your nerves are frayed, but the decision changes nothing, so who cares."

"I've cared for that tiny bit of security, that single guarantee that if the worse came to the worst we could stay here, that they wouldn't drive us away or extradite us to Czechoslovakia. And furthermore, I craved assurance that the way they had treated us back home was not acceptable in decent countries. This way it looks it might be."

"Be quiet!" Jana cut short my laments. "You can discuss questions of morality and justice with Jarda later. Now stop feeling wronged and get back to the real world. They denied us asylum — so be it. We can cope another week without it. Then we have our interview, our chance of being accepted by Canada. Please start thinking ahead."

She knew me well. She knew that the need to concentrate on a future problem would push aside my disappointment.

"Ahead . . . How much have you progressed with your English? Are you able to face the consul?"

"The idea of facing him has haunted me ever since your insane order to learn English in one month. I haven't learned it. I can't. Can't be done!"

Tears of helplessness appeared in her eyes. The passion of her reply caught me off guard. I hugged her.

"I didn't mean it literally."

Jana removed my arm from her shoulder. "Then you shouldn't have said it, because I took it literally and I haven't been able to sleep because of it. It only makes me nervous and hinders my progress."

"I apologize. You don't have to do the interview in English. Still, how far have you got?"

"I've finished lesson twenty-six of the first book. I can converse with the consul about children playing on the beach or the teacher's study."

"How much grammar? Negatives, questions, past and future tenses?"

"I know the theory. I can manage if I use the vocabulary of those twenty-six lessons."

"That won't do. A textbook that meets the special needs of emigrants hasn't been written yet. We'll have to come up with a stratagem."

"You're not coming with me?" Jana asked, disappointed, when I escorted her to the streetcar stop to fetch Ivo from the Czech school at the other end of the city.

"First, we save the fare if you can handle it yourself. Second, since I don't have to work today, I have time to think over and arrange certain matters."

"What kind of matters might they be?"

"I'm going for a stroll in front of the Canadian embassy." I turned on my heel and with long strides headed downtown.

"Would you be so kind as to explain to me what kind of terribly important business you had at the embassy?" Jana was annoyed when we met at home four hours later.

"Espionage," I whispered mysteriously, just to tease her. "I was hoping to run into some people as they emerged from an interview. I thought I could get them to tell me the questions the consul had asked."

"What did you discover?"

"The strategy failed. No interviews this week. It's too bad. If we knew the questions, we could prepare and memorize the answers.

In English. If the bluff works, the consul will award us points for language proficiency."

"And if the bluff fails, the consul will have us beheaded for cheating."

"We have nothing to lose. He might give us half a point for the effort."

Jana was silent for a moment and her expression slowly changed.

"Occasionally you know how to use your brain. Don't just sit there, for Chrissake, work on it! Do something!"

Nobody in our hotel had ever been interviewed by the Canadians. Still, I spread the word I was looking for such a person and the next day I was on the trail. It led me to the Hotel Zum Golden Geld, a cosy, clean hotel beyond the city limits, a few hundred metres from the terminus of a streetcar line. I arrived at dinnertime and found them at home. A young married couple, waiting for departure to St. Catharines in Ontario. They were very welcoming.

"The interview? Sure, I'll tell you everything I know. But it's fun! Don't rack your brains over it."

"You didn't rack yours?"

"Our brains were racking us! The night before we both alternated between having bouts of diarrhea in the washroom and vomiting in the washbasin. Don't do it. It doesn't help anything." As if I had a choice in the matter.

"That's why I came to question you. If I knew in advance what they'll ask me, it would put me at ease and, maybe, I'd be able to limit my body's mutiny to only half of the night and doze off the other half. What happened at the embassy?"

"Informal atmosphere. A friendly conversation. Family, education, jobs, et cetera."

"Could you be more specific about 'jobs' and 'et cetera'?"

"Piece of cake. Let me see . . ." After remembering two questions he slowed down, added a third, and then got stuck. They both thought hard. After a while his wife offered a fourth and fifth.

"You said the interview lasted almost an hour. Try to recall it, please."

"We learned afterwards we had spent an hour there. It's a hell of a problem," he scratched his head in embarrassment, "but all I can remember now is that the consul had a moustache and a scarlet tie."

"Crimson tie and he was clean-shaven," his wife corrected him.

"Scarlet," he held his ground. "It was like being in a dream. As long as I was answering the questions, my mind ran on adrenalin. When he told us we were accepted, the adrenalin turned off, I wilted and couldn't muster my signature. To this day I've wondered what name I signed," he said with an unsure smile.

"How many people did they reject?"

"Four out of sixteen or so, I think."

"Three out of eighteen," his wife corrected him again. "But we weren't there till the end. We left right after the second interview."

"The second!" I cut in. "For crying out loud, is one not enough?"

"A security guy. In most cases it's for men only. About your military service."

I suggested a few questions I supposed the consul might ask. It was just like with the consul's tie. One confirmed the question, the other denied it. After half an hour they began to contradict the questions they had originally agreed on. I wished them good luck in St. Catharines, and left before they confused me out of my wits.

On the way home, their experience of the interview shaped itself in my mind into a formless, menacing, looming monster. A friendly conversation! For the consul, maybe for the interpreter. But for them? Even though they had won, they were subconsciously blocking out at least half of the interview. The subconscious mind, as is well known, censors experiences too terrible to remain in the consciousness. The showdown with the consul at the embassy — that was something for us to look forward to!

★

It was long past midnight when we rose from the table with puffy eyes and a certain degree of resignation.

"Nine answers, forty-two sentences. They cover almost everything the consul should be interested in. If not, here's the answer to fall back on: 'Ask my husband, he'll be able to explain it better.' Try to memorize them. If you can, all right; if you can't, it's all right as well. Each sentence scores. You have more than one hundred hours."

When I came back from work I found the door locked. I went to find Jana and Ivo, or at least the key, at the Landas.

"Jana's got a job!" Tina shouted enthusiastically at the door even before I could hug my son. "An old lady came to the hotel to hire somebody for a big housecleaning. Old Lorelei recommended Jana as by far the best for the job. I don't know when she'll be back. I picked up dinner for you. Ivo has already eaten and has done his homework."

Jana returned after nine o'clock. "Terrible," she laughed, tired but happy. "Major cleaning. Hardwood floors, windows, doors. It looked like the last time they had the apartment cleaned was before they went on their honeymoon, forty years ago. It will take at least three afternoons."

"So when will you memorize your answers?"

"In the morning when I wait for Ivo while he's at school." Jana smiled. "The old lady chatters in German all the time, but it doesn't really disturb me. She doesn't want any reply. Now and then you utter a sound of agreement or disbelief. It's enough for her."

"Damn! For two months there was nothing to do and now, when you need to study, you're crawling on your knees and scrubbing floors!"

"Calm down. I've already learned most of them. Working is good. I don't have to think about the interview and my nerves won't melt down prematurely. Besides, six hundred schillings equals another two hundred kilometres. We're almost above Newfoundland."

★

When I came to pick up Ivo from the Landas in the evening, I could see that Lorenc was burning to share some news.

"Pour a cup of coffee." He pushed the pot at me. "Light a cigarette and listen. Josef has outdone himself today!"

I whistled in appreciation. "Tell me, spin a yarn, exaggerate!"

"About two hours ago his wife burst in here, all in a panic, with a mug. Would I lend her a few drops of rum? Naturally, I delivered the bottle in person. Joe was stretched out on his bed, white as a bedsheet, looking like his own ghost. We had to force the rum into his mouth with a teaspoon. I guessed he must have run into the devil himself or at least Andropov or whoever's heading the KGB now."

"It was half an hour before he could babble out what had happened. In the morning he went to the job corner and was lucky. Somebody picked him up to help whitewash a house somewhere near Vienna. Suddenly, everybody was shouting at him. He couldn't understand, just kept repeating, 'What? What?' till he was hit by a plastic pail that had fallen from the upper level of scaffold. He's all right, nothing more than a bruise on his shoulder. How bad an injury can an empty pail falling from three metres cause?"

"He's turned it into a major tragedy, though. He claims that he might have been killed if the pail had hit him in the head, or if it had fallen from the seventh floor and had been full of concrete. Never mind there was no concrete and no seven-storey building within half a mile."

Lorenc relished his story. Usually we both had a good laugh at the expense of Joe's fears. Every time he decided he would go to the job corner to seek a day job, he wailed he would get hurt at work, that a grave was ready for him or at least a wheelchair, if he were really lucky.

I wasn't able to laugh today. At our site we have a higher scaffold, the pails are metal, and there's plenty of concrete. I felt a surge of sympathy for Josef.

"He's in shock. Not because of the pail, but because of the interview. He has it next Thursday, doesn't he? I bet that with that imagination of his he can't sleep any more. Now the accident has filled him with fears that he could go to the interview with a bandaged head or an arm in cast, and down the drain would go Australia. He realized how thin the tightrope on which his future rests is, and how a little bad luck could ruin his life."

Lorenc scrutinized my face for a full minute and then beamed as if he had discovered what he was looking for.

"Seems to me his fear is contagious. Here, better a shot of prevention than bottles of cure."

Jana lifted her eyes from the paper on which she was writing a list.

"We will have to spend some money. Ivo needs new pants and shoes for the interview. I need hairspray, nail polish, and elasticized panties, and you could use one decent handkerchief."

"Approved. How will we keep Ivo quiet while we're there? With a book? Not enough for an hour, I'm afraid. Lego? He might rattle the pieces and startle the consul."

"How about buying a colouring book? He already has crayons. It's noiseless and should last long enough."

"Excellent idea. One last thing. Understand, I don't object, I'm just curious, why those elasticized panties? Do you think the consul will judge you by the shape of your hips?"

"Probably not. But when I wear them I look good, then I feel good, and when I feel good I'll pass the interview."

"Unbeatable logic. If your panties get us to Canada, I'll buy you a truckload."

The conversation with Jarda took a serious turn.

"I don't dread the interview itself but its potentially catastrophic consequences." I tried to pinpoint my feelings. "Its definitive nature. Try to imagine what it means. You are gambling the lives of three people on the outcome of a one-hour conversation with an unknown person in an unknown language."

"I don't think anybody can imagine this in full," Jarda said, deep in thought. "I didn't have to pass any interview." He brightened and rubbed his chin. "But how about turning it all around. You have a full hour to size him up and convince him. Lots of time. The more time, the better your chances." He fell into silence and his thoughts. "Maybe, if they had given me an hour I could have wiggled my way out somehow. They gave me thirty seconds to sign that fucking condemnation. Thirty seconds destroyed my career and life in Czechoslovakia."

"Do you regret your decision?"

"I bless it. And those bastards, may they all go to hell. It made a lot of things easier for me. The way I am, I would have collided with power sooner or later. The clash came at the right time. I was young, at the beginning of my career, no girl to marry, no property. Their determination to hold my face in the mud forever made the prospect of emigration very favourable. Should I drive a bakery van in Brno or in Vienna? Easy choice to make. When a man has a family, a relatively good job, some property, then the decision is harder. The more you have to lose, the harder it gets. You went through it. You know." He fell silent again, immersed in his memories. Then he rubbed his chin again and slowly continued. "Being rejected for asylum might also be a blessing in disguise. You would be more at ease at the interview if you had asylum and that would be a mistake. Somewhere in the back of your mind you would know you have a place to retreat to. But when you have nothing but an abyss one step behind your ass, you fight tooth and nail for your life, and in the end you slash your way through, even if you were propelled by nothing but pure desperation."

I nodded because he expressed my own thoughts, and then I shook my head in disagreement. But Jarda hadn't finished.

"Even if you pass the interview, you will likely file an appeal just to make sure that you haven't closed any avenue. But listen! I've met a few people who went overseas, then came back, and now regret it bitterly. They hit the bottom there, like everybody does in the first months, regardless of the country. In the gloom of those early days, this hotel and the relative security of welfare here seemed like paradise. Without asylum they could not have come back. They would have clenched their teeth and held on another month or two. Their persistence would have turned the tide and the worst would have been over. But they were lured by the back door that was open to them. They gave up, and it broke them. I would hate to live their future."

"There's a Jesuitical streak in you, you sage."

"It's not slippery logic. It's common sense. And, what's more important, it's the truth, personally dug up and verified. Now I can see it quite clearly." Jarda's voice rose. "You have no way back, *ergo* you bowl the consul over. You leave before your appeal is heard, *eo ipso* you have no other alternative but to succeed there. *Summa summarum*, you are lucky people chosen to succeed by destiny. Do you understand, you dummy?" He slapped my back. "You're chosen by destiny!"

"It sounds so wonderful I wish you weren't a doctor of philosophy, but rather a fortune-teller."

When we emerged onto the gallery later that night, we could hear moans and groans coming from the Kurds' room.

"What's going on in there?" I tensed. "Do they need help?"

"I doubt it!" Jarda suppressed a smile. "It's nothing out of the ordinary. On the third floor lives a woman named Eva. Short, fat, clumsy, not very attractive, to tell the truth."

"The one who spends days at the window with her elbows on a cushion?"

"That's her. Every time we get our allowance she buys a two-litre bottle of cheap wine. That evening she pays a visit to the Kurds. They all get drunk and then they make love to her as long as their virility allows. Afterwards she cries and won't leave her room for a few days. All week she hates those fellows and claims one day she'll kill them. The week after, she hates them less, and the third week they exchange a word or two. When payday comes she buys a bottle and –"

"Today was payday."

"So take it easy. Nothing's going on that requires your intervention or assistance.

"Two Polish guys used to live next door. They are somewhere in Australia now. They wanted to have some fun, too, and when the party was going full blast they called in the night clerk to restore order. The clerk was a tiny guy, so thin that he could hide behind a whip. And he spoke in an incredibly high-pitched voice. He charged in, in the name of the law, demanding they stop disrupting the peace. We heard four loud slaps and then he ran out holding both cheeks. For days afterwards, he told everybody in his high-pitched voice, 'They beat me up.' When he met the girl again, he complained to her, too, but she was in her period of hating everybody, so she slapped his cheeks two more times. The next day he was updating his news: 'She beat me up.'"

Preparation for the interview took a whole week. The physical tune-up of our appearance alone took two days. On the Saturday, when I returned from work, I saw that Jana's washboard from the flea market had been busy. The clotheslines, stretched between the locker and the window, were heavy.

Sunday morning we turned our attention to our bodies. It was easier than we expected. Taking a bath had become a matter of routine. There was enough hot water available in the kitchen passage. Each of us wallowed in the pool as long as we wanted, washing away not only dirt but also the tiredness that had accumulated in our muscles over the week.

Our friends took care of our other necessities, bringing whatever they had. An iron, hair curlers, shoe and clothes brushes. We had our own scissors. Though small, they were good enough to trim hair, nails, and my beard. By the middle of the last afternoon Jana was ready to begin the final procedure – polishing her fingernails.

"Is it worth polishing them?" She looked with contempt at her sore hands, swollen from three days of floor-scrubbing.

"Sure it is. We can't lose on this one. If the consul likes neatness, it will be a plus. If not, the calluses will be a plus."

Nothing more to do but lie down on the bed, even though it was only late afternoon. Our eyes checked again and again the three stacks of underwear and the dress and suit on their hangers.

"Idleness is the mother of sin, they say. And also of a monstrous imagination that preys on one's nerves," I concluded. "We have to keep ourselves busy somehow without getting dirty. Now that we've successfully transformed ourselves into a decent family, how about showing it off on the Mariahilferstrasse? If we stroll all the way to McDonald's, we can reward ourselves with a hot-fudge sundae."

We put Ivo to bed, and when he was fast asleep we went for another walk to get tired. Perhaps the fresh air would help us fall asleep sooner.

"I'd like to know," Jana remarked, "if the consul knows how difficult it is for us to get into presentable shape in these conditions."

"Initially, I thought it wouldn't interest him at all. Why should he care? But I've come to the conclusion that he does care. Looking presentable is required, it's evaluated, it's part of the test. For two weeks I haven't been able to think about anything else. But today, when I managed to get my mind off it, the whole interview suddenly appeared in a different perspective and I understood what it's all about.

"At first I was resentful. It's unfair! Two, even one hundred years ago you simply boarded a ship, sailed there, and became a Canadian. Then I realized that the mere boarding of a ship, some leaky barge with sails, required a certain courage. Yet it was nothing compared with what came after reaching the land. Survival in a wilderness that stretched from ocean to ocean to ocean was no laughing matter. All the adventure books I had read as a boy paraded through my mind this afternoon: fur trappers, the Hudson Bay Company men, whalers, explorers like Mackenzie and Fraser, the first settlers in Saskatchewan who numbered just a few dozen, Arctic explorers. Those forefathers of Canada who survived because of their adventurous nature and abilities."

"Oh my, you're lecturing again! Starting from Adam. What on earth has this got to do with the interview?"

"Do you know why they don't tell their criteria to anybody? I think they have no more than one. They will accept you if you show an adventurous streak, something of the courage that helped the early settlers survive and has to have become a part of Canadian mental makeup. The whole interview probes one thing: Can you cope with an unknown situation? Take a bath without a bathroom? Cut your hair and shave without a barber or hairdresser? Can you keep your quick wit, self-control, and resourcefulness under the pressure of the consul's questioning? He will try to ambush you, throw you off balance, and he will scrutinize not what you're saying but rather your composure while saying it. Are you active? Decisive? Tough? Are you a spoiled brat who needs constant help?"

After some consideration Jana said, "I think my answers are good enough to hold my ground."

"They will help you to be relaxed and that's what counts. You know, at least roughly, what cards he holds."

We walked back to the hotel, and just before I turned off the light we both looked at Ivo. He slept in his bed the way he had done since he had been a baby, on his back, with his fists next to his head. He smiled in his sleep. He looked like a small angel. Jana smoothed his sleeping bag and looked at me with an almost desperate expression. "If for nothing else we must make it for him!"

"My word on it. Tomorrow evening we're going to take a bath in our pool – filled with champagne."

For a long time I stared at the dark ceiling. My emotions were on a roller-coaster ride and I had to wait till they got tired. Finally, they calmed down and I began to sink into sleep. On my closed eyelids a group of people began to take shape: a whaler, settler, explorer, fur trapper. I recognized the team of consuls who were going to interview me. They began to shoot one question after another: How fast can you paddle a hundred miles upstream? How would you build a loghouse using nothing but an axe? How do you keep warm on an iceberg without any wood? You shoot down narrow rapids in a canoe and there's a grizzly bear with her cubs in the stream – what do you do? Are you able to handle childbirth in a sod house? How many beavers can you skin in an hour? How many Indian languages do you speak? Can you train and drive a dogsled team?

Can you become a Canadian?

9

THE INTERVIEW

I WOKE UP without the alarm clock at ten minutes before six. The room, sunk deep in the well of the yard, was still half dark, but through the open window I could see a triangle of sky already lit with sunshine.

The interview. In sixty-six days we've progressed on our tightrope, first with hesitation then with growing self-confidence, towards today's hurdle. We've balanced our way to the point on the rope where the figure of a consul stands in front of us.

He will stop us to pronounce his judgement. He will question us and will weigh our pluses and minuses and decide whether we would be an asset for Canada. Then he will either step aside and let us pass or he'll reach into his pocket, pull out a straight razor, and with one swing cut the rope beneath our feet.

Jana woke up without the alarm clock as well.

"How did you sleep?"

"Better than expected."

"How do you feel?"

"Ready for the fight," she said without a smile. If I'd been in the consul's shoes, I'd have been scared to death.

We dressed with the utmost care. Jana finished her makeup and we ate a breakfast big enough to sustain us for the rest of the day. The sleepy face of Lorenc, our backup alarm clock, appeared in the window across the yard. We signalled him that everything was okay.

"Wipe the floor with him!" he wished us cheerfully and retreated to his room to doze the remaining hour till his breakfast. Before we left, we both drank a big mug of strong coffee. It would keep us alert for at least five hours.

Because I had a job, we could afford to take a streetcar. Through its windows we watched Mariahilferstrasse slowly come to life. Mr. Kukatschka was cleaning his shop window with a long-handled brush; in the delicatessen a fat woman pulled out a red-striped awning against the sun; salesgirls from Herzmansky's department store rolled out stands of dresses and T-shirts on sale. McDonald's was already serving breakfast. Ivo sat with his legs stretched straight in front of him. He was absorbed in admiring his brand-new running shoes, white with dark-blue stripes on the sides and a leaping puma on the heels.

We were as ready as we would ever be. From the résumés to the rehearsed answers to the elasticized panties. My stomach was full of butterflies, but two months earlier it had been filled with exploding dynamite. The streetcar tracks reminded me of the rails converging on the horizon. I smiled. We had passed that impassable point, and now we understood that life is a series of impassable horizons. It's a matter of faith, courage, and the will to reach the horizon and fight your way past it. Positive thinking pushes the rails apart and opens the way. Overcoming small horizons had become a daily event. We were getting used to it. It had made us stronger. Had we lived a single one of those sixty-six days in security? The interview was a huge, potentially disastrous obstacle, but not a completely unfamiliar one. At university we had to pass some forty oral exams, and this was an exam of a kind. An exam in a subject we didn't know, a language we barely spoke, and with a knife at our throats.

★

We got out of the streetcar at Opera Ring and walked the rest of the way. The sun was low above the rooftops, warming our side of the Ring. The air was fresh and cool and kept the flowers in their beds closed while sharpening our readiness. A woman walked her dog alone in the vastness of the park. Sprinklers hummed, moistening the lawns. An old gentleman on a sidewalk bench read a newspaper. The street looked unusually spacious and quiet. In half an hour streetcars and the subway would be delivering thousands of people to their work.

I began to enjoy the stroll. It was a lovely morning, and for the first time in a long while I was once again clean, groomed, in a suit and a tie, with shining shoes. Despite the seriousness of the moment, I felt the light touch of joy. Good, that was what I had been seeking. The pre-examination state of mind I call relaxed concentration. Relaxed on the surface, but the deeper mental strata uncompromisingly focused on the single purpose. All the energy compressed and under control, ready to uncoil and catapult us over the obstacle, our adversary – the consul.

Of course he would be an adversary. Every exam is a duel with an adversary, always has been. If I didn't think of him as an adversary, I wouldn't be able to muster enough concentration, and he'd get me.

"Wouldn't you rather sit in this café, order an espresso, and spend the morning reading a paper?" I sighed when we passed a large window behind which a few people were nibbling on breakfast.

"They're eating with such sophisticated manners they can't be enjoying their meal," Jana commented. "Would you really like to have a conversation with the dowager who's touching her mouth with her napkin so delicately? I prefer the interview."

"You're right. The only guy really alive around here is this apprentice." I pointed to a boy in a red apron who was sweeping the sidewalk and arranging wicker tables and chairs and white-and-red Martini sunshades.

"He still finds fun in life," I remarked when he picked up a glistening fallen chestnut and threw it at a tree trunk. Of course, Ivo had to try his aim as well.

I wondered how they were preparing – the team of consuls. Were they getting a massage and last tactical advice from their coach in the embassy locker room? Putting yourself into the adversary's shoes is a good weapon, but I was straying towards foolishness. Most likely he was still at home, chewing his toast, swallowing his coffee, and cursing the work ahead of him.

His work – *that's us!* I suddenly became the consul, pouring his cup of coffee, dreading the prospect of hours of facing families with scared and imploring eyes, people who would consider him, and rightly so, to be a kind of god who held in one hand the key to the promised land and in the other the razor that would cut the tightrope from under their feet. One single person functioning as destiny. I considered how maddening it must be to have responsibility for shattering a human life. And it was me who'd driven him into this. I chose it, fought for it, but he was assigned to it. Which of us would be the more miserable?

Cut it out. Don't start shedding tears over him. Compassion could cost me my concentration, my determination, and Canada. He is the adversary and that's that!

We were by now within sight of the embassy, but we still had half an hour to spare. We sat on a bench to have one more cigarette.

"Look at him." Jana's chin pointed to a middle-aged man walking briskly down the sidewalk. "He must be a Canadian."

"Could be," I admitted, noticing his checkered suit. "No one in Europe wears that kind of suit, except for the old man in Prague who told us so much about Canada. But his briefcase has a touch of Czech about it. I used to have a baggy, worn-out one like it in public school."

"We could play checkers on his back," Ivo whispered in my ear.

"You'll see. We'll run into him at the embassy," said Jana.

I shrugged. "Why pay any attention to him?"

"To avoid thinking about the interview."

The embassy's waiting room was empty. A spacious, cosy room. Wall-to-wall carpet, sofas, easy chairs, coffee tables strewn with newspapers and magazines, two big rubber plants. The wall opposite the entrance was all glass, one huge window dressed with white curtains. The sun wouldn't reach the waiting room for three more hours, and the darkness and the emptiness began to gnaw at my carefree mood. Slowly, other candidates for Canadian visas wandered in. Everybody in his Sunday best, cleaned and groomed as well as his circumstances permitted. Each of them serious, taciturn, deep in thought. Even though there were soon thirty or more people in the room, including children, it remained unnaturally quiet. Each person sat on the edge of a sofa or chair, staring at the carpet, as if he had lost his tongue. Now and then a woman smoothed her hair or a man adjusted his tie or circled his neck with an index finger, as if his collar were strangling him. The first three families were invited in. Tension began to tighten its grip on my insides. To keep it at bay, I annoyed others by rustling a Vancouver newspaper. Wow, a mansion for $150,000. A photo of a murderer, but I couldn't understand his motives. Seven pages of help-wanted advertisements. There must be plenty of jobs, when they are looking for so many people. More advertising than news –

Jana jolted me with her elbow. "He *is* a Canadian!" she said in triumph as the man in the checkered suit approached.

"Moravec family?" he asked in perfect Czech.

He's a Czech! My eyes sent the message to Jana as we rose and followed him into the inner hallway of the embassy. The craziness of his suit almost made me laugh. He ushered us into an office and spread his arms so that one pointed to us, the other one to the man rising behind the desk. His expression embodied the supreme seriousness of the upcoming meeting.

"Moravec family – Mr. Consul."

In his dual function as the secretary and interpreter, the check-ered man bubbled with activity. He motioned Jana to sit Ivo at a small coffee table and watched her take out the colouring book and crayons. Despite his attention, Ivo, who knew he must remain quiet as long as the consul wished, managed to whisper, "Don't worry about me, Mom."

Then the interpreter pointed us to two comfortable armchairs facing the consul's desk and sat himself down at the consul's right. He had an air of joyful expectation and swung one leg over the other, revealing striped socks.

Nice office. Comfortable, official yet still cosy. Canadian style, I assumed. A portrait of Her Majesty on the wall, Canadian flag in the corner.

The consul. Inconspicuous. In his thirties. Dark-grey three-piece suit. Impeccably groomed. Disinterested, cold, attentive grey eyes. *The adversary.* I focused on him. All else faded away: the flag, the checkered interpreter, my son, the past and future. I shifted to my highest gear. *There's nothing but now.* Me against him. I must walk out of this door the winner.

He speaks. What? It doesn't sound like French, so it must be English. But what kind? A north Yukon drawl? The introduction, I presume. Why? We all know damn well why we are meeting. Go ahead, man, interpret it, I have to catch my breath. How much did I understand? Twenty per cent? Thirty? But I can guess the meaning close enough. My sixth sense is working and I can rely on it.

Do I speak English? Till he spoke I thought so, but if he is speak-ing English, I am not so sure any more. Still, language means points and I have nothing to lose. Good thing I rehearsed the sentence for presenting him my résumé. No, that was stupid. I shouldn't go first. I should show him that I accept his domination here, his superior-ity, and his right to conduct the interview his way. *If I only could understand you better. . . .* I have to guess the question and answer what I think he asked. I prepared the answer and I speak fluently and deliberately. Is something wrong? He isn't reacting. Have I not spoken in English? The interpreter nods, so perhaps I have. The next string of sounds is put in the same unexcited tone but with a rise at the end. Perhaps it is about my occupation. I answer in simple, understandable terms. He makes a note. But not a muscle moves in his face. A tough nut. *Examiners like you were always the worst and you seem to be the very perfection of the type.*

It looks like he's following a questionnaire, similar to the one in Traiskirchen. If so, I have a better chance of guessing the question correctly.

"Yes, sir, it is our first marriage. Our son was born three years after the wedding." *We are a really decent family.*

Watch out, Jana! This one's for you. Fine. Excellent. Now careful with the word "biotechnology." Wonderful, my love. He doesn't even blink. He should have been a poker player, he would be a millionaire. I hope he will ask her a second question from her repertoire. He does. *Jana, you are holding your ground marvellously.* Ouch, I didn't expect this one. I have to think it over and translate at the same time. Not a single move. No gesture, no expression. Is he made out of stone? Am I speaking Swahili or Tatarian, by some chance? What is the interpreter doing? The rascal! He's dozing! A good sign, isn't it? If I were massacring English, he would grimace at my linguistic butchery, wouldn't he?

"We would like to settle in Canada, sir, because it is a free, democratic country with a Western culture. It has both natural resources and highly developed technology. Its dynamic character provides room for growth and, because it is a young, predominantly immigrant society, it offers a chance for newcomers to fully integrate, not like the rigid, old societies of Switzerland or Germany, which leave immigrants always at the fringes. Not to mention that Canada is far away from the Soviet Union."

I might as well have been talking to a stone slab.

"Besides, I can speak both official languages. *Si vous désirez je peux présenter ma langue française.*"

It is a risky proposition, I've forgotten a lot, but I might score additional points. He doesn't take the bait. Back off, back off, don't push it. Maybe he isn't too good at French and this *faux pas* might cost us the interview. Here it comes, the pet question. No, not for Jana, I should answer it. But Jana is already reciting that our son attends school, that his education, his school attendance, is the highest priority for us under any circumstances. Wonderful Frau Doktor. She knew her consuls. *Ivo, you're an angel, hold on, please, a little bit longer.* If I only had a hint whether our answers are getting us to Canada or to hell.

"Yes, sir, we are as healthy as fish."

You son of a . . . Sphinx! Can't you speak more slowly? I'm not your secretary taking shorthand. I should calm down. I must not let him break my concentration. A deep breath helps.

Another one for Jana. What a pounding he's giving her. But she fights back. Thank God, so far he's been asking the questions we rehearsed for. As long as he doesn't ask for a clarification or for more details!

Is he alive? Is he a robot? A scoreboard on a pinball machine, counting the points so that when the limit is reached he'll let us know by ringing and flashing? Shut up! Keep your focus!

One for me. *As you please, Mr. Stoneface.* I don't believe it. How can a career diplomat, posted in Central Europe, ask this question? Doesn't he know that in 1968 Czechoslovakia was invaded by more than half a million troops and is still occupied? How can he judge the applications of Czech refugees? Each of us, one way or the other, is a victim of the invasion. How to translate my answer? Not into English. Into his world. The interpreter! Good luck his ankle is within reach of my shoe. Hurrah! He woke up quite smoothly, what a pro he is. Why not? It could be put that way, I suppose. Simplified, but the substance is there. Did the statue understand it?

"Perhaps, sir, we did have a chance to escape in 1968 like so many others, but we were inexperienced, idealistic. In our youthful naivety, we could not estimate how cruel a disaster socialism is."

Nothing. *Make a move, man, for Chrissake. Shout, hit the desk, fart! Anything to show you're alive.*

"No, sir, I'm sorry, but we don't know anybody in Canada. Of course we'll go happily to any destination you send us."

Is that a routine question or a good sign? This is the last question Jana knows the answer to. Next time, she'll fail. But she's been great, self-confident, pronouncing well. She sounds like she really can speak English. What a performance! Hats off!

Consul, consul, confess! You want to be a robot! You're working hard to be a scoreboard. It's your protection. You're trying to be as impersonal as you can to remain impartial. I cracked your secret, after all, and you immediately became more likeable, though you overplay your role so much you went far beyond being impartial.

"Yes, sir, I work in Vienna as a skilled bricklayer and my wife just last week cleaned up a six-bedroom apartment. We are not afraid of any job." *As proof, I could mention the Traiskirchen washrooms, but you wouldn't understand. If you ever use a washroom at all, you could sell your waste as marble paperweights.*

"No, sir, we have not applied for any other country. We are interested in Canada and only Canada."

Now I'm definitely done for! What kind of long and twisting sentence is this? What has exercising got to do with us? I exercise on a scaffold twelve hours every day, just look at my hands. . . .

My sixth sense is faster than my thinking and sends down my spine a shot of joy that melts my tension in a split second. Then my mind rushes in with its understanding: the consul is talking about exercising the authority vested in him by the government of Canada; because we meet the requirements set by the aforementioned, he, pending the satisfactory outcome of the security interview and the medical examination, is pleased to announce his decision to grant us the status of landed immigrants to Canada!

I do a great injustice to the consul's eloquence by translating it for Jana as: "We're in!"

The surge of joy in her is so sudden and powerful that a tiny bit of it escapes her lips as a muffled squeak. The consul reacts. We move him! Half an inch. That is how much his left eyebrow rises in curiosity, amusement, and indignation. *You asked for it, consul, by giving us the news on which our lives hung as if you were announcing the departure of a train.* If I were consul, I would arrange for a Mountie to spring from that filing cabinet there and run the Canadian flag up the mast; behind that ficus plant a brass band would play "O Canada," and during the last bars a salvo of sixteen-inch guns would explode behind the bookcase. But it doesn't matter. We can hear the jubilation in our minds as we sign some papers the busy interpreter slips in front of us. Something about an interest-free loan for transportation, language courses, and who knows what else. We're signing blank forms. He assures us they won't be misused, but we couldn't care less. At the end, the consul wishes us good luck. His handshake is firm and pleasant.

Next to the elevators in the corridor off the lobby, the smokers gathered. Under the kind auspices of the lion and the unicorn, the heraldic beasts on the coat of arms that adorned the embassy door, I spent the next half an hour.

For a long time I was bathed in the waves of joy that surged in me. There was still plenty of time to gather my concentration before the second interview. According to the interpreter, it wouldn't take place until after lunch. Surrounded by representatives of the families still waiting for their interviews, I answered anxious questions until I let out that we had both done our interview in English. They were aghast, their fingers pulled at their collars as if they had suddenly been cut off from oxygen.

"Really nice going, you bastard," one man said, speaking for all the others.

"You should have been the last ones," another said with a deep sigh. "You've raised the standard so —"

He couldn't complete his complaint because at that moment somebody put a hand on my shoulder. It was the man I had noticed a few seconds earlier, when he entered the lobby. It was impossible not to notice him. Against the background of pale, nervous faces, he glowed with physical and intellectual fitness.

"How about wrapping up the whole business with the security interview without waiting for the interpreter? He won't be available for the next three hours and you would get out of here much sooner."

He led me to the very last door in the hallway, into an office where the desks were covered with papers, files, books, and coffee cups. Clearly, living people, not statues, worked there. He motioned me to a chair, closed the door, and locked it from the inside.

"Nothing personal, just routine procedure," he assured me, though I had made no comment nor had I flinched. In my experience, security offices were usually locked. Besides, he was at home there. He was relaxed. In his short-sleeved shirt, he meant to establish a friendly relationship, to put people at ease and instil in them a feeling of trust. Then they would tell him what he needed to know. I hadn't prepared for this interview. I could only answer his questions truthfully.

Answer the question? Sure. But how when my English is gone? After the stress of the first interview, I had relaxed so much I couldn't conjugate the verb "to be." He laughed and assured me I was neither the first nor the last to suffer temporary brain damage from the stone falling off my heart. He switched to small talk about Vienna and Hotel Zoch to give me time to regain my concentration and stop behaving like a smiling idiot.

He talked more slowly and with more careful pronunciation than the consul. Then he told me, in case I lacked the English word, to use any other I know: French, German, Czech, Russian, Latin. There are plenty of international words and with him it worked. His capacity to combine, understand from a hint, deduce, was fantastic. After we had established that he was not interested in either my military service, because it had been too long ago, or my work experience, because I hadn't had the clearance to work with sensitive materials, we got to the heart of the matter: my father's dissidence and his and my encounters with state security.

That fellow was in a league of his own. What brain power! Each question elaborated on and, at the same time, checked some previous, exact question arising from my answers. Everything fit together like a giant crossword puzzle he solved easily to learn what he needed to know. Here was a real professional of counter-intelligence! Had he been working at the Prague passport office instead of the secret police potato head I dealt with, I would have been safely behind bars.

For the first time in my life I had nothing to pretend or hide. What a marvellous feeling.

The more I was investigated by this intelligent, determined, tough man, the more enthusiastic I became about his abilities. I felt wonderfully safe. There was no way he would let any spy slip through his fingers to Canada, to *our* Canada.

"Now it's your wife's turn," he said, unlocking the door and locking it again when we were back in the hallway.

"There might be a problem, sir. She speaks just a little English," I admitted, concerned that our language scheme would be exposed.

"We'll manage in German, won't we?" he assured me. Only now did I realize that he had scrutinized our application and résumés and that he found me in the lobby without asking because he'd seen our photographs. I had to wait in the hallway until he brought in Jana, to prevent us from communicating. Then he let me go back to my happy son, sitting quietly with those who were still waiting. They were even more mad at us now, not so much because we had jumped the queue, but because, unlike them, the interview was behind us and we had succeeded.

In twenty minutes, during which he cross-examined Jana against my answers, he escorted her with courtesy, as if after a dance, back to the lobby.

"Everything's all right. Wait here for another half an hour, the secretary will give you an official letter confirming your landed immigrant status." With a wide grin he slapped me on my back. This time I understood him perfectly well: "Welcome aboard!"

We burst from the elevator into the ground-floor lobby screaming in euphoria. We thought nobody would be there, and we shocked the uniformed guard so badly he almost fell off his chair. He understood and laughed, and then he jumped up and ran to the heavy glass door to hold it open for us. He could see that in my light-footed state of mind I was going to walk through the glass or pry the door open the wrong way and carry it, frame and all, out to the Dr. Karl Lueger Ring, where magnificent chestnut trees were filtering the sunshine so that it sprinkled the sidewalk in merry freckles. I saluted him in my smartest military manner, except I used my left hand. He tipped his cap and his eyes were laughing.

What now? Which way? To the right, to the WCC to announce the wonderful news to Frau Doktor, or to the left, home, to our friends? It is after noon and the WCC is closed to the public. Frau Doktor might, perhaps, tolerate my dancing and singing there during the working day, but it would be too much after hours. So we make a pirouette towards home, and in the summer air our joy accelerates to intoxicating levels, *if you please, Guv'nor, Mayor, Doktor Karl Lueger, your Ring is until further notice appropriated for our joy.* Beethoven's *Ode to Joy*, carried from below by double basses, begins to rise in full orchestra, rises still further, and thunders – *O Freude* – till Jana laughs and tells me I'm singing slightly offbeat, badly out of tune, and that I am bellowing like a bull. But I'm going to Canada, and Canada is huge and can accommodate plenty of singing like mine.

There you are, Beethoven, in that bronze bust on the building across the street. Ludwig, you marvellous buddy, you wholesale supplier of courage, you supermarket of hope. Now, right now, I understand you to the last note. To be able to write your Ode to Joy, *you must have been terribly beaten. Don't deny it, I know your slow movements from the* Eroica *and the* Fifth *and now I'm one with your joy because I've been beaten down as well, but from now on there's nothing but joy. From this moment we're brothers, and you're going to Canada with me.*

Jana's legs are lightened instead by Mozart, and she is dancing above the sidewalk while I circle around her. Now the third great Viennese, Johann Strauss, enters into the act and it is necessary to pay him homage with some flying turns of a waltz that bring us in front of the posh Burgtheater sidewalk café. Nonchalant patrons lift questioning brows. To make them happy, too, I yell at them in German, "We're going to Canada!" They take it to mean we got a bargain trip and hide behind their newspapers and small talk. For them, everything returns to its habitual track. *Only for you, darlings, never more for us! We've just started a brand-new track and we're dancing in this Elysium occupying the whole sidewalk.* I'm spinning to the beat of the Ninth Symphony, Jana to Mozart's *Eine Kleine Nachtmusik,* and Ivo to "Daring Young Man on a Flying Trapeze."

Watch out! We almost run over two elderly gentlemen crouching by a wall. *What a shame! Such decently dressed people, tipsy so soon in the afternoon.* To put them at ease, I tell them we're going *nach Kanada.* They understand and show us the way to the embassy, until Jana explains that we are not going to the embassy but to Canada, the country, to live there. They congratulate us and, boosted by our joy, shed twenty years from their gaits.

We continue flying. Isn't it beautiful to begin life at thirty-five? Sure it is! It's magnificent! *Hey, you, in that fiacre, yes, you rich tourists. Don't look so bored, as if your life was over at thirty-five.*

What? A streetcar for the ride home? This Ring, this city, is too small to accommodate my joy. I couldn't bear to be confined in any can on wheels.

My wife is beautiful and smart as she dances above the asphalt. Men can't take their eyes off her. To those I catch red-eyed I announce: "That's my Canadian wife and my Canadian son." We barely fit in the wide Mariahilferstrasse. *Celebration? Sure! At McDonald's.* I order in English, but the girl doesn't understand. I repeat the order in German and she asks, "Americans?" No no, my dear, Canadians, and she wishes us a nice holiday in Vienna. *Isn't it wonderful? We are not* Flüchtlings *any more, we're Canadians on holiday. We belong somewhere.* The letter in my pocket confirms that our tightrope is firmly anchored in Canadian soil.

After the celebration we rush to Herzmansky's to buy the biggest box of Lego they have. How long has it been since Jana cried here? In a previous life. Today's laughter wipes it all away, and if the security guard were here I would buy him a drink to celebrate the reversal of our fortune. Back on the street again we take over the whole width of the sidewalk, but people can't frown when they see us beaming with happiness. *You've lost your watch – how marvellous! We would have to throw them away anyway; the old time is lost and that's good. New time calls for a new timepiece from this posh jewellery shop.* We stop to buy a bottle to cheer up our friends. *What do you think, clerk, that we Canadians drink? Sure, Seagram's whisky. Give me a bottle, that big one, and some smokes to go with it. Sure, a pack of Rothmans.*

We stand in the median at the intersection with the Gürtel raising our arms towards the skies like sun worshippers, towards the setting sun, towards the West. There, beyond the ocean, lies our Canada. We still cannot quite believe we are, at least a little bit, Canadians. The vertigo of this vision makes us fall on our backs in a freshly raked pile of golden maple leaves.

10

THE STRANGER

I LEANED MY naked back against the chimney's rough sun-warmed bricks and comfortably stretched my legs along a polystyrene panel. I wouldn't have my lunch anywhere else but on the roof, where I could enjoy the vista of gradually rising Alpine hills, mountains, and peaks visible in the distance through the pristine fall air.

"I wish you had an interview every day." The boss appreciated the quantity of work I had done since morning. No wonder, I had been fuelled with a powerful mixture of immense relief, unburnt adrenalin, and the rosiest expectations.

I'd better cool down or it will backfire because I am expecting too much. That future of ours can't be all that rosy. True, the cornerstone is now in place. Somewhere in the vast nation defined by the names of Victoria, St. John's, Windsor, and Ellesmere Island. For the time being that is sufficient for us, though I suspect that our destination will affect the level of hardship we will have to wrestle with. I wonder where they send newcomers to serve their time. They haven't told us, so that we can continue our guessing game and not get bored. It doesn't matter. Wherever people live, we can survive. We know that we will get the interest-free transportation loan and that the government will sponsor us. Perhaps some kind of Canadian Hotel Zoch?

Am I diluting my exuberant mood? No. Looking at these mountain peaks I know we've already managed to cross them. The Canadians are interested in us, and it means we are living for the future, we are anchored in the future, more than in the past. I'm not spoiling the mood, just trying to return from emotion to reason. We've solved the most important questions, but there is plenty more to deal with. After all, even though we are dancing, we are still on the tightrope, and will be for a long time, even though it now slants down towards Canada.

There could still be three, four months of waiting. We need some strategy to counter our relaxation and impatience or they might do us more damage than the previous high tension. Idle brooding is still dangerous.

I'll need to hold on to my job, not let them fire me. The transportation loan means we can spend some of our money on winter clothing. And the more money I make here, the more we will have to start with in Canada. I can't let myself get injured, especially when snow and sleet make the scaffold slippery. I can't strain myself or get sick, certainly not before the medicals. I suppose I shouldn't die before our departure. But thanks to my work, the time will fly. I can work until I'm dead tired and then sleep like a log. At least on those nights when my emigration nightmares give me a break.

For Jana, it might be worse. Travelling to and from school with Ivo and going for walks with him, the rest of the time spent in the hotel. This is a breeding ground for runaway thoughts about what could happen when we get there. She will have to keep up her English studies and work very hard not to worry too much.

What? The lunch break is over? Just watch out, you Canadian on that Austrian scaffold, or you might bust your Czech ass.

"Guess who called!" Jana greeted me, grinning from ear to ear. "Frau Doktor! You're supposed to pay her a visit tomorrow. Something about work, but I'm not sure I understood her correctly."

At ten o'clock the next day, I was sitting in Frau Doktor's office.

"Judging from your résumé, language abilities, and from what I have heard about your performance at the interview, I believe you might be able to help us here."

"Me? Help you? Of course, but how?"

"A variety of tasks, whatever is necessary, for a few weeks, maybe till your departure."

I kept nodding enthusiastically, of course, sure, anytime.

"I can't pay you much, probably less than the construction job, but to compensate for this we work as long as necessary to process the daily batch." Her eyes twinkled. "Sometimes till five, sometimes till midnight. For us every file is a human life and we must not leave anyone in limbo one day longer than necessary."

"No need to talk about the money," I said. It was the knowledge inherent in this job that fascinated me.

"Second thing. Do you know how to keep your mouth shut?"

"Do you think I could have defected if I didn't?"

"All right. Keep it shut. We don't have any big secrets here, we're not in the same league as the KGB or CIA, but even the small ones might interest somebody and screw up someone's life. Who lives where, when he departs, his destination, and so on. All information, including names, is confidential. Moreover, people will confide many things in you and they must be able to trust you will keep everything they say private."

"I don't do to others what I don't want others to do to me. I have enough of my own worries to brood over someone else's."

"I'm glad we agree. Now go, resign from your job and come back. There's a lot of work today." She pointed to a pile of files the courier had just delivered from the Traiskirchen office.

Holy smokes! Isn't this something? I kept repeating this incredulously while a streetcar carried me from the WCC office to the construction site. Back up from a trowel to a desk and typewriter, doing whatever might be needed: typing, filing, interviews with newcomers, errands around the city, preparation of papers for embassies. I would have a chance to meet interesting people, learn their stories, and positively affect their lives.

But what if I couldn't help? My victory over the consul hadn't made me an expert and adviser. What if I goofed up a letter in German or some Arabic names? The WCC worked in German and English, but its clients spoke half the languages of the world. What if I couldn't understand or if I misunderstood?

If I spoiled a polystyrene panel, I could tear it down and replace it, losing ten minutes. If I made a mistake in somebody's résumé, I would put his future at risk or even damage it. Shouldn't I rather stick to my safe trowel? To whom would I owe loyalty if I found out that an applicant was a crook? To him, a fellow refugee? To Austria? To the U.S.A., Canada, or Australia? To my principles? Hell of a lot of responsibility. And what if people broke into tears? Unloaded their tragedies on me? All the malice of the world could pour on my desk. Would I be able to handle it? Were my nerves strong enough now to cope with another's emotional stress?

Those who are afraid shouldn't venture into the forest, let alone into defection. I could spend the time till departure sitting at home. What difference would it make? None. Except that I would stray towards craziness, like Joe. An idle man is a dangerous man. Frau Doktor should have got a patent for that insight. It was one worthy of Freud's city.

And I should have got a patent for negative thinking. The offer was such an honour! She'd picked me out of hundreds of people. She had more confidence in me than I had myself. Most likely, behind the crescents of her glasses her smart eyes could foresee what was in store for me, and she had solutions to problems I didn't even know about yet. I knew nobody in Vienna who could provide me with stronger support than she.

What was I afraid of? This challenge was sure to come sooner or later. The trowel and mortar had convinced me that my legs could carry me and my hands feed me. Now it was my head's turn. What did I fear? That my new, green, developing head would not be a match for the job. That it would shrivel under the burden of responsibility. But unless I put it under stress, it would never grow strong.

How had Theo expressed it? In the West, I would set my limits myself. But how the hell do I know if they are realistic?

A practical test. Action. Risk-taking.

I dawdled to the construction site. I realized how wrong I had been yesterday. There would be no routine waiting for departure, but another battle instead. A big question mark hovered above its outcome.

Riding high on the crest of the interview wave, I dared to make a phone call home to my parents. I felt strong enough, vindicated. My success had proved my assumptions and calculations to be correct.

In five minutes I stepped out of the booth. Jana had a probing look.

"How bad was it? How are they? How do you feel they are?"

"Still very much down, far from being out of the woods. But the worst emotions seem to have receded and reason is slowly taking over. They were happy to hear from me, to know that we all are safe and sound and healthy. They tried hard to press me to stay in Europe no matter what, and not to move to Canada, though I told them it had already been decided. Before they could get out the heavy artillery of reproaches about emigration in general, I ran out of schillings. They urged me to write more often, and they offered us any help we might need and they could provide."

"It sounds better than I expected." Jana's face cleared.

"I gave them our address."

Her face darkened again. "I guess it had to happen sooner or later. Bye-bye our quiet anonymity. Within a week we can expect trouble."

"Excellent photographs," I remarked to Frau Doktor when I had finished gluing the new batch on immigration applications.

"They weren't always this way. When the photographer opened his business, he was young and had two ambitions: to become an artist and to make big bucks." Frau Doktor leaned comfortably against the windowsill. "In the early sixties he won this government contract and began to photograph the refugees for Traiskirchen. He believed that as an artist he should capture their misery and the trauma they had gone through. He had enough time, in those days fewer people defected. In 1968 the tide rose and refugees began to flood his quiet town. He was shooting thousands of pictures, making big money, but the avalanche was damaging him. He saw it as an avalanche of the desperate, because desperation was what he chose to look for in them. He had many a sleepless night. He told me he was scared by the eyes that rose from his developing bath every evening. Scores of pairs of eyes he had photographed the previous day. He considered quitting the job, moving somewhere to a small village, and going back to shooting pictures of weddings, baptisms, and babies. He had lots of money, but it haunted him. He felt his fortune was somehow tainted, made at the expense of those miserable folk."

"But these little portraits have nothing miserable in them."

"He found peace eventually in those nights without sleep. He began to look in the faces in front of his lenses not for a tormenting past but for a hopeful future. He focused on the moments of hope that showed in their faces. I'd say he stopped seeing his clients as mere objects of his art. Gradually he started taking pictures like these ones. He emphasized the best in people that his experienced eye could find. His photos began to improve people's odds with consuls and immigration officers. He even bought some shirts and ties to dress those who had fled just in a T-shirt. Step by step, he became an important cog in the machine for the resettlement of refugees. He's a wealthy man, but his money doesn't haunt him any more. And I think he became an artist as well."

★

Tina burst into our room without knocking on the door. "Hurry up! Sigi's dying or something!"

A heart attack? Stroke? We knew Sigi had had his interview at the U.S. embassy earlier on and it meant a hellish stress. We ran upstairs after Tina.

Sigi was half lying, half sitting on the floor, trying to crawl onto the bed. Lorenc was watching him, unable to move, petrified, from a chair. Tina was panicking. We hauled Sigi onto the bed. Jana leaned over him.

"What's wrong? What happened to you?"

"My . . . my . . . legs d . . . d . . . died."

"Tina, warm up a glass of milk for him."

"What's wrong with him?"

"Dead drunk."

"I . . . I'm spinning . . . drilling into the ground."

"You'll be okay," Jana tried to calm him down. "Don't worry, you're not dying. We're going to give you some medicine, and in the morning you'll be as fit as a fiddle. Lorenc, don't sit there like a stump, bring a pail or something. Otherwise your bed will be messed up."

Sigi was a bachelor in his thirties. He was fond of fine clothing and today was dressed really smartly. A light-grey suit, matching suede shoes, crimson tie on a snow-white shirt. We took off his jacket so he wouldn't crumple it, but when I wanted to ease his tie he attacked me.

"You want to strangle me. You'll be held responsible. I'm under protection."

"Drink this. It will help you. All of it." Jana poured warm milk into his mouth, supporting his head. "Lorenc, be on red alert."

"My arms have died, too," Sigi babbled, falling on his back again. "I'm spinning faster and faster."

"It will pass, you'll see," Jana comforted him.

Suddenly Sigi's eyes popped open and all the milk flew out of his stomach.

"Mom! . . . Dying . . . Don't want . . . Under the U.S.A. . . ." Poor Sigi was tossing on the bed, kicking his feet in their suede shoes. Then he relaxed a little. Lorenc emptied the pail and brought it back.

"What the hell were you two up to?" I asked.

Lorenc and Tina looked very embarrassed.

"He came here an hour ago, out of his mind with joy that he had passed the interview and America had accepted him. We poured him a shot of rum to toast his success, but he refused, claiming he was a teetotaller."

"I never drink . . . even if I die . . ." announced Sigi.

"Then he hit upon the idea he would celebrate his victory in American style. He ran out and returned with this two-litre bottle of Coca-Cola. He said he had never tasted it before, but Coca-Cola meant America and drinking his fill was the only proper way to celebrate."

"Under the protection . . . American government . . ." Sigi mumbled.

"We knew he had never touched spirits before, but when he wasn't looking we laced his Coke with rum."

"How much?"

"Not even half the bottle."

"Of Coke?"

"No, of rum, of course."

"It won't kill him."

"Whoever kills me . . . responsible . . . U.S.A."

"He took a few swigs, and he went ballistic, singing America's praises and rejoicing what a wonderful country she must be to make such incomparable soft drinks. A veritable paradise for him as a teetotaller."

Sigi interrupted by vomiting again. Lorenc barely managed to catch it in the pail.

"To be on the safe side, fix it over his neck."

We slipped the handle over Sigi's head and propped him half sitting against the headboard.

"He killed the bottle within half an hour, all the time growing more and more ecstatic about Coca-Cola. Nobody but the U.S.A. could make such a beverage! He began to speak more slowly and slur the words, but we didn't realize what was wrong. Such a small drop of alcohol."

"I can imagine. He has eaten nothing since breakfast, a few coffees perhaps, he's exhausted from the interview, and now you've loaded him with almost half a litre of rum!"

"Then he had the idea of buying another bottle of Coca-Cola, but when he got up, his legs gave way. He collapsed to the floor and has been crying he would die ever since."

"A teetotaller doesn't need too much alcohol. And an exhausted one even less."

"Do you think a cup of coffee might help?"

"The two litres of Coke he drank contain enough caffeine to keep him wide-eyed for a week."

But because he was so exhausted after the interview and because he had started to feel better, Sigi calmed down, slightly swaying from side to side, his eyes closed. The yellow plastic pail rested on his snow-white shirt and his beautiful crimson tie dangled into its depths. As he was falling asleep he mumbled something. The hollowness of the pail amplified his words so we all could hear:

". . . Under the protection . . . government of the U.S.A. . . . president . . ."

"Why on earth did you come back from Canada?"

"Everybody there is out of his mind!"

"Didn't you like it there?"

"I liked it very much. But they work like crazy."

"And it was wrong for you?"

"Just wait. It's gonna be bad for you as well. Luckily they paid me enough on that construction job for me to buy a ticket back."

"Do they work less in Vienna?"

"I don't know. I've never had to work here."

"How can you compare, then?"

"No need to compare. I know what I know. If I hadn't escaped, the Canadians would have worked me to death."

I broke off the conversation. Here was the first authentic "Canadian" who could brief me about the first weeks in Canada, and he remembered nothing but terrible work that had nearly killed him. He sowed some doubts in my mind. Even though I thought he was the type of person for whom work is dangerous in any dosage because they are allergic to it, he scared me.

The trouble didn't come a week later as I had expected, but within forty-eight hours. That evening we all gathered at Lorenc's. Only Josef was missing, he had his interview the following day.

"Before we start fretting," said Lorenc, "how do you know he was an informant?"

"A sixth sense. There was just something about him. We both had a queer feeling as soon as he entered the room," I answered.

"Feelings, however queer, prove nothing," Edita remarked.

"He claimed to be an Austrian, he spoke German fluently, but with the kind of mistakes in grammar that Jana, with her high-school proficiency, could identify."

"One strike against him."

"He also claimed he was a wholesale dealer in flowers. The only thing supporting this claim was the soil under his rather long, yellow fingernails. A real businessman would shave more than once every three days, and his suit cried out to be cleaned and pressed. It looked like he'd been sleeping in it."

"Two more strikes," Lorenc decided.

"I also don't believe a well-to-do wholesale dealer would roll cigarettes from the cheapest brand of tobacco."

"Four strikes, though some millionaires are said to do this."

"Why today?" Edita asked. "Is there any connection with your WCC job?"

"The day before yesterday I mentioned my address over the phone to my parents," I admitted. "Of course they tap international phone calls. I didn't mention the WCC. I told my parents, and I later told him, that I was still at the construction job."

"They work really fast," Dan shuddered.

"What else did you tell him?" Lorenc kept probing.

"Plenty. Everything he wanted to know. Except I made it all up. I didn't say a word about any of you, don't worry."

"Is there anything more specific against him?"

"One major thing. As he does business with Czechoslovakia frequently, he's buddy-buddy with the border guards and customs people on both sides of the border. He offered to smuggle out anything. Not money or jewellery, but important documents – birth and marriage certificates or university diplomas."

"I suppose you declined his offer."

"I assured him we already had all our documents, even jewellery, here. I told him we have our own ways. Let them rack their brains over what these ways might be. Maybe they'll become less vigilant as a result, and we really will be able to get them here."

"You're right. He was an agent. Most likely he's waste from a previous emigration wave. He went from bad to worse and then to the dogs, and as an old wino he couldn't resist some pocket money for minor dirty jobs."

"What are we going to do about it?" Tina asked.

"Nothing. We've always assumed they would monitor our moves. Now we know it for sure. At least you were honoured by their attention," said Lorenc.

"They can stuff this kind of honour up their asses."

Lorenc laughed, but quickly returned to his line. "The quality of this agent makes the honour an offence." We thought about this for a moment.

"I've been able to come up with only one explanation so far," I remarked to break the silence. "If they intended to, they could strike without warning. If it was information they were after, I don't think they would target me or they would send somebody smarter. It was impossible not to see through this guy's cover. It means they wanted to scare us, deprive us of sleep by letting us know they're following us."

"Nothing new under the sun. Our sleep is all right, so we can keep going," concluded Edita. "Perhaps you should quit your evening walks, or let me know and I'll come to babysit."

"If he shows up again, send me word." Lorenc hit his big open palm with his fist. "I'll wait for him at the stairs and smash his mug to see whether he calls for his mommy in Czech or German."

Two hours of beating about the bush at Lorenc's solved nothing. That crumpled wino didn't let me sleep, after all. For over an hour I paced up and down the hallway trying to pinpoint what lay behind the whole encounter. Twenty-two steps, turn left, twenty steps, about face. The wino wasn't the issue, of course, those who had sent him were.

Was I being paranoid? Probably, otherwise I wouldn't have haunted the hallway at one in the morning. But wasn't it they themselves who had drummed into us the maxim that where there's a stoolie, there's danger?

Danger. Especially in connection with the WCC. Maybe they really had no big secrets there, but no secret had ever been too small for the secret police. Working there could mean they might focus their interest on me.

What more could they do to me? Not much unless they intended to murder or kidnap me, and I was much too small fry to provoke this kind of revenge.

Why had he come? Really? To check the extent of my bleeding

after cutting myself off their pillory? Not enough motive for them. To find out why this wooden puppet hadn't collapsed yet and to examine whether some strings might have been left? Was he trying to pull those remaining strings to test my old, conditioned reflexes, to make me use my old head, filled with their indoctrination?

They must have realized that I had tricked them by growing a new, private head. Were they trying to pit my two heads against each other? Attempting to throw me off balance, to disquiet me, so that I made a fatal misstep on our tightrope? They knew how destructive man can be to himself. That's why they wanted to breathe down my neck all the time. This was a scheme that bore their signature. They couldn't harm me physically any more; their power lay only in their ability to suggest they still had power. They had lost my strings, so they were trying to establish a presence in my new head and infect it as well.

The more I paced the black and white tiles of the hallway, the more additional meaning this puzzle acquired. Poring over my memories of the past ten weeks, I was stunned by the sharpness and vividness of the images rolling in my mind. I could remember every face, every gesture, every word, every single day distinct from the others. It began to dawn on me that the image of death and rebirth in the Traiskirchen gate was much more than a mere metaphor.

I really had been reborn! Until now, I had been an infant in a huge, unknown world. Everything I'd seen and heard was for the first time. That was why each experience was engraved so indelibly in my memory. That's why our emotions had been so terribly intense. Of course! And just like children we had kept asking ourselves, "Who am I?" No wonder in all our emigration nightmares our search for identity featured every time. We had lost our old one and hadn't yet created, hadn't yet completed the creation of the new one.

Our thinking was timid, insecure, and, at the same time, like a child's, it was very pliable. Whatever imprinted itself in our minds would remain with us for the rest of our lives. That was why they had sent him! That was why they had tried to fool us, to wreak havoc, to stir up panic — to make us fail in some, preferably moral, way we would have to struggle with for the rest of our days. If I resigned my job at the WCC for the safety of myself and my family, I would suffer a moral setback, the loss of integrity. As long as I was convinced I should work there, I had to work there.

It was the truth. Life tests are always right here and right now. Because our childs' minds were so perceptive, whatever we did, or failed to do, would set a precedent for our behaviour in the future. We were laying the foundations of our new identities.

Nothing was the way it seemed to be in the first euphoria. The interview was nothing more than permission to move our physical bodies to Canada. Our minds would follow after a considerable delay. Their shape depended to some degree on us. We had to be attentive to every problem. The way we struggled with life in Vienna over the next weeks would determine the mind-set we would enter Canada with.

Somewhere an alarm clock went off. The first sleepy figures headed for the washroom. My legs ached. I was hungover from too many cigarettes. But it was worth it. Good thing that wreck of a secret agent had come. Those bastards had thought it through quite far, but I thought I had reached one step further.

When I returned to my room, I found that Ivo had kicked his sleeping bag aside. I covered him and he mumbled something in his sleep.

"Sleep tight, my dear, everything's all right." *They came to wake up devils and woke up my guardian angel instead.*

Then a real chilling fright hit me. If it hadn't been for this dirty stoolie, I wouldn't have realized how important the next weeks would be. It was then that we would lay the foundation of our future Canadian existence.

11

———

THE REFUGEE THEATRE

FRAU DOKTOR HAD asked me to come to work fifteen minutes earlier. She briefed me in her office.

"You'll go to Traiskirchen today, to bring new files. Take a subway to Opera Ring and find the stop for the Baden lokalbahn; it looks like a big streetcar or a small motor train. Buy a return ticket at the booth at the stop. Bring the receipt. It takes fifty minutes to get to Traiskirchen. Go straight to our office in the camp, pick up the pouch, and return to the station without delay. You should make it in less than twenty minutes. The return train departs twenty-five minutes after it arrives, so you have five minutes to spare. If you miss it, the next train leaves an hour later and we will all have to wait for you. Now you have half an hour to get to Opera Ring."

I repeated the instructions to make sure I understood them properly.

So far so good, despite light drizzle, I thought, making myself comfortable on the red leatherette seat of the half-empty motor train. It was raining outside and once the motor train got rolling, the window kept fogging up, despite my efforts to wipe it.

Another adventure in the service of the WCC. Something new had happened almost every day and I'd loved every minute of the three weeks I'd worked there. Rubber-stamping letterhead on blank forms, typing long lists of exotic-sounding names and places, learning the fine points of emigration to different countries. Canada and Australia employed government sponsorship in most cases, while the U.S.A. required the would-be immigrant to find a private sponsor. This is what the WCC did through its branch office in New York. This office collected, searched for, and kept the list of prospective sponsors, mostly churches or groups of citizens affiliated with churches, and matched them with applicants. I'd typed a number of letters there. I had also learned that Canada put almost all its emphasis on a refugee's orderly life, stability of his family, and personal qualities. Americans, on the other hand, didn't give a damn about how many divorces the applicant had been through as long as he could prove political persecution. Australian policy was somewhere in the middle. Once, I had even gone to the U.S. embassy to deliver a medical file. The building looked like it was under siege, and Marines searched me with a metal detector because of a Palestinian terrorism scare. New Zealand was also a destination for refugees, but its criteria remained shrouded in mystery. It accepted only a handful of people every year, and it took almost a year to process each application.

What a job! I had never dreamed of anything so thrilling. I was a tiny gear in a huge machine that helped people to find and reach a better place to live. Sure, I was still being helped, but at the same time I was helping others. Compared with the bricklayer's job, this was a test for me, on a higher, much more demanding level, and infinitely more rewarding.

I wiped the window as the train came to a stop. Traiskirchen! I jumped out and ran to the station exit. Something's wrong. There was no camp, only vineyards and a cornfield. It wasn't Traiskirchen! I ran back, but all I could see were the red lights of the departing train. I asked the dispatcher and learned that I had been fooled by the sign at the end of the station that announced the *next* station.

Traiskirchen was about one kilometre down the rails. I would see it if it weren't raining so heavily. But I must not go along the tracks, it was strictly prohibited by law. The highway I have to follow is winding, about a three-kilometre walk. The next train departs in fifty-nine minutes. Good day, sir.

I had twenty-three minutes to make it to the office and back to the station. I thought about taking the path along the rails. No. I couldn't afford to get caught doing anything illegal. It could cost me Canada, asylum in Austria, and might lead to my deportation back to Czechoslovakia.

What a moronic idiot! They entrust me with something important and I screw up like the dumbest nincompoop. Get going, imbecile, on the double! Make it triple, stupid!

The road was winding indeed, and I made it to the office at about the time I was supposed to board the return train.

"Thank God you're here safe and sound, although wet," the boss greeted me with visible relief. "What was the problem?"

He phoned Frau Doktor with my explanation, to calm her. When I hadn't arrived at the right time, he had called her to tell her that I had failed to show up, as was the routine safety procedure.

"What a mess I've made," I sighed when he hung up.

"No apologies needed. It can happen to anybody."

"Is there any other way to get back to Vienna earlier than in one hour?"

"Only one. An express bus will pass on the main highway in thirty minutes. But it's a fifteen-minute walk to the stop and it's still raining cats and dogs."

"I can't get any wetter. If there's a chance to recover a few minutes, I must take it. Please."

"All right. I guess it's important to you. Still, you've got fifteen minutes. Have a cup of tea and a smoke."

He offered me a cigarette because the rain had turned my pack into a handful of damp tobacco.

"Was Frau Doktor angry?" I asked.

"No, worried. Listen, man, don't take it too hard. We understand you are under a lot of pressure and can make mistakes. You are living and working under extreme conditions, in a foreign country, in two or three foreign languages, and your future still appears to be rather foggy. You have spirit to share but little security. Now, grab the pouch, make it safely back to Vienna, and don't worry."

Thanks to the express bus, I arrived back at the office only twenty-five minutes late.

"Here he comes!" Frau Doktor greeted me in the hallway. "Where were you? Trying to plug Niagara Falls?"

"I'm terribly sorry. I was plain stupid. I will make it up in the evening."

"The last thing you need now is to indulge in self-reproach and guilty feelings. Something like this was bound to happen sooner or later, and you should consider yourself lucky it happened now and not on your way to Canada." For a moment she focused her eyes on the growing puddle around my running shoes. Her voice became sterner.

"About face! Go home! You don't need to catch a cold or even pneumonia before your Canadian medicals, do you? Dismissed!"

When she saw I was still hesitating, she added, "When you're dry you may come back."

My job offered me one fringe benefit: unlimited use of the washroom.

Who would ever have thought that such a lowly, commonplace room could be a source of intense happiness? Clean — splendid, sparkling clean all around. A small window let in plenty of sunlight all morning and pampered the user with an excellent view. To the left, I could see the high spire of St. Stephen's Cathedral and the old city; to the right, almost within reach, was the back wall of the Canadian embassy.

It felt good to have the embassy as a neighbour. Every time I passed by, it cheered me up. I would run my fingertips over the

Canadian coat of arms, engraved on the solid-brass sign next to the entrance, to assure myself Canada existed and I wasn't dreaming. A couple of times I caught a glimpse of the Canadian ambassador being chauffeured in or out in a big black Chevrolet with a small flag fluttering above its hood. Canada has a beautiful, joyful flag. Sometimes I could see parked cars with exotic licence plates: Beautiful British Columbia, Wild Rose Alberta, Friendly Manitoba. My imagination soared, fed by the adventure books I'd read as a boy. Which one of these plates would adorn my car one day? What corner of that marvellous land of adventurers would they choose as our destination? Where would we live out the adventure of our lives?

During these sunlit days of early fall, I ate my lunch sitting on one of the benches lining the Ring, under the mighty chestnut trees that were slowly turning red and yellow. I had the embassy at my back and a shining stream of colourful traffic in front of my eyes to enjoy.

Once, I even had the honour of having lunch with our consul, though he didn't know it. He brought his lunch, an apple strudel, and sat down a few benches from me. He was dressed casually this time in a corduroy jacket with heart-shaped leather patches on its elbows. He looked much younger. After he had finished his pastry, he lit a pipe, sipped his coffee, made himself comfortable, and looked across the Ring at the pretty young women climbing the steps to the university gates.

It must have been some kind of magic this city exhaled. So little can make a man happy: a lovely day, lovely young women, a lovely washroom.

A ripple of excitement came from the end of the breakfast line. We turned our heads. Pale as a whitewashed wall, stiff, with his hands stretched forward as if he were swimming the breast stroke in slow motion, Josef made somnambulic progress. His eyes were focused somewhere at the end of infinity, his lips moved. Not until he passed us did we understand the spell that cleared his way.

"Let me pass, let me pass. I'm flying to Australia."

"Bullshit," commented a seasoned veteran, who had already done a return trip. "Today to Traiskirchen. There you're going to spend the night. Tomorrow, maybe, you can talk about flying. Don't be silly."

But Josef could neither hear nor see him, so overwhelmed was he by the vision of what lay ahead. He let the cooks fill his tray, and like a ghost he hovered back towards the stairs. He still mumbled, though nobody stood in his way. "Let me pass, let me pass. I'm flying to Australia."

I answered the office doorbell. Nobody I'd ever seen around the WCC looked so downcast as she appeared. As if she had run out of energy, determination, hope, and even tears. Though she was from my country, her case was clearly beyond my competence, and I ushered her into Frau Doktor's office.

I expected a storm to break out. Frau Doktor didn't like weaklings who came in, sobbing, for some consolation and comfort. What they got instead was a thunderstorm of ironic, sarcastic, and even contemptuous words. Her maxim about idle men being dangerous was famous. At first I felt embarrassed hearing Frau Doktor unleash her thunder, but by this time I understood it was her way to get them back on their feet and into a fighting mood again.

There was no thunder this time. What came, muffled, through the door was more like a soothing melody played on a cello. When I escorted the young lady back to the door, she even managed the hint of a smile in the corners of her mouth. She looked in my eyes and with absolute seriousness whispered, "Is she an angel?"

I wished that one day I could manage the transformation of a human wreck into a being capable of smiling. Frau Doktor performed those miracles daily – two, three times a day. But where did she find the strength in those tides of misery rolling through her door, day after day, for some thirty years? From where did she draw so much strength that she could give it away?

Half an hour later Frau Doktor stopped at my desk. She looked satisfied.

"Poor girl. She had really hit the bottom."

"What had happened?"

"They couldn't get permission to travel out of the country as a complete family. So her husband and their four-year-old daughter went to Yugoslavia when she was sent to Austria on a business trip. He tried to cross the mountains to Austria but was caught. Next he paid a fisherman to take him and the child across the sea to Italy, hoping they would make it from there. But the Italian Coast Guard seized them and sent them to a refugee camp near Rome. She had no news from them for twelve days. You know there's a rule that a refugee must make his claim in the first free country he reaches. Now the father and child are refugees in the Italian camp and the mother is a refugee in Traiskirchen. Neither can move because it would mean forfeiting his or her refugee claim. To them it seems hopeless."

"No wonder she looked the way she did." I shuddered. "But you know a way out, don't you?"

"I phoned our office in Rome. We will have to conduct some high-level negotiations to make the bureaucrats on both sides bend their rules for the sake of humanity. It will take some time, but in a couple of weeks they should be together." She rubbed her hands in satisfaction.

"May I ask you a personal question, Frau Doktor?"

She nodded.

"Are you an angel?"

For a moment she looked stunned. Then she called in her secretary and in a big voice ordered, "Inge, give him some typing. Lots of typing! We've got here a dangerously idle man!"

But her eyes were smiling.

"I wonder where our Calamity Joe is right now," Lorenc said with a twinkle in his eye.

"Some thirty thousand feet above the Indian Ocean, I guess."

"What a height! I bet the attendants are having to change his diapers every half an hour because he's shitting his pants continually. His kind should sit at home and never defect."

"I don't think so. In the end I came to the conclusion that Josef had more guts than both of us combined."

"Hold it, man!" Lorenc flew at me. "A decent guy, yes. A straight shooter, granted. Hard-working, I'll give him that, too. But courageous? You can't be serious!"

"I don't know what he's been through to consider all news bad news, to see everything as if it were a looming calamity. But think of the torment he must have suffered before defection, before Trais, every job he had, before the interview, and his departure. And yet he always carried on. He did defect, went to Trais, worked even after the pail mishap. He succeeded in the interview, even though he was scared witless he would not find the embassy, would suffer a heart attack there, that he would wish the consul 'good moron' instead of 'good morning,' that he would stammer, lose his voice, or forget his name. Before his departure he couldn't sleep because he imagined he would miss his plane, the plane would crash into the forest at the end of the runway, or somebody would plant a bomb on it, or the plane would run out of gas, or both pilots would die at the same moment, and if no other tragedy happened, he would fall out of the plane while in the air. Right now he's scared to death because, if by some incredible miracle he makes it to the Sydney airport, for sure he will be killed by his own suitcase, ejected by a terrible force from the luggage carousel that will go berserk just as he gets there. I'm telling you, he almost died of fright a thousand times, but a thousand times he conquered his fear, rose again, and did what was necessary. We have it easier because we're less susceptible to fear."

"I've never seen him from that point of view," Lorenc admitted reluctantly.

"He's going to win there as well. He will shit his pants a few more times, then he'll discover that everything has its sunny side, too, and his condition will improve; he will only wet his pants now and then. In the end he'll calm down completely and he'll be fine. We laughed at his expense often enough, but I tell you, he's one tough guy."

We raised our half-empty coffee mugs towards the Indian Ocean.

"Here's to your courage, Josef."

Shit! That nightmare was an extra nasty one. I couldn't sleep any more. It would have come back.

In the dim glow of the forty-watt light bulb on the gallery I checked the time. Half past two. Jarda's lamp was still on. I knocked. He raised his eyes from the book he was reading in bed.

"Another nightmare? Brandy? Coffee?"

"A few human words, if you don't mind."

"Make yourself comfortable." He closed the book and with his foot offered me his only chair.

"I'm running out of nerves for them. Everybody tells me they subside with time. Normal guys have one a month. I have at least one a week. What's wrong with me?"

"The thing wrong with you is that it's good to be with you. Why, do you think, so many people drop in for a cup of coffee with you? First, Jana made your room so cosy that everybody feels at home. Second, you behave like you are at home, that is, not in limbo. They draw a sense of security from you."

"Nonsense. My mind is a battlefield where everything fights everything else around the clock. I can't make it out myself, so where's the security?"

"They can't see through you. They get strength not from who you are but from who you appear to be. For everybody here, you're confidence incarnate. The rock. They feel that if Zoch collapsed, you would still hold its roof above their heads. When the bugaboos haunt them, they come to tell you and you sweep their ghosts away."

"A bugaboo repellent . . . What a great role. Thanks a lot."

"It's an enviable one."

"And what about those nightmares?"

"Everybody fills you with his worries, doubts, homesickness, anger, misery, desperation, you name it. Only you have nobody to vent them to. Or you don't want to. You've got no wall to wail at. You listen, carry, keep silent, and smile. When you've accumulated too much, you discharge it through a nightmare."

"I'm glad to hear those dreams might be good for something, after all. If they didn't have any redeeming value, I would be really pissed off."

"Knowingly or not, you're doing a lot of good here. You're kind of a benefactor to the people."

"Except that being a benefactor is not worth shit."

"Never has been. But you've got no choice. You're not doing it for them but for yourself. It's your way of coping with emigration. Clench your teeth, suppress everything, and steam-roller through. The others follow."

"Bugaboos . . . There does exist one I would like to talk about. It haunted me even before the defection. And since I escaped, I've been waiting for it to ambush me and finish me off. The guilt. Abandoning my motherland, mother culture, mother tongue."

"You shouldn't have said that." Jarda jumped with joy in his bed. "Now I'm going to lecture you to death. Make some coffee, it's going to take till morning.

"World literature has been full of guilt for the last century. A metaphysical guilt, so to speak. My subject, German literature, has been focused on specific historical guilt. Neither can help you much because socialist guilt is a special category. I call it ideological guilt. Its distinguishing feature is the fact that it is a political cate-gory, not a moral one. It happens when an ideology is elevated to be the judge of traditional morality and ethics."

He sat in his blankets and gestured animatedly.

"What is guilt? A feeling that you have violated some moral commandment or norm. Why politicize it? Because man, feeling guilty, is more manipulable, controllable, because he tries to atone for his guilt, real or imagined. Our comrades devised a great many commandments so that we would feel guilty all the time, to make guilt inescapable, even if your only guilt was that you were born to your parents.

"They identified their ideology with what they called the scientific concept of historic progress. Do you object to some point of their teachings? Don't you like comrade Vonasek? You're obstructing the course of history – aren't you ashamed? Are you politically neutral? You're not helping to develop the socialist paradise. Shame on you! Do you support communist ideology? It's not enough, you could do much more. Think about it!"

Jarda couldn't stay in bed. He got up and in pyjama pants began to pace his cubbyhole of a room.

"It's not binding for them, of course. They created it and appointed themselves the interpreters of a whole system of morality which has been, naturally, developed to get them to power and keep them there.

"They have turned the whole moral system inside out by connecting it, through ideology, to their power. It has one single constant, the one they themselves follow: The end justifies the means. Whenever you hear this in history, there's always plenty of blood and endless dirt, I can guarantee this. They set the ends – their power – and it sanctions their using any means any time, so they don't have to feel guilty. Just remember what they taught us in schools: To kill for the sake of revolution is not only moral but desirable. To turn your parents in to the police is your duty. The same with lying, stealing, and so on. Do you think Stalin felt guilty when he murdered sixty million or so of his own people? Do you believe our so-called leaders felt any guilt when they betrayed our country and invited the Russians to take us over, so they could be appointed their lieutenant-governors?"

"Shut up there!" A sleepy voice yelled from outside.

"Consider this absurdity," he went on, lowering his voice. "They keep you in a concentration camp. At least for me, a country fenced around with barbed wire is a concentration camp of a kind. You're in the camp because you were born in it. Since childhood they have indoctrinated you to feel guilty if you don't like it there, if you think about escaping, even if you do escape. When we defected, it was we who felt and were supposed to feel guilty of treason, not they, who turned the country into a concentration camp."

He took a gulp from his coffee, thought for a moment, and continued.

"Did you ever take home a few sheets of onionskin paper from your office?"

"Sure, like everyone else, to use it instead of toilet paper, which was in short supply at the time."

"Did you feel guilty?"

"A little bit. Thou shalt not steal."

"Do you think those who stole the whole paper mill after the revolution felt remorse? Of course not. They were stealing in the interest of revolution, while you stole in the interest of your clean ass."

"I think people should judge revolutions less by their slogans and more by their ability to ensure that their citizens can have clean asses."

"And the paper mill was only a part of it. They stole everything, both from the rich and the poor, from everybody who had worked his whole life. Remember our grandparents, their small savings, pensions. They lost everything. You may notice that revolutions are never led by working people, always by the idle ones, people who are either rich or work-shy. That's why every revolution indulges in stealing on a mass scale. The leaders turn their deficiencies into a virtue and make a crime of honest, responsible living."

"And they hammered their ideology into us from nursery school onward. Thirty-five years. Successfully, I have to admit," I said.

"Not quite. Otherwise we would not have defected. There is something left in us, after all, something we got from our parents, good literature, philosophy. That something is the good old moral code rooted in the Old Testament, if not even deeper in history. The morals of the Judeo-Christian-Hellenic tradition on which the whole of Western civilization has been built." He held out his mug for me to pour him more coffee.

"Naturally, their morality clashed head on with this older and deeper code. We got drawn into the conflict. To honour one code meant violating the other. They were not reconcilable. Each and every day we faced moral dilemmas. By our defection we, *de facto*, chose the older morality in which the ends do not justify the means. The morality that reconnected us with at least four thousand years of history.

"Two moral codes, two sets of guilt. It would be serious if you transgressed the old, the just one. You haven't done this, though they've forced you. You have to cope only with the guilt that stems from transgressing their morality. A man-made morality, unless you consider the Interior Ministry a department of hell. And as it's man-made, it can be rationally explained and neutralized. Tell me the truth. Are you afraid they won't let your nephews and nieces enrol in university?

"It was a nightmare even before we defected," I exclaimed.

"You see, they got you! And all the others who would hold you to blame. Think a moment! Who decides about enrolment? You or a comrade at the university, or the Ministry of Education or the Interior? Who will stamp Rejected on your nephew's application? He will, therefore he's responsible and he bears the guilt. You have nothing to do with it."

"I never saw it in that light. It's interesting how much people are fooled," I admitted before he caught his breath. "They don't blame the terrorist practising blackmail and hostage-taking, but the few individuals who refuse to go along."

"Their propaganda has been very successful, I have to give it to them." His arms rose in a gesture of desperation.

"The state of morals in the nation is abysmal."

"You see, and the same comrades who devastated the nation would like you to feel guilty because you have slipped beyond the reach of their power. From the point of view of your integrity, of your child's future, you had to escape. They drove you to abandon the motherland, mother culture, mother tongue. Who is guilty then?"

He was right. When I left his room, day was dawning. In the sky as well as in my mind.

Ivo couldn't fall asleep. When he succeeded at last, he didn't sleep long. At half past one he was awake and crying that his ear hurt.

We could have expected it. During the last two months he had had a sore throat twice and for the last two days, a cold. The causes were beyond our control. Damp fall weather, unhealthy living in the hotel, air polluted by heavy traffic on the Gürtel. And most of all, he had been weakened by long-term tension, a strange environment, and the stresses he sensed in us. Too many new things were confronting him and it was too much for his child's mind to handle. We had noticed the gradual loss of his playfulness over the previous two months. He had begun to be more withdrawn, ill at ease, taciturn. His eyes were often sad. Why had he had to abandon his room, his bed, toys, friends, grandma and grandpa? The reasons were hard to explain to a six-year-old.

As he wavered, so did Jana. Unlike me, she spent whole days with him in the hotel or on walks. Her state of mind has been the reflection of his, aggravated by her feelings of helplessness, of not being able to do the only thing that would really help – to fly to healthy Canada and away from Zoch, the Gürtel, the troubles and nervousness.

"I've given him an Aspirin. I don't have anything stronger."

"He doesn't seem to have a fever," I said, touching his forehead.

"It could be an inflammation of his middle ear. If it is, we should see a doctor as soon as possible."

"Where can we find a doctor now? It's half past one in the morning. Old Lorelei has to issue us a voucher for medical treatment. We'll have to wait at least till seven o'clock."

"We can't risk waiting." Jana's voice was irritated and ready to explode. "You'll have to deal with it somehow!"

"I know, I got him into this; it's up to me to help him out. Still, let's wait for a while. Perhaps it will get better by itself."

At half past three it was clear we had to find a doctor.

"I'll take money in case they want a cash payment. They might reimburse us later. How much will it cost?"

"Take everything. If it's not enough, we'll have to bargain. Don't forget to take a city map."

Jana dressed Ivo warmly, I lifted him on my shoulders, and we walked out into the deserted night streets. It was chilly, close to freezing.

"The nearest hospital is on the other side of the Gürtel. Will we give it a try?"

The iron gate was closed, but in the adjacent booth there was a small, lighted window. Once the porter understood what we were looking for, she explained something in fast vernacular Viennese. Then Jana said something. The porter slowed down. We learned this hospital had no emergency room. We had to go to the General Hospital, about three kilometres down the Gürtel.

"There's nothing to do but go there," Jana decided.

"No streetcars at this hour. We have to go back to Westbahnhof and take a cab."

Jana stopped me as we approached the cab stand. "Wait a minute. Careful now. He's fallen asleep on your shoulder."

"Too tired, I guess. Or, is it possible the pain has receded?"

"It is possible. I've heard that sometimes cold air helps more than a doctor. Let's walk for a while and see if the relief lasts. Walk softly."

The cold air proved to be an effective medicine, and in half an hour we put Ivo back to his bed without waking him up.

"Why? What has he done to deserve this?" Jana looked at him in near desperation. "He's already had antibiotics twice and this looks like yet another case."

"I can't do anything. Neither can Frau Doktor. And probably neither can the embassy. It's in the hands of the Canadians on the other side."

"How many more weeks? We can endure anything, but how long will he have to wait?"

While someone fetched a representative of the Kadlečka family to the phone in a small hotel somewhere in the Alps, Frau Doktor briefed me. Then she handed the phone to me.

"Kadlečka" sounded in the earpiece. A tentative voice apprehensive of hearing an avalanche of German or English words. Using a phone in a foreign language is one of the most dreaded things you can't avoid. I nicely surprised him by speaking Czech.

"I'm calling from the WCC, and I'm pleased to tell you that next Thursday you fly to Orlando, Florida, via New York."

"Yahooo, man! Where did you get this?"

"In today's mail from the U.S. embassy."

"Jesus Maria . . . Florida . . . I could never dream. . . . What on earth am I supposed to do right now?"

"To begin with I'd suggest a bear hug for your wife and kids, then you can dance a jig if you wish. A new life begins for you in a week. You will get details and instructions in the mail."

"You must be kidding! Who are you, anyway? I need to know whom to praise forever."

"Never mind. The WCC arranged everything."

"When I visit Vienna one day, I'll come to kiss you all over."

"Slim chance. I'm heading for Canada."

"We'll be neighbours! Listen, we must meet somewhere there."

"Sure. The recognition sign is a grin from ear to ear and the password is the WCC. Agreed?"

"My wife will be out of her mind with joy – "

"So hurry up and tell her."

"Good night," he shrieked with happiness though it was still afternoon, and because he couldn't have cared less about hanging up the phone I could hear him rushing helter-skelter up the stairs to hug his wife and kids.

Frau Doktor smiled. "He speaks some German and English, but I wanted you to enjoy a reward for so many hours of work. I bet he didn't say, 'thank you,' but his forgetfulness is more eloquent than any words."

Saturday evening. From somewhere a few bars of a Mozart concerto floated into our room and we tuned in on our transistor radio. We were sitting in the window enjoying a last cup of coffee on what was an unseasonably warm evening.

"What a pity we couldn't go to a concert," Jana sighed, "or to a theatre."

"Why? We've got a theatre right here, and a better one. From the first row, with the comfort of coffee and cigarettes."

"There's no substitute for a real theatre," Jana objected.

"Just watch for half an hour."

Mozart's music soothed our souls.

Watch:

Somewhere on the upper floor a door opens and two quarrelling voices fall into the yard.

The Iranians are cooking again. By the smell it is lamb with rice, as usual. Now they are placing the pan on the windowsill to let the meal cool a little before adding the final ingredients.

From the Kurds' room comes faint moaning.

The door upstairs bangs open again. A surge of draft rocks the Iranians' window and the pan begins to topple. At the last moment a hand catches the handle. Upside down, unfortunately, and lamb risotto splashes on the concrete floor of the yard.

What is that? *Da da da daaa.* Beethoven's Fifth? No, it's just somebody banging at a washroom door. Once more. The second one is occupied as well. A beastly howl in perfect counterpoint to the winds in Mozart, slippers clapping on the stairs, and a man bursts onto our floor. Bad luck, buddy, ours are busy, too. Look at him tapdancing. One hand supporting his pants, the other swirling above his head. Just as his performance reaches a crescendo, the door opens. He darts in and a long, triumphant fart, positively in A major, bounces between the walls, a joyful report commensurate with the magnitude of relief it brought to the tormented body and with the way Mozart's music lifts the worried soul.

One of the Iranians comes into the yard with a dustpan and a broom.

Who is this beautiful princess in a fancy nightgown descending the stairs carrying her toilet bag and a towel? Ah, the youthful Hungarian newlywed. I met the couple at Traiskirchen yesterday. They escaped on their honeymoon, which they interrupted so they could continue it one day in Niagara Falls, Canada. She's going to the washroom to make herself beautiful for her new husband, to smell of soap and cleanliness.

Watch what happens when she sees all the slime and filth. She closes the door. Turns on the light. What a shriek! As if she had seen a dead body in the bathtub. She flies straight back to her room – except she's one floor too low. The door is locked. She bangs at it and yells, "Let me in! Let me in!" The door opens and there's a mountain of a man with a hairy chest, in just his underwear. The bride shrieks again and backs off, as if she saw the murderer of the corpse in the bathtub. He understands, laughs, points to the number above his door, and then to the ceiling. Now she turns and sprints towards the stairs. Up, two at a time. We hear the bang of a door and the rattle of a lock. Her towel lies abandoned across the stairs.

From the small washroom window a ribbon of aromatic smoke winds up. The victor is enjoying his pipe and is not about to relinquish his captured territory.

Mozart increases his tempo and so do the Kurds around the corner.

The Iranian has already swept the remnants of his dinner into the dustpan. He shakes his head, bends backwards to search the black sky, and raises his arms. He doesn't shout, but I know what he wants to say: Why me, O Lord? I just wanted to make a dinner the way my mom used to cook it back home. Why, O Lord? But as he spreads his arms, the dustpan empties onto his head and shoulder.

Another door bangs, letting loose a burst of the quarrel. Somewhere the Voice of America announces that Andropov might be seriously ill, but Mozart ignores the news, as do the Kurds. Their moaning and groaning is now laced with sobbing. The Iranian, humbly on his knees, sweeps up his spoiled dinner for the second time.

Somebody shouts, "You old fart, your feet stink like hell! When did you wash them the last time?" Another voice yells back, "Last Friday and it's none of your business. There are no taps in the bathroom." The first voice gets shrill. "How could there be any taps if you keep stealing them?! For Chrissake, wash your feet! How can I live here with you when you smell so terrible."

An awful scratching sound. Somebody is pushing the main gate open too far and it's scraping on the concrete. Who is it? Here he comes, flying, almost crashing into the night clerk's door. The next swing might bring him into the hallway. No. He's missed and has shot into the yard. Our valiant army captain has scored another great victory over a bottle of vodka. What's he doing? Hey, Captain, that's the boiler room, there's no bed for you there.

The quarrel upstairs is louder. They've opened their door, and our Mozart is spiced with Arabic music.

The Captain barely avoids strangling himself in the clotheslines. If he's lucky, his next sway will get him to the stairs. Almost. His knee and elbow hit the corner and spin him in a pirouette. He's chasing his centre of gravity down the hallway towards the kitchen. He can't catch up with it. He's swirling towards the floor tiles like an auger.

Now! Impeccable timing. The sound of flushing water fits into the violin variations so precisely it's as if the flusher, who now briskly steps out zipping up his pants, could see the conductor's baton pointing at him on the toilet. The harmony of violins and flushing water is accentuated by a percussive shout from one of the Kurds and hiccups from the captain.

He has more brains left than I thought. He doesn't try to get up but, on all four, conquers one step after another on his quest for his bed.

"The best thing of all," I tell Jana, "is that we don't just have to watch, we can join in. '*O dolce Napoli, o sol beato . . .*'" I sing at the top of my lungs into the yard.

"Shut up, dummy! You'll wake up Ivo."

"Or I can go down there and act for you the balcony scene from *Romeo and Juliet*."

"Kneeling in your pyjamas in the remnants of the rice? Better stay here. This is a crazy farce and I had in mind serious theatre."

"You wouldn't like it. We have changed. We're down to real basics. In a theatre all you would see is some remote aspects of the absurdity of life that the playwright has followed for thirty years from his desk."

"But there would be art in it."

"There's more art in what you've just seen than in all the Viennese theatres in a season. It's in a raw, unrefined form, I concede, but it's got everything that makes theatre art."

"Except for the art."

"Nonsense. What else are Eva and those Kurdish stallions if not a drama of desire and loneliness? That newlywed? The drama of disillusion: the idealism of innocent youth running into the sleazy reality of life's bathrooms and, seeking solace, finding only the apelike, hairy chest of a stranger. How about the Iranian? Wasn't his

the immortal gesture of a dialogue with God? Tell me, what's more
of a torment: the pressure in your bowels when all the washroom
doors are shut or the pressure of guilt or alienation? The single-
minded determination of the captain crawling towards his bed, is it
really less heroic than Captain Scott's at the South Pole? Those two
upstairs, yelling at each other. They need to get away from each
other. But there's no place for them to go, so they are condemned
to stay with each other and their quarrel."

Mozart was still lovely.

"Then let's join in this theatre," says Jana. "Close the window
and come to me. Make up a nice bedtime story. Let's say . . . about
Romeo and Juliet. The morning after their wedding night they
both fled Verona, and after wandering for a long time they made it
overseas. In Canada they founded another Verona, built a house
and . . . you tell me how it continues."

"What language do they speak?"

"Neither German nor English. That's why I can't phone them,"
said Frau Doktor. "That's why you must find a way to communicate this message."

Though we'd met from time to time in the hallways, I had never
spoken with the three Iranians. The language barrier kept them
apart. I knocked at their door. It opened slightly and searching eyes
appeared in the crack. When I showed the eyes the letters WCC on
a piece of paper, the whole man let me in.

Their room was surprisingly clean and tidy, considering that
three young men lived here. An English textbook and a dictionary
lay open on the table.

"In ten days you fly to Duluth, Minnesota, U.S.A."

They didn't understand. Sign language is more international: I
raised all ten fingers, waved my arms to show flying. The effort to
comprehend distorted their faces. Then realization exploded! They
roared as if they were at a football game. The one who was studying English asked for silence.

"Repeat, please."

"You fly, ten days, Minnesota, U.S.A."

They slowly began to believe it. They slapped my back and thanked me as if it had been my decision. One dragged me to the table, the second one put a tea kettle on a hot plate, the third searched the closet. He brought back a small bottle of bourbon and their three toothbrush cups. We lifted the cups.

"Hurrah for the WCC!"

"Hurrah for Minnesota!"

"Hurrah for the U.S.A.!"

The English-speaking one asked me, "Where Minnesota is?"

I drew an approximate sketch on a piece of paper.

"What country is like?"

"Flat, woods, plains, many lakes. Good country." I wrote the words down rather than saying them, so they would understand better.

Before we finished our drinks, there was a quick exchange in their language. Then the English student consulted his dictionary and soon handed me a piece of paper: You come tomorrow, nine o'clock, celebration dinner.

Could I ever be more honoured for my tiny contribution to their fate?

Frau Doktor was about to leave and had just put on her coat when two young men came in. She listened to them for a few moments in the hallway and then took me into her office.

"They are not registered with us, but take a look at his case. As far as I can make it out, it's a crazy story. Other supporting organizations have refused to get involved, presumably because they fear they might become a laughingstock if they took him seriously. If you can find a plausible way to present it, prepare a draft. I'll be back around four."

Two Hungarians. One had a problem, and the other interpreted for him in broken English. He didn't know what to do. Everybody had had a good laugh over his story, but nobody had advised him on how to present it seriously to the U.S. embassy consul. His helplessness was driving him crazy.

The story was as simple as the man himself. He had been a railroad worker in a small town controlled by party hardliners. A few days ago there had been some horseplay with friends on the street. He had lost his balance. Falling, he tried to grab hold of something and accidentally tore down a poster celebrating the Russian Revolution. It wouldn't have been so bad if somebody, a notorious informant, hadn't seen him. The poor guy was already under a suspended sentence for defacing the giant of world revolution. The new offence would send him to jail – for both acts.

His first offence occurred in the late evening a year earlier. Disgusted with all the hype surrounding the anniversary of the revolution, he had gone to the city park. There he spread the party newspaper on the ground, dropped his pants, and emptied his bowels onto it. He picked up the newspaper and with a mighty swing threw the shit at the face of the bronze titan, Lenin. That very moment a plainclothes policeman, who was guarding the statue, emerged from a bush and arrested him on the spot. He couldn't run because his pants were still down. The trial was a quick affair. They considered the act to have been premeditated and gave him a sixteen-month sentence, suspended for three years.

"Was it premeditated?" I asked.

"Sure as hell it was. I experimented with my diet for a month before I reached the right consistency. I wish you could have seen it splatter on his face and drip so slowly onto his chest," he said with a spark in his eyes.

"I have to think this over, prepare a first draft, type it, and consult with Frau Doktor. If you drop in between five and six it might be ready for you to sign."

What on earth was I supposed to do? No wonder nobody had taken him seriously. Was this the basis of his claim to be a political refugee? Couldn't he have come up with something better?

Throwing shit is half-vandalism, half-practical joking, the act of a grade-school child. But he hadn't been punished by spanking, as would have been fitting, but by a sixteen-month jail sentence. The authorities considered it a political act, and he thought it was political. For him that statue was an incarnation of evil, a symbol of the system that was driving him down without offering him an oppressor he could trash with his fists.

Technically speaking, he met the criteria for a political refugee. He couldn't return home because he would be jailed. But how on earth could I explain to the Americans, with their freedom of expression, that in socialism even shit can be politics?

If the system stifled him to such a degree that the only way to express his political opinion he could come up with was with shit, it cast a bad light on the political system, not on him. At least it was less harmful than assassinating somebody or setting off bombs. He had been more courageous than ninety per cent of the people whom we helped here. They suffered in silence, without revolting and fighting back. Not he. He had dared to speak out. He had expressed his contempt. When they took away his freedom of speech, he reached for his freedom of expression. He hadn't let them turn him into a piece of shit.

A few hours later Frau Doktor raised her eyes from the draft and looked at me intently above her glasses. "You've managed to get him into the U.S.A."

I was ready to challenge any consul in Vienna. Finally, I understood how Frau Doktor drew her strength from the weak by giving strength to them.

Though evil knows no seasonal ups and downs, the chance of escape does. Now, in the first days of November, the summer torrent of refugees has slowed down. Most days we're finished work shortly after three p.m. Today is Friday. I am paid two thousand schillings from the iron cashbox and kindly dismissed for the weekend.

The lower you descend in this building, the posher the standard. From the fifth floor down, there are mahogany doors, at the third floor the granite steps change to marble. There's a publishing house on the second floor. I once peeked in and from the look of the lobby I felt certain it published nothing but thick, leather-bound volumes with golden stamping. The carriage entrance is still paved with hardwood blocks to muffle the wheels of long-extinct horse-drawn carriages.

A pristine, cold fall afternoon. The descending sun casts a tan on the naked, sandstone giants supporting the Empire-style architrave above the entrance. Fall is here, and soon the days will be grey and melancholic. But the summer was good to us. Hot, dry, long. It's easier to keep up one's spirits in sunshine than in grey drizzle. On Tuesday we received the letter from the Canadians advising us that our destination is a city named London, in Ontario. We will leave in four to six weeks.

I look around at what I will be leaving behind. The cold shine of steel and glass of the modern embassy building. Its high-tech style doesn't quite fit in this neighbourhood of stately centenarians. Maybe it would fit better if it had sported sandstone giants. Is it true that in America the higher the floor, the more prestigious the office?

A sweet smell from the small bakery with the semi-circular window. The best apple strudel in town. If the other shops bake strudels half as good as theirs I wish I could taste them, too.

The narrow sidewalks paved with red, grey, and white cobble-stones, small like the toy bricks I had as a child. Behind a curve the street unexpectedly widens into a miniature square dominated by the baroque façade of an aristocratic palace. Its heavy wooden gate is closed. Above the entrance is a coat of arms, but there's no name-plate at either the bell or the mailbox. No need. The family has been at the same address for some three hundred years. An impos-ing chestnut tree in the centre of the square shades three empty benches. The benches and the pavement are littered with yellow and brown leaves that spread the odour of damp decay.

A much stronger scent lures me to the tiny Eduscho coffee shop. Here they serve a cup of wonderfully aromatic espresso for just five schillings. You can sip it slowly, leaning on the elbow-high marble counter, and watch people hustling along outside.

The Graben. Vienna's Champs Élysées or Fifth Avenue. A pedestrian-only zone. You don't have to enter the shops to know they are very expensive. An unmistakable sound, though I've never before heard it live. A barrel-organ. Our grandparents' world coming alive. But the organist isn't begging. Maybe because he doesn't have a wooden leg, as a First World War veteran would. He turns the handle simply to please passersby. Most likely, he's paid by local merchants.

At a shop entrance stands a rack of the most beautiful children's snowsuits I've ever seen. Vivid colours that would look merry against the whiteness of fresh snow. I could buy one on the spot. Cash. I've not been idle. I've been working like all the people around me. I could afford it if I wanted. But I don't. Some self-protective mechanism has shut off any desire for material goods. Shops loaded with everything imaginable to us are just exhibition halls. Their displays don't make our hearts beat any faster. Like the canvases by Breughel, Cranach, and Vermeer in the Kunsthistorische Museum, they are for admiration only. You really need very little in life, much less than you think.

Twilight creeps in. The remains of light from the ice-blue sky blend with the colourful neon signs, brilliant shop windows, and electric streetlights that copy the shapes of those that burned gas a century ago. None of the buildings looks less than two hundred years old. Most of the shops were established around 1850, but some are much older. Maybe from the time the first settlers built log cabins in London.

At the corner there's the stamp dealer's shop where Edita landed a job last week. She sorts out piles of worthless stamps and stuffs them into envelopes: "100 different – overseas" or "50 – animal kingdom." A far cry from fashion design, but it's a paying job. As future Austrians, she and her son were granted asylum in the first round. Dan attends preparatory language courses offered by the business school at the university. They are back on track.

Our feelings about Vienna have kept changing. On the first day she was a tourist attraction. After Traiskirchen, we perceived her as a perilous and treacherous jungle we had to survive in. After the interview, the city seemed much friendlier, offering us almost comfortable ease. Now, since we've known about our upcoming departure, we're almost sorry we have to leave her behind. A touch of nostalgia has tinted everything.

Could it be my parents are right? They have pressed us hard to remain in Europe. They've tried to convince us we're Europeans inside out and we will never be happy in the New World. But they have never been to North America. They just want to keep us as close as possible. I know that, but their distress makes me feel guilty.

What kind of place is our London, Ontario? The circle on the map indicated a city with over 250,000 inhabitants. Must be a lot of industry there to support a city that big. It should mean jobs. It means a chance for us to get back on track, too. Great!

I descend into the Opera Passage. A small underground mall, full of stores, under the busy intersection at Opera Ring. At its centre is the circular snack bar where patrons sip their drinks separated from the chaotic pedestrian traffic by a curved glass wall. On a TV, close to an escalator, promotions for new movies run continuously. The uncompromisingly optimistic theme from this fall's hit, *Flashdance*, never fails to lift my spirits. What a feeling!

I climb the steps back to the sidewalk. Across the Ring is the old Opera House. I am sure that in the New World there are state-of-the-art concert halls with unbeatable acoustics, but no technology in the world can provide Beethoven's fingerprints on a conductor's stand, the echo of young Mozart's whistling, or the ghosts of legions of capricious prima donnas.

The Air Canada office. A six-foot high model of the CN Tower. I could drop in and ask if they have something about London. Sorry, sir, nothing. London is not a tourist attraction.

The Lorenz Büchner bookstore. No need to go in there tonight. I visited it twice when I felt the overwhelming urge to be among books for a few minutes, to touch their spines and inhale the distinctive scent of fresh print.

At this hour the McDonald's on Mariahilferstrasse is crowded. Has it really been less than four months since we were here with Uli and Theo? How full of memories the city is now! Every corner powerfully reminds me of something. That's why we feel at ease here now, almost at home. Memories are what transform a place into a home.

If we could take off for Canada tomorrow, we would do so happily. Still, our looking forward is not pure, there's a touch of sadness in it and more than a touch of apprehension. We'll miss this city. We'll sorely miss our hard-won relative security, especially in the first weeks and months in the new city, new land. Another packing up, another uprooting, another jump into darkness. But it should be a short-term anxiety. We're going to fill London with our memories, too. We'll make it our city. I don't think I will lose Vienna. I don't believe I have lost Prague. I am a lucky man who will have three cities he's deeply attached to.

London. I hope we can get there before Christmas. The celebration of Christmas, still magical for little Ivo, would fit poorly into the raggedness of Zoch. I pray he can have an unforgettable white Christmas in Canada.

In a niche of an oddly shaped building a big-bellied man in a white apron is selling chestnuts from his stove-cart. He puts them into brown paper cones he rolls skilfully on the spot. Another unmistakable sign of the oncoming winter.

We haven't yet bought winter clothes. If we fly after November 25, we'll get them free from Traiskirchen.

A team of Kurdish men in yellow raincoats sell the evening paper to drivers waiting for the green light at the Gürtel. Though none of them is from the hotel, they give me a friendly nod, wink, wave. It seems I enjoy some reputation within the Kurdish community. It feels good.

In the tobacco shop at Westbahnhof, I buy one pack of cigarettes, each time a different American or Canadian brand. The bonus for a work-filled week. A morale booster. There is intense joy in one good cigarette.

The deeper in shit you are, the less you need to be happy.

As I cross the street towards the hotel I see Jana and Ivo's silhouettes in the distance. They are returning from the Emperor's summer palace – Schönbrunn. It's a comfortable walking distance from here. Large French gardens and a park. Its flower beds, bushes, and even some trees are shaped and trimmed in geometric symmetry. In the pond where a fountain falls there are golden fish. People feed them, and some fish weigh ten pounds.

We spent last Sunday afternoon there. Just before leaving we heard the noise of a jet. Low, very low, flying so slowly it almost looked as if it were suspended in the air, a huge, red and white Boeing 747 was on its final landing approach. On its red rudder there was a white maple leaf in a circle, shining in the last rays of the setting sun. We watched its slow, majestic glide until it disappeared behind the treetops. Despite all the letters and procedures, actually flying to Canada has been just a dream. But since the moment we saw this Air Canada beauty, we have known with rock-hard certainty that Canada does exist, and that we will fly there.

It is true, I will miss this city, but nothing will make me happier than flying to London, Ontario, Canada, the New World. For it, we will leave behind a continent filled with a long-living tradition and mementos of its great past.

But we are looking for the future.

12

THE END OF THE TIGHTROPE

WE FINALLY GOT the letter. Our departure was set for Tuesday, November 15. A three-leg flight, a transatlantic triple jump: from Vienna to London, England, to Toronto, Canada, and then to London, Ontario. We were as ready as we could ever be.

Jana had become an expert at knowing all the inexpensive stores in our neighbourhood, their prices, sales, and specials. Within a few hours we were dressed from head to toe for the most Canadian of all winters. I wouldn't have to wait for what somebody would give me. I bought the clothes myself with the money I had earned using my hands and head.

The next day we rode – for the last time – to Traiskirchen. In exchange for our travel arrangements we had to waive our asylum claims. Though our signatures meant closing the door to Austria, we signed with peace of mind and lightness of heart. We wouldn't need to come back. Whatever challenges awaited us in Canada we could tough out. We had already been tested under fire and we had passed with flying colours. We were certain we could muster whatever it would take to make it.

As he had foretold, I did meet our first roommate from Traiskirchen, the Romanian doctor, again. The day before he flew to Calgary he dropped into the WCC with a bouquet of dark-red roses to pay his respects to Frau Doktor. His hotel had been much better than ours, but in a small town that offered no chance of a job. He had managed to keep himself busy, anyway. A couple of days after he arrived there from Trais, he borrowed a portable blackboard from the local school. Since then he'd run free language courses for his fellow refugees. Seven days a week from breakfast to dinner he taught German and English. At night he worked on his own grammar and vocabulary. He was ecstatic about flying to Canada. In two days he would be able to start procedures to extricate his son from the grip of the Romanian secret police bureaucracy.

Theo, who has supported us tirelessly through his letters packed with good advice and humour, sent us a "goodbye and welcome" postcard. From the turn of the century, hand-coloured, it featured a young tightrope-walking Miss Speltrini high above the biggest waterfall in the world, Niagara Falls. I had never told him about my image of a tightrope crossing, but after so many years our imaginations were tuned to each other.

Saturday and Sunday we spent packing. We had to buy two additional suitcases to accommodate a sudden increase in our worldly possessions. In the end, my parents accepted our decision and sent us several parcels of books and clothes. More important, they sent our certificates and diplomas. They had five sets of official copies made and sent them all. Two of the sets eluded the surveillance network and reached us. But no more envoys from the secret police appeared in Vienna, at least none we encountered.

Monday morning we delivered our luggage to the office of the Intergovernmental Committee for Migration, which organized our transportation. We fit exactly into the weight limit prescribed by the airlines.

Once more we were lucky. We would be given a ride to the airport from the ICM's office and not from Traiskirchen. As a routine procedure the Austrians brought all departees to Trais for the last night and accommodated them in one huge dormitory. Thank God, we would miss the Merry Traiskirchen Night, the last night on the old continent. *It calls for a drink! For a party! Here's to a future in Australia! Here's to rinse away the past! Here's to quell the fear of the future!* Drinking, talking, smoking, singing, dancing, yelling, lovemaking, you name it, till dawn, when buses pulled in to deliver one batch after another to the airport.

On our way back from the ICM we made a detour to Thalia Travel. Colourful, snow-covered Whistler was gleaming in its window. A strange feeling. Today Whistler is an inaccessible place on the opposite side of the globe; tomorrow evening it will be a mountain *in our country.*

For long minutes I meditated silently and then, with a slight bow, I whispered, "I hadn't expected any, but there's been a lot of comedy. Thank you, O lofty one!"

Thalia didn't answer. Of course. The mighty muse of comedy would not answer the whisper of a mere mortal. But I could not erect an altar to sacrifice a lamb or a goat on a busy Vienna street.

And yet, as we walked away, I had a distinct feeling that I heard, "Good laughs in Canada."

How could I express our thanks to Austria? Should I shake the hand of every person I met in the street? Should I shout thank you from the spire of St. Stephen's? Yell it from the open door of the aircraft? There was no real or adequate way to convey our gratitude.

Nothing more to do for the rest of the day. We made our rounds in the hotel with a bottle of Seagram's that Frau Doktor had given me. Thanks to her wisdom, our parting had been swift, though not painless. We stood at the main door, she shook my hand and said, "You've proven to yourself you're worthy of something. Good luck. And one more thing you should know. In that sea of refugees, you've been one who deserved our efforts. You've revived my faith that what I've been doing is worth it." She gently pushed me out and rather abruptly closed the door.

In the hotel, most of the people we were close to had already left. We had another cup of tea with the Kurds; this time we could talk a little, as they had started German-language courses.

Ahmed was confined to bed. The cold, damp weather did him no good. "Perhaps I should have applied for Canada," he commented bitterly, seeing our beaming faces.

We had already downed our goodbye drinks with Lorenc and Tina. He had started his first steady job. As a co-driver with a big trucking company, specializing in moving households, he had gone to Bologna, Italy, and wouldn't be back for three days.

Our "furniture" was gone. Our friends made sure nothing usable was left in the room. It looked almost as desolate as when we had first walked in. Desolate, but clean.

Jarda had been on the road for the past two weeks. All I could do was slip a note under his door.

After the last dinner we returned to Old Lorelei everything she had issued us: the bed linen, tableware, and leftover meal tickets. We had to do without it all for one night. A short one. We had to wake up at three-thirty to make sure we would be at the ICM before five.

Edita acted as our backup alarm clock this time. She surprised us by making a big breakfast for us in the middle of the night. Again, the pain of saying goodbye, most likely forever, to someone with whom we had become quite close friends.

At five-forty we entered the empty lobby of Schwechat International airport. An official from the ICM approached me. Would I be willing to act as a courier for them and deliver a big manilla envelope containing a list of next week's immigrants to the Canadian immigration authorities at the Toronto airport? Frau Doktor had recommended me. No problem, one more service in a good cause.

A few minutes later a busload of fellow travellers pulled in from Traiskirchen. The men, pale, tired, hungover or still drunk; children sleepy, mothers nervous and irritated. A sleepless night there wouldn't have done Ivo any good. He had just finished his third batch of antibiotics in six weeks.

It's over. The battle, not the war. The war is going to be for life. If my emigration is to fulfil its purpose, I will have to achieve in a spiritual sense the heights I could not achieve in Czechoslovakia. That's why I defected. Of course, I will have all the handicaps of an immigrant. I'm going to be disabled in language, culture, education; I'll lack the solid ground of shared heritage under my feet. But I must not allow it to put me on the defensive. It would mean living in a mental ghetto and slowly withering.

I've changed from thinking negatively to thinking positively. A major transformation from a defensive crouch to grabbing life by the horns. It is freedom. I've breathed my first lungfuls of it in Vienna, how wonderful it will be when I'm breathing it all the time in Canada, year after year. It will obliterate the shit I'm still carrying in my head. Yet I can keep the good aspects of my old head, have two heads, each providing a different perspective. Emigration is not so much about losing, it's more about enriching; the old experience remains, enriched by the new one. We are being uprooted, but, with the exception of our families, our friends, and our language, we are losing only the shallow roots. In return we've re-established a connection with the deep roots of our civilization.

During the months we've been at our lowest, we've also been at our highest, closest to our true selves. Our stereotypes, prejudices, and ideological crap were left flapping on the border's barbed wires. We have learned what really counts and what are frills.

Maybe once in a lifetime everyone should hit rock bottom. It would help them set their values and priorities straight.

It's over. And as a motto to sustain us I'll remember the answer I gave to Zoli, our Hungarian friend. When he examined the downcast-looking photos on our Traiskirchen IDs, he sighed deeply.

"You must have gone through hell!"

"Hell? No! Hell is without hope. We've had full backpacks of hope. Purgatory is more like it. Purgatory with an occasional swing to paradise. But hell? Never. We have never been without hope."

For its last twenty metres our tightrope took the comfortable shape of the flexible corridor leading to the open door of a huge Air Canada Lockheed 1011.

Propelled by his inquisitive nature, Ivo rushed a few steps ahead and entered first. Rightly so, Canada is to be his country and he deserved to go first for his perseverance, patience, and courage. Then Jana and I, hand in hand, beaming triumphantly, made the Step. The first step onto Canadian territory and, at the same time, the first step down from our tightrope. We made it! The unbelievable had come true!

For a second I felt a sentimental urge to get on my knees and to kiss the crimson carpet representing Canadian soil. But the pretty attendant at the door would have thought I'd had a heart attack and would call for a doctor. Besides, there were scores of people behind us, pushing forward, anxious to make their first step. Their eyes already focused on the other shore of the Atlantic, they would overlook my kneeling body and trip over me, one after another, creating an American football pile-up, and this is no time for such a delay. So I just stored the moment in a special compartment of my memory and followed the attendant to hospitality class, row thirty-two. Though we hadn't asked for it out loud, our last wish was granted. Ivo took the window seat, Jana sat next to him, and I made myself comfortable just across the aisle.

While we taxied to the runway, six attendants performed a kind of morning workout that had something to do with emergency landing procedures and lifejackets.

Absolutely not, sir! We've already crossed the Atlantic to the Canadian shore on our tightrope. There's no way this mighty three-engine aircraft will go down, and no chance we will have to swim the rest of the way.

Now we're waiting at the end of the runway. I can imagine what the pilots see. A long, concrete strip with parallel tire marks, converging on the horizon. But I know for sure, as the pilots do, that long before we reach the horizon we will be airborne. We'll fly over it, on the start of one huge, eight-thousand-kilometre jump into the future.

"What are we waiting for? Let's go!" Ivo shouts and all the would-be Canadians enthusiastically join in. Let's go! Let's go!

The engines rev, and we can feel their harnessed power. The whole plane vibrates. More and more power. I feel in sync with the plane, filled to the brim with controlled energy, vibrating with impatience to fly to our new life. Let's go! Canada is waiting for us, Canada draws our plane.

Finally, the force of Canada, combined with the power of the engines and the desire of our hearts, overcomes the resistance of the brakes. Acceleration thrusts us back into our seats. We're moving. Faster and faster we charge. Canada is reeling in a tiny piece of her territory, with us inside, tiny elements of her future. Faster and faster!

The nose rises skyward.

We've lost touch with the Old World.

Acknowledgements

When we landed as immigrants at Pearson International airport in Toronto, my dream of becoming a writer was all but dead. Language is the writer's only tool, and second-language writers are exceedingly rare. It was the freedom and the "can-do" attitude of Canadians that prevented me from allowing my dream to die completely.

My friend Bohumil (Theo) Košťál initiated me into creative writing and then into emigration. For a number of years our letters were the only creative writing we did. Some of the ideas expressed by Theo in Chapter Two are quotations from or paraphrases of his letters.

Stan Dragland, who edited my first "Canadian" short story, encouraged me to pick up serious writing again. He has been the driving force behind this memoir. His support, encouragement, and trust kept me going when the whole project of being an English-as-a-second-language writer seemed just too absurd.

Doug Gibson and the other people at McClelland & Stewart were magnanimous. They were not put off by the stylistic roughness of the manuscript in its original form. The difficult task of harmonizing my voice with proper English fell to my editor, Dinah Forbes. I think she has succeeded marvellously, and I wish to express my gratitude for her extraordinary editorial skills. I am also grateful to Heather Sangster for straightening out residual stylistic, factual, and typographical flaws.

My wife, Jana, and my son, Ivo, were in a very real way co-authors of the book. They co-created the story by living it; then they helped me in every imaginable way to tell it.